A CONCISE HISTORY
OF THE THIRD REICH

WEIMAR AND NOW: GERMAN CULTURAL CRITICISM

Edward Dimendberg, Martin Jay, and Anton Kaes, General Editors

A CONCISE HISTORY
OF THE THIRD REICH

WOLFGANG BENZ

Translated by Thomas Dunlap

UNIVERSITY OF CALIFORNIA PRESS

Berkeley / Los Angeles / London

University of California Press

Berkeley and Los Angeles, California

University of California Press, Ltd.

London, England

First paperback printing 2007

© 2006 by The Regents of the University of California

Library of Congress Cataloging-in-Publication Data

Benz, Wolfgang.
    [Geschichte des Dritten Reiches. English]
    A concise history of the Third Reich / Wolfgang Benz : translated
by Thomas Dunlap.
        p.   cm.— (Weimar and now ; 39)
    Includes bibliographical references and index.
    ISBN 978-0-520-25383-4 (pbk. : alk.)
    1. Germany—History—1933–1945.   2. National Socialism.
  I. Dunlap, Thomas, 1959–. II. Title. III. Series.

DD256.5B38313   2006

943.086—dc22   2005025768

Manufactured in the United States of America

15   14   13   12   11   10   09
10   9   8   7   6   5   4   3   2

CONTENTS

GLOSSARY

Anschluss   "Union," used by the Nazis to describe the annexation of Austria in March 1938.

DAF   Deutsche Arbeitsfront, German Labor Front. A monolithic labor organization officially set up on May 10, 1933, by the Nazi party to take the place of the unions of the Weimar Republic. It was headed by Robert Ley.

Enabling Act   The law that provided the constitutional underpinning of Hitler's dictatorship, promulgated on March 24, 1933. The law essentially emasculated the Reichstag (s.v.) by allowing Hitler's government to pass laws outside of the constitutional legislative process.

Gau, pl. *Gaue*   The main territorial division superimposed on Germany after the National Socialists came to power. Eventually there were forty-two *Gaue,* or districts, each headed by a gauleiter who was appointed by Hitler and answered directly to him.

Gestapo   Geheime Staatspolizei, Secret State Police. The secret police force dedicated to preserving the Nazi state domestically.

Gleichschaltung   "Coordination," used by the Nazis to describe the process of bringing all social, political, and economic organizations and activities in line with the regime's goals and ideology.

Kristallnacht   The Night of Broken Glass, or Crystal Night. Refers to the night of November 9, 1938, when the Nazis launched coordinated attacks on Jewish synagogues and stores.

NSDAP   Nationalsozialistische Deutsche Arbeiterpartei, National Socialist German Workers' Party, Nazi party. Originally the German Workers' Party, the name was changed in February

1920. The party was re-founded by Hitler in February 1925. From July 1933 until Germany's surrender in May 1945, it was the only legal party in Germany. Hitler was its dictatorial leader, or Führer.

OKW   Oberkommander der Wehrmacht, High Command of the Wehrmacht (s.v.).

Reichstag   The German parliament. Hitler retained the Reichstag, but it was deprived of its legislative powers by the Enabling Act (q.v.) of March 1933.

Reichswehr   Germany's standing army during the Weimar Republic and the early years of the Third Reich. The Reichswehr was the 100,000-man army to which Germany was limited by the provisions of the Treaty of Versailles (s.v.). In 1935, the name was changed to Wehrmacht (s.v.), the armed forces of the Third Reich.

RSHA   Reichssicherheitshauptamt, Reich Central Security Office. The chief security office of the Nazi government. It was created in 1939 and given oversight of all the various police forces (Gestapo, criminal police, and the SD [Sicherheitsdienst], the security service of the SS). One of its subbranches, Office IV, was headed by Adolf Eichmann and charged with carrying out the Final Solution (Endlösung).

SA   Sturmabteilung, Storm Detachment (more commonly known as Storm Troopers), the name given after 1921 to the private militia of the NSDAP (q.v.). In January 1931 the organization was taken over by Ernst Röhm and assigned the task of winning the street for the party. By 1932 its ranks had swelled to 400,000. Internal struggles over the distribution of power within the party and differences over the future role of the SA, especially as it related to the Reichswehr (q.v.), led to the bloody purge of Röhm and other SA leaders on June 30, 1934. Thereafter, the SA ceased to play an important political role. The uniform of SA men was brown with a red swastika armband.

SD   Sicherheitsdienst, Security Service of the SS (s.v.). Headed by Reinhard Heidrich.

SS   Schutzstaffel, Guard Detachments. Originally the black-shirted personal guard of Hitler, these units were later transformed by Heinrich Himmler into the most feared and powerful organization of the Third Reich. Originally a subdivision of the SA, the SS carried out the bloody purge of SA leadership and was subsequently established as an independent organization. Virtually a state within the state, it was the backbone of the

Nazi system of terror. The SS controlled the Gestapo (q.v.) and the SD (q.v.) and was in charge of both the concentration camps and the notorious *Einsatzgruppen*, task forces that carried out mass killings in the occupied territories.

Stahlhelm	"Steel helmet." Nationalist ex-servicemen's organization hostile to the Weimar Republic. Founded and led by reserve officer Franz Seldte, it played an important role in politics in the 1920s and early 1930s.
Treaty of Versailles	The treaty concluding the First World War, by which the victorious powers forced Germany to acknowledge its war guilt, imposed ruinous reparations, severely reduced Germany's military forces, and removed certain territories from the sovereignty of the Reich. Contemptuously referred to as the *Versailles Diktat* by the Nazis and other ardent nationalists and right-wing forces, who saw the treaty as the symbol of Germany's humiliation.
Volk, völkisch	*Volk* is usually rendered as "nation" or "people," *völkisch* as "national," but these terms do not capture the emotional weight carried by the original. For the Nazis, these terms were fraught with elements of a racial blood-and-soil nationalism that was deeply antagonistic to outsiders, especially Jews.
völkisch movement	By the end of the First World War, there were about seventy-five *völkisch* (q.v.) groups in Germany promoting an extremist form of nationalism. The movement advocated a racial mysticism, pseudo-biologistic views, often intense anti-Semitism, and a vision of history as a racial struggle between superior and inferior peoples. The *völkisch* movement formed the powerful undercurrent that fed a good deal of Nazi ideology. Hitler wrote in *Mein Kampf,* "The basic ideas of the National Socialist movement are *völkisch* and the *völkisch* ideas are National Socialist."
Wehrmacht	The official name of the combined military forces in the Third Reich (army, navy, air force).

Map of the occupation areas. Münchner Stadtmuseum, Munich.

CHRONOLOGY

1918	November 9	Abdication of the German emperor; republic proclaimed
1919	January 5	Founding of the German Workers' Party in Munich
	April 4–May 1	Soviet Republic (*Räterepublik*) in Munich
	June 28	Signing of the Treaty of Versailles
	July 31	Adoption of the Weimar Constitution
	September 16	Hitler joins the German Workers' Party
1920	February	German Workers' Party changes its name to National Socialist German Workers' Party (NSDAP)
	March 13–17	Right-wing Kapp-Lüttwitz Putsch in Berlin
1922	August	Beginning of collapse of German currency; onset of rapid inflation
1923	January 11	French and Belgian troops occupy the Ruhr
	September 26	German government ends campaign of passive resistance to occupation of Ruhr
	October 23	High point of inflationary spiral: $1 worth 4 billion marks
	November 8–9	Beer Hall Putsch in Munich
1924	December	Hitler released from prison

1925	February	Hitler reestablishes the NSDAP
	April 26	Hindenburg elected president
1931	October 11	Formation of the anti-Weimar Harzburg Front
1932	January	Unemployment in Germany surpasses 6 million
	March 13	Hindenburg reelected president
	July	Reichstag elections; NSDAP becomes the largest parliamentary party
1933	January 30	Hitler appointed chancellor by Hindenburg
	February 27	Reichstag fire
	February 28	Reichstag Fire Decree
	March 13	Ministry for Public Enlightenment and Propaganda established
	March 20	Dachau concentration camp established
	March 24	Passage of the Enabling Act
	April 1	Nationwide boycott of Jewish businesses and professionals
	April 7	Passage of Law for the Restoration of the Professional Civil Service
	May 10	Nationwide book-burning
	June 22	Banning of the German Social Democratic Party (SPD)
	July 14	Passage of Law against the Founding of New Parties
	July 20	Signing of Concordat between the Vatican and the Third Reich
	September 22	Reich Chamber of Culture established
	October 14	Germany withdraws from the League of Nations and the Disarmament Conference
1934	June 30–July 2	Night of the Long Knives: Hitler and supporters eliminate Röhm, the head of the SA, along with his supporters and members of the conservative opposition

	August 1	Passage of law combining the presidency and the chancellorship
	August 2	Death of Hindenburg; Reichswehr swears oath of loyalty to Hitler
1935	March 16	Government reintroduces compulsory military service
	September 15	Passage of the Nuremberg Laws
1936	March 7	German troops occupy the demilitarized Rhineland
	August	Olympic Games in Berlin
	October 25	Formation of the Berlin-Rome Axis
	November 25	Signing of Anti-Comintern Pact between Germany and Japan
1938	March	Annexation of Austria
	September 30	Munich Agreement: Sudeten region of Czechoslovakia ceded to Germany
	November 9	Kristallnacht pogrom
1939	March 15	German troops occupy and extinguish rump Czechoslovakia
	August 23	Signing of German-Soviet Non-aggression Pact
	September 1	Germany invades Poland
	September 3	Great Britain and France declare war on Germany
1940	April 10	Germany attacks Norway and Denmark
	May 10	Germany invades the Netherlands, Luxembourg, and Belgium as a prelude to war against France
	June 14	German troops occupy Paris
	September 27	Signing of German-Italian-Japanese Tripartite Pact
1941	June 22	Germany invades the Soviet Union
	December 7	Japan attacks Pearl Harbor
	December 11	Germany declares war on the United States

1942	January 20	Wannsee Conference
1943	February 2	German army at Stalingrad surrenders
1944	June 6	D-day: Allied forces land in Normandy
	July 20	Attempted assassination of Hitler
1945	April 30	Hitler commits suicide
	May 1	Goebbels commits suicide
	May 8	VE Day: end of the war in Europe
	June 5	Allied Control Council assumes full control of Germany

MAJOR POLITICAL PARTIES IN WEIMAR GERMANY

(listed from left to right on the political spectrum)

KPD	Kommunistische Partei Deutschlands [Communist Party of Germany]
SPD	Sozialdemokratische Partei Deutschlands [Social Democratic Party of Germany]
DDP	Deutsche Demokratische Partei [German Democratic Party]
Zentrum	Zentrumspartei [Catholic Center Party]
BVP	Bayerische Volkspartei [Bavarian People's Party]
DVP	Deutsche Volkspartei [German People's Party]
DNVP	Deutschnationale Volkspartei [German National People's Party]
NSDAP	Nationalsozialistische Deutsche Arbeiterpartei [National Socialist German Workers' Party, Nazi party]

The SPD, the largest party until the elections of July 1932, was the bedrock of the Weimar Republic and with the pro-Republican DDP and Zentrum formed the so-called Weimar coalition.

Seats Won by the Major Parties in National Assembly (1919) and Reichstag Elections
(1920–1933)

Date	KPD*	SPD	DDP	Zentrum/BVP	DVP	DNVP	NSDAP
January 19, 1919	22	163	75	91	19	44	
June 6, 1920	88	113	45	86	62	66	
May 4, 1924	62	100	28	81	45	95	
December 7, 1924	45	131	32	88	51	103	
May 20, 1928	54	153	25	78	45	73	12
September 14, 1930	77	143		87	30	41	107
July 31, 1932	89	133		99	7	38	230
November 6, 1932	100	121		90	11	52	196
March 5, 1933	81	120		92	2	52	288

*Through May 1928, includes seats won by the USPD (Unabhängige Sozialdemokratische Partei Deutschlands, or Independent Social Democratic Party of Germany).

PREFACE TO THE GERMAN EDITION

The twelve years of the Third Reich, along with its prelude and aftermath, are among the best-researched and best-documented periods of modern German history. Yet another book about National Socialist ideology and rule calls for justification. This study is directed at readers who are looking for concise but reliable information, who wish to use the insights of historical scholarship in formulating their own judgments without retracing in detail the scholarly efforts behind those insights. The text therefore contains no notes or source references; the select bibliography at the end of the book provides access to more detailed literature, standard scholarly works, and recent studies.

The pictures are a critical part of the book. They are not meant to illustrate the text but to provide information about the Third Reich in their own right. Selecting these images was difficult, since most photographs from the Nazi period are affirmative in character, reflect the perspective of the rulers, and were intended to solidify the myths provided by Nazi ideology.

Recounting the rise and fall of the Third Reich in such a concise format was a gamble. I would like to thank the book's German publisher, Verlag C. H. Beck, for presenting me with that challenge, and editor Detlef Felken for his company and help on the difficult journey.

FROM THE FIRST REICH
TO THE THIRD REICH:
A BRIEF HISTORICAL EXCURSUS

An Introduction to the English Edition

GERMANY AT THE END of the eighteenth century, at the time of the French Revolution, was constitutionally and politically a highly heterogeneous entity consisting of more than one thousand independent territories, secular and ecclesiastical principalities, and the two monarchies of Austria in the south and Prussia in the north, absolutist and enlightened Great Powers by contemporary standards. Not all of the lands of the monarchies belonged to the German Reich, while other regions governed by foreign sovereigns—the kings of Denmark and the Netherlands—*were* part of the imperial realm. An emperor functioned as overlord of the entire territory, known since the Middle Ages as the Holy Roman Empire of the German Nation.

The political and constitutional fragmentation of the first, the "old" Reich, did not prevent a rich diversity of cultural currents from flourishing; on the contrary, competition between courts, prince-bishops and dukes, between monasteries directly subordinate to the emperor and free imperial cities, produced an unparalleled flowering of literature, music, art, and science. The brilliant intellectual era of German Classicism was at the same time the era of Germany's greatest political fragmentation and powerlessness.

The French Revolution and its aftermath—the Revolutionary Wars and the rise of Napoleon—profoundly affected Germany. The defeat of Prussia and Austria at the hands of France resulted in a territorial reorganization by French dictate. All territory west of the Rhine was ceded to France in the Peace of Luneville (1801) and the map of Germany was redrawn: ecclesiastical lands were stripped of their sovereignty and constitutional independence and given to secular lords as compensation for their losses on the left bank of the Rhine. The dissolution of small and minuscule lordships was above all an act of modernization.

The fragmentation of the German political landscape with its countless currencies, weights and measures, political boundaries, and customs borders, the jumble of exclaves and widely separated territories—all this was ended in favor of medium-sized states like Baden, Bavaria, Saxony, and Württemberg, which emerged larger and stronger from the consolidation of 1803. To be sure, alongside Prussia and Austria there were still more than thirty independent states, and the formal end of the old German Reich was still to come. In 1806, the medium-sized states formed the Confederation of the Rhine (Rheinbund) under Napoleon's protectorate and left the German Empire, which had thus reached the end of its long history. German Emperor Franz II had taken the title of emperor of Austria in 1804; on August 6, 1806, he laid down the imperial crown and declared the Holy Roman Empire dissolved.

Germany was now only a geographic term, and, following the catastrophic defeats of Prussia and Austria, it was also an occupied land dominated by France. The states of the Rheinbund, the "third Germany" alongside Prussia and Austria, modernized under French influence: privileges of the nobility were abolished, the liberation of the peasants was begun, state administration was organized more effectively, the tax system and the military were reformed, the educational system was overhauled, and the road to industrialization was prepared through the elimination of traditional constraints placed on crafts by guild ordinances. The reforms had only just begun and there was still a long way to travel on the road to the modern constitutional state, to the emancipation of the Jews, to liberty and equality as principles of social order, when Napoleon's star started to descend following the disastrous collapse of his campaign against Russia on the outskirts of Moscow in 1811–1812.

In the Wars of Liberation that followed, national and liberal movements in Germany joined hands against France. Napoleon was defeated in 1813 by a coalition of the great powers of the European continent—Prussia, Austria, Russia—and Great Britain. Diplomats assembled at the Congress of Vienna in 1814 to reorganize Europe. Despite the stated intent of the congress to restore Europe to the condition it was in prior to the revolution, the German Empire was not reestablished; the mid-sized German states held on to their gains and above all their sovereignty. The two great powers, Prussia and Austria, were enlarged: Prussia expanded westward, which enhanced its weight within Germany, and Austria expanded to the southeast, which weakened its position in Germany and Europe. In place of the old German Empire with an emperor at its head, there now arose the German Confederation, a loose league of German princes and city republics. The confederation had no leader; its only organ was the diet, the plenary assembly of all its members.

The German nation remained fragmented in a multitude of sovereign territories and principalities sandwiched between the two great states of Prussia and Austria. The entire nineteenth century was marked by the longing of Germans to unite in a national state. It would be a long and tortuous road. Nationalism, as the striving for unification in a single state, and liberalism, as the striving for individual autonomy within society, became the most important forces opposing the powers and currents of political reaction in nineteenth-century Germany.

The liberal bourgeoisie and academic youth in Germany became the standard-bearers of this longing for a national state. The establishment of the German Confederation as a loose association of sovereign states whose chief focus was on external politics came as a profound disappointment to German patriots who had fought against French hegemony in the hope that a unified German state would emerge from the victory over Napoleon. To them, the constitutional definition of the German Confederation that was codified in 1820—"a league of German sovereign princes and free cities for the purpose of preserving the independence and inviolability of the states encompassed within the Confederation and maintaining Germany's peace internally and externally"—was quite unsatisfactory.

The July Revolution in Paris in 1830 gave a boost to the liberal and national movements in Germany. In May 1832, twenty thousand people gathered at the three-day Hambach Festival in the Palatinate to agitate for a united Germany. Students were joined by burghers, craftsmen, and workers. Germany's political patchwork quilt of small and miniature states clashed with the dream of new German greatness in a Second Empire, the historical symbol of which was the medieval emperorship; as a political vision, however, that emperorship was imagined as a modern constitutional state, a liberal community. The symbols of the national movement included the colors black, red, and gold, which harkened back to the Wars of Liberation and which, after 1919, would come to symbolize the republic and German democracy.

In 1848, Europe was convulsed by a wave of revolutions and national uprisings, beginning in France in February and reaching Germany in March. Prince Metternich, until then guarantor of the restoration, was toppled and forced to flee to London. In Berlin, the capital of Prussia, the people rose up on March 18. The uprising was put down by military force, and at least two hundred civilians and about fifty soldiers were killed. The revolutionary situation threatened to turn into civil war. The Prussian king, Friedrich Wilhelm IV, gave in to prevent the worst from happening, even though his troops were in control of the situation. On March 21, 1848, he addressed his people and "the German nation," offering his assurance that henceforth Prussia would "merge into Germany." Now the individual states of the German Confederation agreed to call a pan-German parliament charged with drafting a common German constitution. This national assembly convened in the Church of St. Paul in Frankfurt am Main.

On March 28, 1848, the delegates of the Frankfurt assembly adopted a constitution and elected the king of Prussia emperor. A delegation traveled to Berlin and offered Friedrich Wilhelm IV the crown on April 2, but he declined it. This put an end to the effort to unite Germany through parliamentary-democratic means. Over the next two decades, the German national state was established by other means, as the product of power politics and the instrument of the Prussian army.

In 1862, Otto von Bismarck became minister-president of Prussia. He pursued German unification under Prussian hegemony by fanning the flames of opposition between Prussia and Austria to the point of military conflict. The technologically superior Prussian army defeated Austria and its allies (Bavaria, Württemberg, Saxony, Hannover, Baden, and others) in the German War of 1866. This also spelled the end of the German Confederation. Bismarck made peace with Austria on lenient terms, though he was tough on Austria's allies in northern Germany, where the kingdom of Hannover was annexed by Prussia. The North German Confederation, composed of twenty-two small and medium-sized states, was formed under Prussian leadership. The model of the second German Reich was thus in place, with individual member states remaining sovereign under the Prussian king. The Prussian minister-president became chancellor. Treaties of alliance were signed with the southern German states of Bavaria, Württemberg, and Baden, while Austria was excluded from German affairs.

All Bismarck needed to complete German national unification by monarchic-authoritarian means was a confrontation with France, which came about in 1870. A claim to the Spanish throne by a Catholic line of the Hohenzollern dynasty provided the casus belli. The union of the southern German states with the North German Confederation into the German Reich after their joint victory over France was the constitutional culmination of a national euphoria. The Prussian king was proclaimed emperor of Germany on January 18, 1871. Henceforth the Prussian minister-president was also chancellor of the German Reich. Bismarck strove to secure the new national state in the center of Europe with alliances and to dispel neighbors' distrust of the new power.

Society in the German national state, the empire that was proclaimed at Versailles in 1871, was from the very outset in a state of imbalance and burdened with many unresolved problems. These included an undeveloped parliamentarism and in some respects the federalist structure of the German Reich, with its particularist tendencies and Prussia's dominance. Also problematic was the existence of a party system that was not integrated into the concept of the state. Most troubling, however, were the social tensions.

The social foundation of the state was made up of the nobility, especially the Prussian Junkers; the military; the Protestant church; and the patriotic middle class. Politically, these groups encompassed both conservatives and liberals. Conservatism, oriented toward the Prussian monarchy or the other territorial rulers, had its prototypes in the large landholding nobility and the middle class. Rooted in tradition, the conservatives opposed industrial modernization and cultivated the values of a tradition-bound agrarian society. The liberals, from the outset split into a moderate and a progressive wing, were embodied in the class of bourgeois entrepreneurs and in the intelligentsia. But the commitment to a German nation, the conviction of being part of a common national culture in an ethnically largely homogenous national state, were values both political camps could agree upon.

The role of outsider was played by two parties that represented important segments of the population, Catholics and Socialists. One reason these two groups were cast in the role of the internal enemy was that doing so allowed the majority to define and stabilize itself by excluding minorities. The Social Democrats perceived the monarchically constituted state primarily as a feudal state that treated organized workers as enemies. Catholics looked upon the empire as an authoritarian state with a Protestant and dynastic orientation, a state that regarded them with suspicion because of their cultural and religious identity and foisted on them a conflict of loyalty created by the clash between the spiritual leadership of the Vatican and the secular sovereignty of the German Reich.

Bismarck believed the state was in a position where it needed to defend itself. Instead of acting defensively, however, Bismarck went on the offensive, forcing through laws by which the majority demarcated itself from the minority. Rudolf Virchow, one of Bismarck's liberal opponents, was right on the mark when he coined the phrase "clash of cultures" to describe the war of Bismarck's state against the Catholics. Virchow waged that battle on the side of the state against the churches; in his eyes it was a battle "for the freedom of culture and humanism." While the social and cultural tensions within German society in the last third of the nineteenth century were made clear by the lines drawn between the hostile camps, the majority was unequivocal in assigning blame for these menacing anxieties to the minorities.

During the 1880s, the clash between state and church eased. Although the conflict was not entirely resolved, the opposing sides arrived at a degree of reconciliation. Yet the wounds of exclusion suffered by the Catholic population would not completely heal until after the Second World War, and would do so only against the backdrop of much larger political and social catastrophes.

The other group identified by the state as a domestic enemy were the Social Democrats. They were reproached for a lack of national consciousness, which in turn formed the core of other accusations that sprang from a fear of upheaval and revolution. Concealed behind the charge of a deficient sense of nationalism was an emotional opposition to modernization. The Anti-Socialist Law of 1878, promulgated by Bismarck to combat Social Democracy, changed the legal status of the Social Democratic workers' movement to that of domestic enemy, which is exactly how the Junkers east of the Elbe, industrialists, and the conservative bourgeoisie thought of it. The fact that the Social Democrats continued to gain importance in spite of this, that the party gained votes in the face of persecution and bans, emerging as the strongest one in the Reichstag as early as 1890, merely deepened the fault lines in the German Reich.

Within the social structure of the empire, the most important force was the military, which stabilized the system. It set the tone for society as a whole, enjoyed special privileges, and was considered the guarantor of order both at home and abroad. The army was the symbol of national unity and unanimity, and as such it exercised an integrative function.

The self-awareness of the Germans as a nation was symbolized by the fact that the empire had been proclaimed on foreign soil, as a sign of triumph over the external enemy France, which thereby became the traditional foe. The hour of national unity was to be celebrated at the same time as the hour of the humiliation of France, when the Prussian king was proclaimed German emperor in Versailles. This event would characterize the German nation-state for the entire duration of its existence. It was based on unity through the exclusion of enemies and foreigners and derived stability from its images of the enemy, but also, and quite essentially, from a feeling of cultural superiority.

Still, allegiance to the German national state formed a common denominator even among the minorities, including the Social Democrats, as was demonstrated by 1914 at the latest. It was something even assimilated German Jews believed in, even though they were the most zealously pursued target of exclusion. Formally, they had won long-sought legal equality in the constitution of 1871, but this emancipation, a demand raised by the French Revolution, had been late enough in coming, and resistance to it was potent and persistent.

The national awakening of Germany brought with it a qualitative change in the way other Germans regarded the Jewish minority. Alongside religiously motivated enmity, which had shaped the relationship of the non-Jewish majority to Jews since the Middle Ages, the nineteenth century saw the rise of a new hatred of Jews based on racist arguments, a hatred that claimed to be a science and called itself anti-Semitism. The transition from traditional religious bias to the new anti-Semitism was not abrupt: religious anti-Judaism and its stereotypes remained a force and strengthened the new, pseudo-rational arguments of racial anti-Semitism.

At the end of the nineteenth century in Germany, hostility toward the Jews was a tool of communication for social protest as well as for reactionary endeavors, and it served as an exclusionary affirmation of allegiance to a German national culture. Anti-Jewish agitation was pursued vociferously and publicly by third-rate writers and narrow-minded zealots. However, this agitation was accompanied by a debate over "the Jewish question," a debate that appeared more respectable because the participants, for example composer Richard Wagner, were esteemed because of their achievements in other spheres. The scholars, artists, and writers who commented on "the Jewish question" made the topic socially acceptable. Hostility toward the Jews at the end of the nineteenth century was a stance tacitly agreed upon by conservative society.

The demand for colonies expressed by Germans in the second half of the nineteenth century was driven by the desire to win Germany greater influence and power in the world. Bismarck, now chancellor, had a realistic assessment of the dangers of colonial possessions given the imperialistic competition between the European states, and tried to contain the push for colonies. But while he regarded the acquisitions and treaties that German merchants made in Africa and the South Seas primarily as private economic matters, he could not and would not prevent the African territories acquired in 1884 and 1885, German East Africa, Togo, and Cameroon, from being placed under the protection of the German Reich. Germany was now a colonial power because it possessed a few rather small and economically unimportant overseas territories.

During the transition from the Bismarck era, which ended with his resignation in 1890, to the era of Emperor Wilhelm II — the years leading up to the First World War that embodied Germany's grasp for world power, the militarization of all spheres of life, and the institutionalized arrogance of Germany's craving for recognition — the idea spread that Germany had been shortchanged in the distribution of the world's riches and would have to make up for what it missed by competing with the imperialism of the other nations of Europe. The great power politics of Germany's second Reich led to the First World War, which Germany entered with illusions of winning a glorious victory. The discussion about Germany's war aims started from the German claim to superiority, which had to be rewarded. The general goal was to weaken France enough to prevent it from rising again as a great power, and to push Russia far eastward. Other goals included annexation of large tracts of French and Belgian territory, France's economic dependence on Germany, subordination of Belgium and the Netherlands to German rule, and annexation of Luxembourg. Colonial acquisitions and the establishment of Germany's economic dominance in central Europe were to round out the project of the future greatness of the German nation.

The First World War, however, ended in disaster for Germany. The collapse of the empire in the revolution of November 1918 became a national trauma, characterized externally by territorial losses, oppressive reparations, a loss of status, and military impotence. At home Germans failed to understand the defeat, regarding it as a humiliation and national disgrace. The military defeat and its aftermath triggered the longing for new German greatness in a Third Reich.

PROLOGUE

ON JANUARY 5, 1919, machine-fitter Anton Drexler and journalist Karl Harrer founded the German Workers' Party (Deutsche Arbeiterpartei) in a Munich tavern. This anti-Marxist and anti-Semitic organization, an offshoot of the obscure, *völkisch* Thule Society, was one of many radical right-wing political sects on the German political stage at the time. In the late summer of 1919, Private First Class Adolf Hitler attended a meeting of the party at the behest of the Reichswehr, which had sent him to investigate the organization. Hitler took a liking to its goals, joined the party, and became its propaganda chairman. The political climate in Munich after the First World War was a breeding ground for extremist organizations like the German Workers' Party, which changed its name to National Socialist German Workers' Party (Nationalsozialistische Deutsche Arbeiterpartei, NSDAP) in February 1920. Two thousand people packed the Hofbräuhaus beer hall in Munich for the NSDAP's first mass meeting on February 24, 1920. They cheered the proclamation of the Twenty-Five Points of the party's program and became acquainted with Hitler, who modestly presented himself as the "drummer" of the movement but soon left the party's founders behind on his way to becoming Führer. In July 1921, a special meeting of party members elected him chairman with absolute powers.

By the end of 1920, the party, with help from the Reichswehr and private supporters, had acquired the *Völkischer Beobachter* as its official organ; beginning in February 1923, the paper was published daily (interrupted by the occasional ban).

After the First World War, Munich was the stage on which nationalist

NSDAP delegates demonstrate their contempt for parliament by turning their backs on the government bench, leaving the chamber while Goebbels remains behind as an observer, and then returning in their prohibited party uniforms. Erich Salomon, at the time a famous Jewish photographer, captured this ominous scene in 1931. He died in Auschwitz in 1943.

disappointments and passions were played out with greater intensity and passion than anywhere else in Germany. The collapse of the Wilhelminian monarchy and the revolution of November 1918 had engraved themselves upon the consciousness of the leading political and social circles primarily as acts of violence against the traditional ruling house of Hapsburg, acts without justification and essentially incomprehensible. Order and law seemed shaken to the core. Kurt Eisner, the leader of Bavaria's

revolutionary government in the spring of 1919, was seen as an outsider and an intellectual, a person onto whom the people could project all their pent-up discontent over the war, their despair over its outcome, and their fears of the future. The anger directed at Eisner, a Jew from Berlin, was an outlet for the disappointment felt by civil servants and professors, entrepreneurs, tradesmen and merchants, military men, the nobility, the clergy, and peasants as they compared the present with the prewar years, now bathed in the bright sunlight of hindsight and nostalgia. The short-lived Munich *Räterepublik* (Soviet Republic), proclaimed in April 1919 following the assassination of Eisner in February and put down by force of

The ringleaders of the Hitler putsch were put on trial in Munich between February 26 and April 1, 1924. The right-wing conservative presiding judge allowed the defendants to use the trial as a pulpit for nationalistic demagoguery. The sentences were lenient: Ludendorff was acquitted, and Hitler, though not a German citizen, was not deported and served only eight months of his five-year term. DIZ, SV-Bilderdienst, Munich.

arms in May, traumatized the citizenry, and its aftershocks were felt for decades.

The political reaction had begun immediately after the November revolution, the episode of the *Räterepublik* notwithstanding. It was well under way by March 1920, which saw the failed Kapp-Lüttwitz putsch, an attempt by right-wing forces to overthrow the Weimar Republic in Berlin. Although the putsch failed in its primary objective, it had successful repercussions in Bavaria, where Minister-President Gustav von Kahr charted a right-wing political course: supported by militias and other right-wing groups, veterans' associations and officers' organizations, his program of government integrated all the nationalist passions and anti-democratic emotions that were stirred up in rallies and marches, at flag dedications and "German Days." Munich regarded Berlin with even greater suspicion than before. The slogan *"Ordnungszelle* Bayern" (order cell Bavaria) gained currency: people saw themselves as a bulwark against Prussianism and Bolshevism, were preoccupied with what they regarded as Bavaria's special qualities, and at the same time suffered from the hu-

Hitler at the Landsberg prison, surrounded by his faithful followers (from left to right): Emil Maurice, Hermann Kriebel, Rudolf Hess, and Friedrich Weber. DIZ, SV-Bilderdienst, Munich.

miliation imposed on Germany by the provisions of the Versailles treaty. First World War General Erich Ludendorff settled in Bavaria, joined the *völkisch* movement, and soon became the figurehead and idol of all radical patriots.

"This party knows how to call attention to itself again and again by means of posters that denounce the Jews and international capitalism in harsh language and invite everyone to meetings that are generally well attended," wrote an official observer of the political scene, the Württemberg envoy in Bavaria, about the young NSDAP in August 1921. Hitler was "regarded as a pathological personality, though possessed of a rousing oratorical talent." At about this time, the unit of the party that provided security at meetings, the Sturmabteilung (SA), was reorganized and fashioned into a paramilitary force. Twenty thousand NSDAP members attended the first Reich party convention in Munich in January 1923. The NSDAP was no longer a fringe movement, but it did not wish to be a party that sought to exert influence through parliamentary means. Instead, as one of the Fascist movements that sprang up all over Europe in the inter-war period, it sought to capture power through radical action in order to refashion state and society on the model of a strong man who led

Poster announcing a mass rally on the occasion of the re-founding of the NSDAP on February 27, 1925. Three thousand people filled the hall; another two thousand had to stand outside.

and masses who obeyed. When Benito Mussolini, leader of the Italian Fascists, marched on Rome in October 1922, he awakened expectations of a national revolution in Germany as well.

The year 1923 was one of crisis for the Weimar Republic: the government's decision to end the passive resistance to the occupation of the Ruhr region by French and Belgian troops was seen by jingoists as a declaration of political bankruptcy; hyperinflation caused ordinary people to fear for their very existence; Berlin declared a state of emergency against the unruly and reactionary Bavarian government. The mood seemed favorable and the time ripe for a coup against the Weimar democracy. Hitler, as the political leader of a so-called German *Kampfbund* (combat league) whose shock troops came from the NSDAP, staged the "national uprising" on November 8–9, 1923. It began when Hitler and a group of sup-

porters ousted the Bavarian government at gunpoint from the Bürger-
bräu beer hall on the evening of November 8, and it ended the following
day when police stopped the putschists with a volley of gunfire outside
the Feldherrnhalle in Munich.

Following the trial of the instigators of the coup, Hitler spent nine
months in prison while his comrades dispersed to successor organizations
and quarreled among themselves. Released in December 1924, Hitler
reestablished the party in February 1925. Its consolidation was helped by
external circumstances, especially massive unemployment and an economic crisis, which provided the party's radical propaganda with plenty
of ammunition for assigning blame and offering simplistic global explanations and promises of salvation. During the so-called struggle period
of the movement, the second half of the 1920s, the NSDAP revealed itself as an organization fixated on Hitler, one in which discussions of a
political program and factual statements were irrelevant in the face of the
Führer's charisma. Hans Frank, a follower from the early days who would
rise to the post of Reich minister and governor-general of Poland, described the impact of Hitler's rhetoric: "He spoke for more than two
hours, often interrupted by virtual storms of frenzied applause, and one
could have listened to him on and on. He spoke everything that was on
his mind and what he said came straight from all our hearts."

Although the NSDAP rejected parliamentary democracy on principle,
for tactical reasons it pursued a legal path to power after its reestablishment. Hitler vehemently affirmed this policy of legality before the supreme
court in September 1930, but he added that once he reached his goal, he
would completely change the nature of the state. Hitler was a candidate
in the presidential election in 1932, winning 30.1 percent of the votes in
the first round of balloting and 36.8 percent in the second round. In January 1930, the NSDAP joined a governing coalition for the first time when
Wilhelm Frick assumed the post of minister of the interior in the state of
Thuringia. The minister-presidents in the states of Anhalt (May 1932), Oldenburg, Mecklenburg-Schwerin (July 1932), and Thuringia (August 1932)
came from the ranks of the NSDAP. In the Reichstag elections the party
raised its share of the votes from 2.6 percent in 1928 to 18.3 percent in 1930;
in July 1932 it became the largest single parliamentary party, with 37.3 percent of the votes and 230 seats in the Reichstag.

Still, after internal fights and in the absence of a concrete political program, the NSDAP was in a precarious state, faced with a financial and
personnel crisis. The party had a dangerous public presence, thanks to
the agitation and terror tactics it employed in street battles such as the

Bloody Sunday of Altona, a deadly clash between the Nazis and their opponents on July 17, 1932, that reportedly left nineteen people dead. In opposition to Gregor Straßer, the leader of the party's left wing, who had been advocating participation in an authoritarian government (possibly supported by the unions) since the summer of 1932, Hitler, with backing from Joseph Goebbels and Hermann Göring, insisted that the party aim for absolute power. This led to a split with Straßer, who resigned all his party offices in December 1932 and withdrew to private life. The success of the NSDAP in the state elections in Lippe on January 15, 1933 (39.5 percent of the votes cast) was seen as a sign that the party was stabilizing. The chancellorship was now within Hitler's grasp, and it was his German-national allies who set the final steps in motion.

The conservative enemies of the Weimar Republic, those who despised parliamentarianism, parties, and democracy, had thoroughly prepared the ground for the Third Reich with their glorification of the war experience, their invocation of the spirit of 1914, their ultranationalism, and their belief that the Germans had a sense of mission and were a master race. In the fall of 1931, the nationalist enemies of the republic and democracy put on a military parade in Bad Harzburg to demonstrate their unity and their common will to achieve power. This Harzburg Front was an alliance between Alfred Hugenberg's German National People's Party (Deutschnationale Volkspartei), Hitler's NSDAP, Franz Seldte's Stahlhelm, and patriotic groups, and it operated with the tacit consent of Reichswehr generals. But the only thing front members agreed on was the rejection of the "system," and in the spring of 1932 they were unable to field a joint candidate in the presidential election. The rival allies all intended to use each other for their own purposes and insisted on their own independence. The leaders Hugenberg, Seldte, and Hitler came together again in the cabinet that assembled on January 30, 1933. The Young Conservatives, who saw their ideal government realized in the cabinet of Franz von Papen in 1932 and failed to recognize in time that Papen was merely holding the stirrup with which Hitler would mount to power, also had a share in the downfall of the Weimar Republic. Like the reactionaries of the empire, who were bent on reestablishing the era of the Wilhelminian emperors, the Young Conservatives originally despised the Hitler movement. However, following the movement's success in the spring of 1933, opportunism impelled them to join the NSDAP, cast aside their contempt for parties, and replace a state based on the rule of law with the cult of the Führer.

The term "Third Reich," used to propagate and popularize National

NSDAP rally in the Berlin Sportpalast prior to 1933. The upper banner reads, "Give Hitler the power—Germany awakes!" The lower banner reads, "No workplace without a Nazi cell!" Bundesarchiv, Koblenz.

Socialist rule, came from the ideological laboratory of the Young Conservatives. "The Third Reich" was the title of a tract published by Arthur Moeller van den Bruck in 1923, the same year Hitler first attempted to seize power. In van den Bruck's vision, the Christian-medieval utopia of the ideal state would find fulfillment in the myth of the third and final Reich (following the medieval Holy Roman Empire of the German Nation and Bismarck's establishment of a unified German state in 1871, which had ended with defeat in the First World War). As a doctrine of redemption, the longing for a Third Reich included a revision of the Treaty of Versailles as well as the *völkisch* idea of a Greater Germany, a Germany in which a *Volk* community would be realized with the help of ideas about a corporate, hierarchical, and equalizing state that were based more on social romanticism than concrete political vision, more on emotion than rationality.

Using the simplistic slogans of an ideology built on images of the enemy, the movement of Adolf Hitler—a political savior driven by megalomania and paranoia, by fears and fantasies of omnipotence—was able to unite, with the help of the magic formula of National Socialism, the discontented and the déclassés, the traumatized and the despondent left behind in the wake of the First World War. The term "National Socialism" promised a synthesis of opposing political ideas and a third way out of the misery of the unpopular Weimar Republic. Of course the anti-capitalist ingredients of this ideology were no more than decorative frills, while the social Darwinist, anti-Semitic, and *völkisch* elements constituted its fundamental building blocks. The cult of the Führer, meanwhile, represented the fulfillment of the longing for a strong man, which was typical of the period, and it served as the vessel for national hubris.

1

THE "NATIONAL REVOLUTION"

"WHAT WE ARE WITNESSING BELOW, these thousands upon thousands and ten thousands upon ten thousands of people, who, in a frenzied delirium of exultation and enthusiasm, are acclaiming the new leadership of the state—this is truly the fulfillment of our dearest wish, the crowning achievement of our work. We are fully justified in saying Germany is awakening!" The man who spoke these elated words into the microphones of the radio stations of the German Reich in the late evening of January 30, 1933, was Joseph Goebbels, the propaganda chief of the NSDAP. Hitler had been named chancellor that same morning. Goebbels was standing at the window of the chancellery in the Wilhelmstraße in Berlin. He was enjoying the torch parade that the SA, the paramilitary unit of the party, and the Stahlhelm were putting on between the Brandenburg Gate and the Wilhelmstraße on the occasion of the party's assumption of power, ostensibly in honor of President Paul von Hindenburg but mostly for their own leader, the new Chancellor Adolf Hitler.

This staged outpouring of jubilation, which would be followed by many state spectacles organized by Goebbels, was the origin of the legend of the national revolution, of Hitler's "assumption of power" (*Machtergreifung*). Goebbels was a tireless disseminator of this phrase, using it to divert attention from the fact that Hitler had been named chancellor at the head of a coalition government in which his own NSDAP was only a minority, represented by Wilhelm Frick as the new minister of the interior and Hermann Göring as minister without portfolio. None of these men had any prior experience in public office, with the exception of Frick, who had served as a minister in Thuringia for fourteen months.

Postcard from the Publishing House for National
Pictorial Art, Rudolf Bischoff, around 1933. The
words read, "Under full sails into the Third Reich."
Sammlung Karl Stehle, Munich.

The new chancellor and his two fellow National Socialists in the Reich
cabinet were in the company of experienced and self-confident conservatives. These included Alfred Hugenberg, media tycoon and German-
national minister extraordinaire (of economics and food and agriculture).
The posts of deputy chancellor and commissioner for Prussia fell to Franz
von Papen (a former member of the Catholic Center Party), who acted
as the kingmaker of this government and who had brought four experts
from his prior "Cabinet of the Barons" into the new "Government of National Concentration": Foreign Minister Constantin Freiherr von Neurath, Minister of Finance Schwerin von Krosigk, Minister of Justice Franz
Gürtner, and Postmaster General Eltz von Rübenach. The leader of the
anti-Republican Stahlhelm, Franz Seldte, joined the cabinet as minister

of labor, while General Werner von Blomberg became minister of defense. Papen, who, in a grandiose misreading of the political situation, had persuaded the senile, eighty-six-year-old president to appoint Hitler chancellor, was deeply satisfied with this triumph of his statesmanship. The keys to real power seemed to be in the hands of those who stood for conservative values—the German National People's Party (DNVP), the Reichswehr, and the Stahlhelm—while the Hitler party would be used only for the rough stuff of politics.

Many observers, even abroad, shared Papen's belief that Hitler and his party could be tamed. Some were hoping that high office would transform Hitler from a demagogue into a statesman—the same Hitler who as the head of his movement had always demanded absolute power and who had left no doubt about his will to radically change state and society once he had attained it. Others simply had faith that the nightmare could not last that long. In the face of the NSDAP's radical nationalist slogans, some forgot the explosive power of the movement, which was resolutely ready to wage civil war and had demonstrated as much for years in meeting hall brawls and street battles. Others argued that things would not turn out as bad as all that, taking comfort in the belief that the excesses perpetrated by the SA and its subdivision, the SS (the NSDAP's praetorian guard, which in January 1933 comprised at least 600,000 uniformed men), had been committed in the frenzied aftermath of their party's assumption of power. "If the Führer only knew about that," people told themselves, he would surely put a swift end to these unchecked activities.

What many considered national exuberance—militant National Socialists settling scores with their Marxist enemies, which they understood to be the Communist Party (Kommunistische Partei Deutschlands, KPD), the Social Democratic Party (Sozialdemokratische Partei Deutschlands, SPD), and the Republican organization Reich Banner Black-Red-Gold, and the harassment of Jews as targets of racially based hatred—was in reality the beginning of state terror. Soon this terror was no longer spontaneous but was carried out with the help of an increasingly effective apparatus of oppression.

A cleansing of state and society seemed necessary, tough action natural to all who believed in the dawn of a new era, in the rebirth of national greatness and glory. In February 1933, Hermann Göring, in his capacity as Prussian minister of the interior, set up an auxiliary police force, transforming 40,000 SA and SS ruffians into an organ of the state. He emphatically encouraged them to employ the "harshest measures," which meant the use of deadly force in the interest of "the national population,

Hitler greets the crowd from the window of the chancellery on
the evening of January 30, 1933. Österreichisch Gesellschaft für
Zeitgeschichte, Vienna.

which is being continually constrained in its activities." Under the eyes
of conservative "tamers," Göring applied the instruments of power to the
fullest extent possible.

During his first twenty-four hours in office, Hitler himself had destroyed
another part of the political framework by prevailing upon his coalition
partners to agree to a dissolution of the Reichstag and to new elections.
Electioneering in those days meant confrontation to the point of civil war,

Franz von Papen (shown with the Stahlhelm leaders Seldte and Duesterberg) was not up to the job of chancellor, which he held from June to November 1932. He was successful in preparing the way for Hitler but had no clout as his vice chancellor. DIZ, SV-Bilderdienst, Munich.

and the NSDAP, now a governing party, would use every means, including terror and violence, to expand and solidify the power it had just been given. This meant war against all parties, against the democratic system, against the Communist left as well as against German national rivals, whose parliamentary basis (52 of 584 seats, or 8.9 percent of the vote in the November 1932 election) was weak. Hitler had his way. Reich President Hindenburg dissolved parliament on February 1, with new elections scheduled for March 5. These five weeks were put to good use. On the basis of Article 48 of the Weimar Constitution, which gave the president the power to declare a state of emergency, other parties were obstructed, freedom of the press was restricted, and civil servants were dismissed. This was called a "cleansing of public administration" (the victims were chiefly Social Democrats and other supporters of the parliamentary system) and "securing of national concerns." In actuality it was the prelude to the establishment of a dictatorial system and the dismantling of the rule of law.

One particular incident, so fateful and fraught with symbolism that many believed it had been instigated by the National Socialists, accelerated all these developments. In the night of February 27–28, 1933, the Reichstag in Berlin caught on fire. The building, if not a symbol of democracy at least a symbol of state power and of German unity following the establishment of the Reich by Bismarck, was the target of an attack by a single individual, the Dutchman Marinus van der Lubbe. The arsonist was quickly apprehended, though some thought it much more plausible that this was the work of the Communists, whom Goebbels effectively blamed in the public media, while others believed it was a National Socialist coup. In point of fact the Nazis were completely caught by surprise. Hitler was a dinner guest at the house of his propaganda chief Goebbels when news of the fire reached him. "I consider this a crazy, fabricated report and refuse to inform the Führer," Goebbels noted in his diary. Eventually he did tell him, and they hurried to the scene of the fire.

Word went out that the fire was evidence of an attempted Communist coup and justified a state of emergency. That same night, the decision was made to go after the Communists (who were the third-largest party, with 100 seats and 17 percent of the votes) and to suppress the Social Democrats (121 seats and 20.7 percent of the votes in the election of November 1932). On February 28, President Hindenburg put his signature on the Decree for the Protection of the People and the State (also known as the Reichstag Fire Decree). The decree suspended important basic rights such as freedom of speech, freedom of the press, freedom of assembly and association, and postal and communications privacy. It did away with the principle of the inviolability of a person's home and tightened penalties for certain offenses. The death penalty could now be imposed in cases of high treason and arson.

"Protective custody," a phrase that would take on crucial importance for the suppression of any stirrings of opposition in the years ahead, was legalized for the detention of political enemies and was soon put into practice in the new institution of the concentration camp. In the days immediately following publication of the decree, protective custody was used first against Communist functionaries and elected officials. The Reichstag Fire Decree established a state of emergency that would last until the end of the Nazi regime and that was constitutionally formalized in March 1933 by the so-called Enabling Act. The critical point was that the decree of February 28 placed the instruments of power directly in the hands of the chancellor and the National Socialist minister of the interior and did not link the state of emergency to the authority of the president. Hitler's coalition partners from the DNVP and Papen, who as a confidante of the president fancied himself in the role of influential behind-the-scenes power broker, did not realize the extent to which they had tied their own hands by agreeing to the state of emergency, which they regarded as very much in the tradition of the presidential emergency decrees by which Hitler's predecessors had governed since the fall of 1930.

The National Socialists knew how to take full advantage of the emergency decree and made it very clear during the electoral campaign what they wanted. During an electoral speech in Frankfurt on March 3, Göring declared that the measures he was taking as Prussian minister of the interior would "not be afflicted with any kind of legal concerns," and that his job was not to exercise justice but "only to destroy and exterminate." War against the critics and enemies of National Socialism, at first especially against Communists and Social Democrats, meant terror and despotism, mistreatment, illegal detention, and murder. In spite of the elimination of the KPD and the intimidation of the SPD and the Catholic Center Party (Zentrumspartei), the only meaningful opponents, in the last election in which multiple parties were allowed to participate and which took place under more or less legal conditions, the NSDAP won only 43.9 percent of the vote. Together with the DNVP, the coalition, with 52.5 percent of the vote and 340 of the 647 seats, held a parliamentary majority (against 120 deputies of the SPD and 92 of the Catholic Center Party; the 81 elected Communist representatives were no longer able to take their seats in parliament), a majority it disdained. Hitler did not wish to be dependent on the Reichstag, he wanted dictatorial powers: he had said as much in countless speeches over the years, and in March 1933 he made good on that demand. Following the so-called Treachery Law, which the president had issued as a decree for "defense against treacherous attacks on the government of the national uprising" and which made criticism of the Hitler government punishable by law, the Enabling Act was intended to suspend parliament and all other constitutional checks and balances of the government and establish a dictatorship, initially for a period of four years.

Passage of the Enabling Act by the Reichstag on March 23, 1933, had been prepared by actions that employed enticement and coercion, terror and national apotheosis in a way that would become typical of National Socialist rule. Political enemies were silenced and intimidated through the terror of the SA in the streets and in improvised detention and torture chambers that sprouted everywhere like mushrooms. Sympathizers and traditional elites were offered a national spectacle in the "Day of Potsdam," an event intended as an emphatic demonstration that the goals of the revolutionary National Socialist movement, as represented by Adolf Hitler, were in harmony with Prussian virtues and civic-conservative patriotism, as embodied in First World War Field Marshal Paul von Hindenburg.

The director of this state event was Joseph Goebbels. Following the electoral success of the NSDAP, on March 13 Goebbels was named minister of public enlightenment and propaganda, an appointment that marked the Führer's creation of a new department—the first of its kind in the world—dedicated to controlling public opinion and orchestrating acclamation of the regime. In Potsdam, Goebbels introduced sentimentality and kitsch as forms of National Socialist self-representation. The backdrop for the Day of Potsdam, the goal of which was to situate the Hitler movement within the tradition of the Bismarckian Reich, was provided by the delegates of the new Reichstag. Following the constitutive ceremony with the president in Potsdam, the delegates met in the Kroll Opera House, the parliamentary quarters that replaced the burned-out Reichstag. It was highly symbolic that the few sessions of parliament held between 1933 and 1942 took place in an opera house. Once the Reichstag had completed its self-emasculation, when passage of the Enabling Act placed all power in the hands of the Hitler government, it was left with the theatrical function of offering applause and a background chorus in homage to the dictator's sway.

Passage of the Enabling Act required a two-thirds majority in the Reichstag. The eighty-one delegates of the KPD were no longer able to participate in the March 23 session. Moreover, twenty-six Social Democrats had also been arrested or were on the run. Göring, who was president of the Reichstag, used procedural maneuvers to control the session. Above all, the Hitler government needed the consent of the Catholic Center Party and the Bavarian People's Party (Bayerische Volkspartei). These two parties, representing political Catholicism, were internally divided and in the end decided to support the Enabling Act. The prelate Ludwig Kaas, chairman of the Center Party, believed that a "no" vote by his party would not change the balance of power, while a "yes" vote would at least protect ecclesiastical and religious concerns, such as influence on the schools and the education of the young, and ensure the survival of Catholic organizations. To "prevent even worse" and to improve their relationship with the NSDAP, the Catholic delegates, many of whom had vigorously opposed the Nazi party only a short while before, submitted to the demands of the National Socialists, only to discover soon after that the promises they were given in return were worthless.

The meager remnants of the middle-class liberals put aside their "serious misgivings" in the "interest of the *Volk* and the fatherland and in expectation of lawful development," as Reinhold Maier declared on behalf of the German State Party (Deutsche Staatspartei), and likewise approved the granting of unlimited power to the Hitler government.

The 444 "yes" votes were opposed by merely 9 "no" votes from the

Social Democrats. Otto Wels, the chairman of the SPD, justified his rejection of the proposed law in one of the most stirring speeches ever delivered in a German parliament. The governing parties of the NSDAP and
the DNVP, Wels argued, held the majority and could govern in accordance with the letter and spirit of the constitution. Where such a possibility existed it had to be taken. "But we stand by fundamental principles
of the constitutional state, of equality of rights, of social justice. . . . In
this historic hour, we German Social Democrats solemnly affirm the principles of humanity and of justice, of liberty and Socialism. No enabling
act gives you the power to destroy ideas that are eternal and indestructi-
ble. . . . We salute the persecuted and the harassed. We salute our friends
in the Reich. Their steadfastness and loyalty deserve admiration, the
courage of their convictions, their unbroken confidence guarantee a
brighter future." These were words of departure, to be followed in short
order by the emigration of the party leadership and the withdrawal of the
intimidated party members from the political stage.

Hitler had called the vote on the Enabling Act a "decision about peace
and war" when he appealed to the delegates with his typical mixture of
threat and pathos, which he cultivated as an air of statesmanship. At an
election event in the Berlin Sportpalast in February, he had stepped "before the nation" as a tribune and praetorian and had beseeched it: "German *Volk!* Give us four years' time—then judge and pass sentence on us!"

But any possibility of judging and passing sentence on Hitler and his
NSDAP was deliberately, swiftly, and thoroughly eliminated in the spring
of 1933. In the *Völkischer Beobachter,* the central organ of the NSDAP, one
could read how quickly the conservative "taming" concept had fallen apart,
how the illusion of making use of the Hitler movement to establish an authoritarian state as envisioned by Hugenberg and Papen had vanished into
thin air: "For four years Hitler can do whatever is necessary to save Germany. Negatively in the extermination of the *Volk*-corrupting Marxist powers, positively in the building of a new *Volk* community." In plain language
this meant that Hitler was on his way to a totalitarian dictatorship—the
authoritarian ideas of his coalition partners were no longer a topic for serious debate.

Soon the talk was not of a national but of a National Socialist revolution. Another new term in the German vocabulary was *Gleichschaltung,*
roughly, "coordination." It appeared for the first time in laws that enforced
conformity with the NSDAP and its goals by removing ministers, civil
servants, and deputies in states that were not yet under Nazi control. These
were primarily the Hanseatic cities of Hamburg, Lübeck, and Bremen,

"The Potsdam celebration was the first to be held in the National Socialist style," Goebbels confided to his diary. After the event he expressed his satisfaction because everyone had been "profoundly moved." Hindenburg had even had tears in his eyes: "All rise from their seats and pay jubilant tribute to the aged field marshal, who extends his hand to the young chancellor. A historic moment. The shield of German honor has been washed clean once again."

along with the states of Saxony, Hesse, and in the south, Bavaria, Württemberg, and Baden. Beginning on March 5, the minister of the interior appointed commissioners to replace the constitutional governments. The preliminary Law for the Gleichschaltung of the States with the Reich required that the composition of the parliaments reflect the results of the Reichstag elections; the same was true for all self-governing bodies at the

district and communal level. This move provided many National Socialists with positions and offices and prepared the ground for the centralization of every kind of authority. The development was made definitive
on April 7 with the Second Gleichschaltung Law. Commissioners with
dictatorial powers were dispatched to all the states (with the exception of
Prussia, where, since Papen's coup d'état against the democratic government on July 20, 1932, state commissioners operated simultaneously as
Reich ministers). These commissioners functioned as governors of the territories, which had lost their political autonomy and soon maintained the
names and institutions of their former statehood merely as decoration.

Gleichschaltung was also extended to organizations: henceforth they
were compelled to march in lockstep with the NSDAP or, in anticipatory
obedience, did so voluntarily. Another measure of the Gleichschaltung campaign was the Law for the Restoration of the Professional Civil Service,
passed on April 7, 1933, and used to purge civil servants whose political
loyalties were suspect. Though Social Democrats were the chief victims of
the law, it also affected other committed supporters of the Weimar Republic
and especially Jews, who, in accordance with one of the demands of the
NSDAP's program, were to be excluded from the civil service. The "Aryan
paragraph" was formulated for the first time in this law: it demanded that
civil servants of "non-Aryan" descent be sent into immediate retirement.
Initially this paragraph applied only to public service and, through a separate law promulgated the same day, to lawyers; later it was gradually expanded to include many professions, though at first it granted exemptions
for First World War veterans who had fought on the front lines. But a broad
social trend of adaptation to the new times became visible very quickly, as
sports and bowling clubs, singing clubs, student fraternities, and social organizations began, without any compulsion by the state, to exclude their
Jewish members. And the definition of who was a "Jew" was entirely a
matter of National Socialist racial ideology: the self-definition of those affected, many of whom had been Christians for a long time and had no cultural bonds to Judaism, made no difference in this drive toward exclusion.

With Hitler's assumption of power, anti-Semitism, the NSDAP's racially
based hatred of the Jews, became state doctrine. What began as rowdy
scenes and excesses in the streets, carried out by the SA and other Nazis
and aimed at individual Jews, became—without a word of protest from
coalition partners or the public and excused by the majority as the side
effect of national euphoria—an official, nationwide action against German Jews. The NSDAP had called for a boycott of Jewish stores, businesses, doctors, and lawyers on April 1, 1933, and had issued appropriate

The boycott of Jewish stores, lawyers, and doctors on April 1, 1933, was reinforced by SA sentries. The large placard in the middle reads, "Germans! Defend yourselves! Don't buy from Jews!" Bildarchiv Preußischer Kulturbesitz, Berlin.

slogans. "Germans, defend yourselves! Don't buy from Jews!" was written on placards and banners that SA men held up to passersby whom they prevented from entering Jewish shops and department stores—or tried to prevent from entering, for there were many examples of solidarity with the harassed minority on that day. Many shoppers refused to be intimidated and ignored the action, which had been launched in response to alleged anti-Hitler agitation by the foreign press. This coercive action against Germany's Jews was called off on April 3, in part for economic reasons, in part because of diplomatic repercussions, and in part because of the indifferent response of the public. One example of the latter is the course the boycott took in the town of Wesel on the lower Rhine. There the owner of the Jewish department store, Erich Leyens, adorned with his First World War medals, distributed a leaflet to passersby asking whether this was the gratitude of the fatherland for the 12,000 German-Jewish soldiers killed in the war. His action won support among residents and forced the SA to withdraw.

Two other events in the spring of 1933 sent a powerful signal and had a profound impact. The Reich government had declared May 1, 1933, National Labor Day and for the first time a legal holiday. This traditional celebration of the international labor movement was usurped by mass rallies of the NSDAP invoking a worker-friendly "*Volk* community." The next day the offices of the labor unions were occupied by government forces, headed by the SA and the National Socialist Shop Cell Organization (Nationalsozialistische Betriebszellenorganisation, NSBO), the NSDAP's surrogate for the labor unions. The unionists offered no resistance; their fainthearted leaders, taken by surprise, were paralyzed. As they had done on July 20, 1932, when then-Chancellor Papen had deposed the Social Democrat–led Prussian government in a coup d'état, the leaders of the labor movement urged their members not to budge an inch from the path of lawfulness and not to seek confrontation through a general strike or militant action.

The crushing of the unions and the theft of their assets ended with the compulsory incorporation of their members into the German Labor Front (Deutsche Arbeitsfront, DAF), which was established on May 10. Under the leadership of Robert Ley, the DAF, an "allied organization" of the NSDAP, was built up into a monolithic organization of "all working Germans," a compulsory association of employers and employees. With roughly 23 million members by 1938, the DAF was the largest Nazi organization, developing into an empire of its own with enormous financial resources but without any real competence in social or economic policy. The DAF did not have authority over the pay scale, which had been the core power of the unions. Instead, beginning on May 19, 1933, so-called public trustees of labor regulated labor contracts by way of state coercion.

The other event that proclaimed the spirit of a new time was the solemn burning of books by authors who had fallen into disfavor. On May 10, 1933, students in every university town, with the active participation of rectors and professors, spouted condemnatory "fire speeches" and hurled the works of Karl Marx, Sigmund Freud, Heinrich Mann, Erich Kästner, Erich Maria Remarque, Carl von Ossietzky, Kurt Tucholsky, and others into the flames. These "bonfire celebrations" had been organized by the National Socialist German Student Association (Deutsche Studentenschaft). The proclamation "Twelve Theses against the Un-German Spirit" was part of the ritual everywhere and made it very clear that the universities were not offering any resistance to National Socialism. In Berlin, this action, to which the public generally responded with indifference, re-

Deutfche Studenten marfchieren wider den undeutfchen Geift

12238

"Burn me!" demanded the writer Oskar Maria Graf, who felt disgraced that his books were not part of the auto-da-fé against the "un-German spirit" on May 10, 1933. The banner on the back of the truck reads, "German students are marching against the un-German spirit." Bildarchiv Preußischer Kulturbesitz, Berlin.

ceived a special blessing in a defamatory speech made by the minister of propaganda against the banned authors. Not only was the book-burning an obvious act of barbarism, it also demonstrated the NSDAP's claim to cultural hegemony. In literature, the arts, and the sciences, opinions that diverged from those of Nazi ideology were spurned—the auto-da-fé made this clear and that is how it was understood.

The Nazis tolerated political competition only for as long as it was unavoidable. The parliamentary mandates of the KPD delegates had been annulled on March 9. Functionaries of the party had either been arrested or were in hiding. Party members had prepared themselves for a political battle that would have to be waged from a position of illegality, and for a long time they continued to make their presence known—while incurring heavy losses—with resistance actions, leaflets, and slogans painted on walls. The SPD, while determined to adhere strictly to legal action vis-à-vis the government, took the step of sending its leading functionaries out of the country to safety. Under the leadership of Otto Wels and Hans Vogel, an exile executive committee of the SPD was established in Prague, from which it maintained contact with the party in Germany through "border secretariats" and couriers. When the SPD group in the Reichstag voted in favor of a foreign policy declaration by Hitler on March 17, it triggered a conflict with the émigré members of the party leadership, who disapproved of the accommodation and did not share the hope that Hitler would reward this kind of loyalty. All further illusions came to an end when the SPD was outlawed on June 22, 1933. Other parties preempted a similar fate by dissolving themselves. For those that failed to see the light, Nazi terror proved persuasive. On June 27, Hugenberg, leader of the DNVP, Hitler's coalition partner, a double minister and in a very strong position in January but by now driven into a corner by the Nazis, asked to be relieved of his offices. The Ministry of Economics was given to Kurt Schmitt, the Ministry of Agriculture to NSDAP ideologue Richard Walther Darré. The DNVP's delegates in parliament switched to the NSDAP and the party dissolved itself on June 27, as did the national-liberal German People's Party (Deutsche Volkspartei). The German State Party (the last incarnation of the German Democratic Party, Deutsche Demokratische Partei) followed suit on June 28, the Bavarian People's Party disappeared on July 4, the Center Party the following day. The NSDAP's claim to political monopoly was no longer in question. There was now only a single party in Germany, and all other associations that could possibly compete with it were "coordinated." On Hitler's orders, the Stahlhelm, allied with the NSDAP in the Harzburg Front since October of 1931, was subordinated to the SA leadership on July 1.

The Law against the Founding of New Parties, promulgated on July 14, 1933, put the finishing touches on the Nazis' monopolization of power. In September a Party Day of Victory was held in Nuremberg, which would henceforth be known as the "City of the Reich Party Days." Here the NSDAP celebrated itself with a parade of all its branches and associations. In the years to come this parade would evolve into the most important ritual of National Socialist self-representation.

2

THE CONSOLIDATION
OF POWER

OPPORTUNISTS JOINED THE HITLER MOVEMENT in droves once the NSDAP had become the governing party. Membership in the party rose from 1 million at the beginning of 1933 to 2.5 million within a few months. The "old fighters" (those with a gold party insignia, which people with membership numbers below 100,000, indicating they had joined by about 1928, were allowed to wear) and the "Old Party Comrades" (those who had joined prior to January 30, 1933) gave the sarcastic name "March casualties" (*Märzgefallene*) to those who joined only after Hitler's accession to power, induced by the prospect of advancement and sinecures. ("March" because they recognized the way the tide was flowing after the elections in March of 1933.) A moratorium on membership was declared on May 1, 1933, though it was not entirely absolute. When the moratorium was lifted in 1937, the number of party comrades (*Parteigenossen*, commonly abbreviated "Pg.") eventually rose to 8.5 million.

The situation was difficult for those who had fought against the National Socialists politically and in their published statements, and who had sought to warn against the consequences of a Hitler regime. Intellectuals, artists, and writers had offered resistance to Hitler and his National Socialist movement. Their weapons were irony and satire, derision and ridicule, and in the end the pathos of despair.

In 1923, Ernst Toller, who was serving a prison term for his participation in the Munich Soviet Republic of 1919, wrote the comedy "Der entfesselte Wotan" (The Unbound Wotan), in which Adolf Hitler figures as a demonic hairdresser. The play, which premiered in Berlin in 1926, was

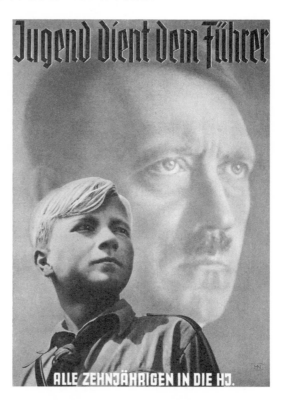

The Hitler Youth, as the NSDAP's organization
for the young was called after 1926, was a crucial
instrument of Nazi rule. The introduction of
compulsory youth service in 1939 was an attempt
to marshal all of Germany's "state youth." The
poster reads, "Youth serves the Führer" and "All
ten-year-olds join the Hitler Youth." Deutsches
Historisches Museum, Berlin.

not a success—no one had taken Hitler seriously since the comic opera
putsch in Munich in 1923—but Toller had a premonition of the career of
the future Führer. Another early work was Paul Kampffmeyer's tract *Der
Faschismus in Deutschland* (Fascism in Germany), also published in 1923.
Lion Feuchtwanger, in his novel *Erfolg: Drei Jahre Geschichte in einer Prov-
inz* (Success: Three Years of History in a Province), published in 1930,
painted a detailed picture of the political landscape in Bavaria. The novel's
Hitler figure, Ruper Kutzner, the Führer of the "true Germans," comes
across as both ridiculous and dangerous. Hitler's rise, the attempted putsch

of 1923, his bravado at the trial in 1924, and the enthusiasm and support of his followers are portrayed as a pitiful and despicable pastiche of nationalistic fervor, disorientation, and longing for a perfect world, preached by a barnstormer whose gesticulations are rehearsed, a loudmouth driven by ambition and a sense of mission: "Speech-making was the meaning of his existence." But Feuchtwanger's portrayal also includes the murder of the maid Amalie Sandhuber, who as a presumed traitor was the victim of a Nazi *Fehme* murder (the phrase was used to describe murders committed in the early 1920s by members of right-wing paramilitary *Fehme* bands).

From the beginning of the Weimar Republic, right-wing murders had been a topic of interest to the scientist Emil Julius Gumbel, since 1923 a lecturer in statistics at the University of Heidelberg and a well-known pacifist and belligerent journalist. A member of the German League for Human Rights, a committed Republican, and an advocate of reconciliation with France, he wrote about right-wing extremist secret societies, about the Black Reichswehr, and repeatedly about the number of *Fehme* murders. In 1931, at the request of the League for Human Rights, he produced a pamphlet, "Let Heads Roll: Fascist Murders 1924–1931." The title was a quote taken directly from Nazi propaganda. The pamphlet listed and described sixty-three murders committed by National Socialists prior to 1931. Gumbel left Germany before January 30, 1933. A worse fate awaited the philosopher Theodor Lessing, who had in effect lost his associate professorship at the Technische Hochschule in Hannover as early as 1926 because of his criticism of Hindenburg and because he was an open leftist, pacifist, and enemy of right-wing radicalism. In the spring of 1933, Lessing fled to Prague; at the end of August he was murdered by Nazis in Marienbad in Czechoslovakia.

Various forms of resistance to National Socialist ideology and its proponents were also found in the bourgeois–left liberal camp. The most prominent figure was undoubtedly Theodor Heuss. To be sure, Heuss, like his party comrade Reinhold Maier, fell silent following Hitler's assumption of power, and after the fateful approval of the Enabling Act in March 1933, he withdrew into "internal emigration." Heuss early on opposed the anti-Semitism of the NSDAP. As a delegate of the German State Party he gave a Reichstag speech in May 1932 in which he locked horns with Göring and criticized Nazi ideas about foreign policy. His book *Hitlers Weg: Eine historisch politische Studie über den Nationalsozialismus* (Hitler's Path: A Historical-Political Study of National Socialism) had been published at the beginning of 1932. Of course the liberal political journalist Heuss lacked the imagination to conceive of the brutality and bloodthirstiness with which the NSDAP program, and much more, would be put into practice. Still, the work contained passages like this one: "The destruction of Jewish cemeteries is a profound blow to a community in which, contrary to all the blather about the individualistic corruptive force of Judaism, the family represents a vital bond to the past. It sullies all of us. We are all bear a stain, ever since such a cowardly and irreverent act became possible in Germany."

Another opponent, the liberal writer Konrad Heiden, irritated the Nazis even more than Heuss. In 1932, Heiden published a book entitled *Geschichte des Nationalsozialismus: Die Karriere einer Idee* (A History of National Socialism: The Career of an Idea), a well-researched and objectively analytical polemic that made its mark. The author, a former correspondent for and editor of the *Frankfurter Zeitung* and a staff member of the *Vossische Zeitung*, emigrated in April 1933. He continued his opposition to National Socialism from the Saar region with further books: *Geburt des Dritten Reiches* (Birth of the Third Reich, 1934) and two works published under the pseudonym Klaus Bredow, *Hitler Rast* (Hitler in a Rage) and *Sind die Nazis Sozialisten?* (Are the Nazis Socialists?, both 1934). Heiden was also the author of the first large-scale critical biography of Hitler, which was published in two volumes in Zurich in 1936–1937, with simultaneous editions appearing in England, the United States, and France.

Among the most committed defenders of the Weimar Republic was Theodor Wolff, editor-in-chief of the liberal paper *Berliner Tageblatt*. In the last months before the fall of the Republic, he struggled in vain to win over Thomas Mann as an advocate of reason and a public champion against Hitler. The idea was to have Mann take the stage as the speaker for a "Republican cartel." Theodor Wolff left Germany in the spring of 1933; his flight from Hitler ended ten years later in Nice, where the Italian occupying police handed him over to the Gestapo. After spending some time in prison and a concentration camp, he died an agonizing death in the Jewish Hospital in Berlin. Public opposition to the NSDAP in its quest for power resulted, in the best of circumstances, in emigration— unless the Nazis preempted such a move. In the spring of 1933, Thomas Mann did not return to Germany after a lecture tour; he spent several years in southern France and Switzerland and after 1939 lived in the United States. In 1936, the government revoked the citizenship of Germany's most prominent writer, as well as his honorary doctorate from the University of Bonn.

Along with critical artists, writers, and scientists, the list of those who were vulnerable and in danger included functionaries of other parties,

The anti-Fascist prints and pictures of George Grosz are legendary, but no less so the photomontages of John Heartfield. Both artists were members of the KPD and saw themselves as class warriors and fighters against reactionaryism and Fascism in the Weimar Republic. Heartfield's media were the political poster and the *Arbeiter-Illustrierte Zeitung* (Worker-Illustrated Paper), or *A-I-Z*. He and Grosz also worked for the Malik Publishing House of Heartfield's brother Wieland Herzfelde, the most important literary and artistic forum of the revolutionary left until 1933. Malik also published Ernst Ottwald's analysis "Deutschland erwache!" (Germany Awake!), which attracted little attention because of its unorthodox Marxist perspective. The figure shows the front page of the *A-I-Z* of October 16, 1932: "The meaning of the Hitler greeting: Motto: Millions stand behind me! Little man asks for big donations." Deutsches Historisches Museum, Berlin.

unions, and political organizations, pacifists, and committed democrats, chief among them Communists and Social Democrats. Many fled in the first months of the new Hitler regime without having made any preparations for a life in exile. During a second phase of emigration that began in the middle of 1933, leftist parties took steps to save their most important officials, who were supposed to carry on the political struggle from outside the country—in the case of the SPD and other Socialist splinter parties, initially from Czechoslovakia and France; in the case of the KPD, from the Soviet Union. A third wave of emigration lasted until the outbreak of war and included mainly members of resistance groups.

Until the referendum of January 1935, the Saar region, which the Versailles treaty had removed from the German Reich and placed under French administration, was an important home to many refugees from Germany. All in all, not a great number of people left the country for political reasons. At the end of 1933, the number of émigré labor unionists and Social Democrats was estimated at 3,500. In 1935, 5,000–6,000 unionists and Social Democrats left Germany, along with 6,000–8,000 Communists and 5,000 opponents from other political camps: all told, roughly 20,000 émigrés who, as refugees out of political conviction, as voices warning of the rule of the Hitler movement, were able to save their lives and little else by crossing the border into another country. What lay ahead were years of loneliness and hardship, rage and helpless despair. Most ended up living a meager existence. Ludwig Quidde lived in very modest circumstances in Geneva; the other grand old man of the German peace movement, Hellmut von Gerlach, eked out a less than comfortable existence in Paris. Ernst Toller moved around restlessly, finally taking his own life in a New York hotel in 1939, at the age of forty-six. Some did better in material terms, such as Graf Harry Kessler or Lion Feuchtwanger, who emigrated to France, but they were the exception.

With the help of the Law for the Cancellation of Naturalizations and the Revocation of German Citizenship, promulgated in July 1933, the National Socialist regime was able not only to punish individuals it disliked, but also rob them of their personal wealth. This law was invoked 39,000 times against emigrants, "because by their conduct, which violates the duty of loyalty toward the Reich and the people, they have harmed German interests." Proscription lists with the names of the expatriated were published in the *Deutscher Reichsanzeiger* (German Reich Gazette) and the *Reichssteuerblatt* (German Tax Journal); in addition, the Ministry of Foreign Affairs sent lists to all German embassies and consulates. The first expatriation list, published on September 1, 1933, included the names Rudolf

Breitscheid, Friedrich Wilhelm Foerster, Kurt R. Grossmann, Albert Grzesinsky, Emil Gumbel, Heinrich Mann, Ernst Toller, Berthold Jacob, Kurt Tucholsky, Lion Feuchtwanger, Philipp Scheidemann, Friedrich Stampfer, Otto Wels, Georg Bernhard, Alfred Kerr, and Leopold Schwarz-schild. The subsequent lists add up to a nearly complete "Who's Who" of democratic-republican notables from the fields of literature, politics, science, and journalism.

The political exile movement was a lonely one for two reasons: it felt isolated both by the growing acclamation Hitler received in Germany in response to his successes, and by his regime's growing reputation abroad. The possibilities of fighting Hitler from abroad were limited. This was the result not only of restrictions that the countries of exile put on political ac-tivities; continued ideological differences within parties and groups also hampered the effectiveness of the exiled opposition. The party landscape of the Weimar Republic lived on in the groups and organizations in exile; little changed in the constellations and positions. The SPD and KPD were unable to come together in a popular front, and the leftist splinter parties and the diverse camps of the labor unions continued to lead separate lives, as did bourgeois-democratic or conservative-Christian organizations such as the German Freedom Party (Deutsche Freiheitspartei).

In the years between 1933 and 1938–1939, outside resistance to Hitler and the National Socialist regime could do little more than educate the world and the Germans about the true character and goals of the regime, to warn and beseech. This was done in papers such as the *Pariser Tage-blatt* and the *Pariser Tageszeitung* (1933–1940), *Deutsche Freiheit* (1933–1935 in Saarbrücken), and *Die Zeitung* (London), and in weeklies such as *Neuer Vorwärts*, *Gegenangriff*, *Neues Tage-Buch*, *Neue Weltbühne*, *Zukunft*, and many others. Added to these was a wealth of cultural and literary jour-nals, only a few of which are mentioned here: *Die Sammlung*, published in Amsterdam beginning in the fall of 1933; *Maß und Wert*, from the fall of 1937 in Zurich; *Neue Deutsche Blätter*, from September 1933 in Prague; *Das Wort*, from July 1936 in Moscow; and *Orient*, 1942–1943 in Haifa.

Legendary publishing houses such as Bermann-Fischer in Stockholm, Querido in Amsterdam, Oprecht in Zurich, Malik in Berlin, and others provided an outlet and forum for the political and literary writings of the exile community. Of course, the effect of this publishing effort was mod-est, and often its sole purpose was the self-affirmation of the exiled de-mocrats. The better part of the world and especially of the Germans was fascinated by Hitler, and few were interested in being educated about the real nature of the regime, its crimes, the terror in the concentration camps, the persecution of the Jews, the predatory intentions toward the neighboring states of the German Reich.

While the National Socialists would have been only too happy to expel the Jews from Germany, the emigration of prominent artists and writers was not something they welcomed. For politicians who were not too severely compromised, there was the possibility of integrating themselves into the Nazi state. Anyone who withdrew into private life, into "internal emigration," refrained from statements critical of the regime, and was willing to accommodate himself or herself to the new "*Volk* community" had little to fear after the excesses of the first months of Nazi rule.

The churches did not reject National Socialism on principle. The idea of a strong authority and of a close bond between throne and altar, of the kind that existed in the empire between 1871 and 1918, was in keeping with Protestant tradition. Many Protestant Christians were plunged into a profound personal crisis by the collapse of the Bismarck Reich in the First World War. Most of them had reservations about the democratic Weimar Republic and sympathized with political forces—such as the German National People's Party—that idealized the past.

Catholics had other memories of the empire. In those days their church opposed the state in an effort to preserve its religious rights and cultural autonomy. Like Social Democrats, Catholics were considered unreliable in their nationalist attitudes. Almost by default, this placed the parties of political Catholicism, the Center Party and the Bavarian People's Party (BVP), in a situation in which they played the role of pillar of the state in the period after 1918. As long as Hitler needed majorities, he sought a good relationship with political Catholicism. Persuaded by Hitler's prochurch assurances, in a panic because of the radicalism of the NSDAP, and appeased by the prospects of the Concordat between the government and the Vatican, which guaranteed the rights of the Catholic Church in Germany, the Center Party and BVP voted in favor of the Enabling Act in March 1933.

Many Christians found themselves in a paradoxical situation: the majority of church officials had recently made it clear at meetings and rallies that Catholics had to oppose Hitler with their conscience and their vote; now, in an announcement on March 28, 1933, the Catholic bishops officially retracted their warnings against Hitler and their condemnation of the ideology of the NSDAP. One had to acknowledge, they argued, that the head of the Reich government and Führer of the NSDAP had publicly and solemnly guaranteed the inviolability of Catholic doctrine and the rights of the Church. Without retracting the previous "condemnation

Initially the churches had no reservations about the Third Reich. Abbot
Schachleiter and Bishop Ludwig Müller at the party rally in 1934. DIZ, SV-
Bilderdienst, Munich.

of certain religious-moral errors," the Catholic bishops signaled a certain degree of trust in the new situation and admonished the faithful to show "loyalty toward the legally constituted authorities."

Initially, dissent based on a theological or religiously grounded rejection of the authoritarian-dictatorial state was confined to marginal groups and individuals in both the Protestant and Catholic churches. On the Catholic side it was the *Rhein-Mainische-Volkszeitung* as the center of a circle of social activists (Friedrich Dessauer, Walter Dirks); men of the Catholic workers' movement, such as Jakob Kaiser; and pious Christians who listened to their priests and wanted nothing to do with "neo-pagan" Nazi politics. On the Protestant side there were theologians such as Dietrich Bonhoeffer and Karl Barth who had misgivings about a dictatorial regime because they rejected its implicit claim to exercise total control over human beings.

Beginning in the spring of 1933, representatives of the Protestant churches clashed with the state, a conflict that subsequently escalated into the *Kirchenkampf* (struggle between church and state). The churches resisted efforts to "coordinate" them, efforts aimed against the traditional structures of self-government of ecclesiastical organizations. The National Socialists were intent on pushing through a church reform that would have combined the twenty-eight independent Protestant churches of the German states in a single, uniform Reich church governed by a Reich bishop in accordance with the "Führer principle"—subjugation of the individual as part of a *"Volk* community" to the absolute will of a strong man who was shown cultic veneration. Many Protestant Christians had joined National Socialism; under the name German Christians, they contested elections for ecclesiastical synods in an effort to secure a majority, often with success. Beginning in the fall of 1932, the German Christians, under the leadership of Nazi pastors, also took to the public stage. They were opposed by Protestant Christians, both pastors and laity, who at first adhered to the maxim that the church should not get involved in affairs of the state and the state should not interfere in matters of the church. In the struggle over the tradition and organization of the state churches, this stance gave rise to opposition to the Nazi state, first driven by religious concerns and then increasingly by political ones.

In its fight to fend off the German Christians, who, with massive support from the NSDAP, had won more than 70 percent of the votes cast at the church elections in July 1933, the ecclesiastical opposition gradually organized itself into what was called the Confessional Church. The nucleus around which it took shape was the Pfarrernotbund (Pastors' Emergency League) founded by Martin Niemöller in September 1933. A third of the Protestant pastors joined this league out of opposition to the "Aryan paragraph," which required Protestant churches to exclude any member who could not establish an Aryan ancestry two or three generations back, and which the German Christians were also propagating. In May 1934, the Synod of the Confessional Church in Wuppertal-Barmen formulated a set of principled objections to Nazi doctrine. The Theological Declaration of Barmen contained the core statement that even the totalitarian state encountered its limits in God's commandments, and that it was the task of the church to remind everyone of the "responsibility of those who govern and those who are governed." This kind of protest against the secular authorities was still directed primarily at the Nazi regime's ecclesiastical policy. The representatives of the Confessional Church could have thwarted Hitler's plan to integrate the Protestant church into the Nazi system by the stance they took. But for a long time they were caught in the dilemma of, on the one hand, the loyalty toward the state that was demanded of a Christian, and, on the other, the state's transgressions against Christian commandments.

The Confessional Church as a whole did not offer resistance in the political sense, with the intent of bringing down the National Socialist regime. It fought first to keep its organizational structures intact and then to preserve the independence of church doctrine, according to which the Christian commandments were not to be subordinated to Nazi ideology. However, the regime often felt politically and ideologically attacked by this ecclesiastical and theological contrariness. Henceforth a rupture ran through all the churches of the German states: the adherents of the Confessional Church found themselves increasingly in a state of principled opposition to both the state and the German Christians, who were committed National Socialists. In many Christians of the Confessional Church the oppositional stance eventually evolved into political resistance. Duty bound by conscience and often entirely on their own (and at other times supported by fellow congregants), they fought with the means at their disposal—sermons and the written word—first against state intrusion into church life and then against National Socialist ideology in practice, for example when it targeted the handicapped. Moreover, they also opposed a Christian faith that was blended with anti-Semitism and "neo-Pagan heresies." The latter included the call for a "heroic Jesus" as well as the desire for a "true to type" faith founded on "race, national characteristics [*Volkstum*], and nation."

As for the faith the Catholic Church had placed in Hitler's assurance in

The Concordat between the Vatican and the German Reich, signed on
July 20, 1933, guaranteed freedom of religion to the Catholic Church,
but at the same time enhanced the standing of the Hitler regime. DIZ,
SV-Bilderdienstthe, Munich.

the spring of 1933, it also quickly gave way to disenchantment. National
Socialist demonstrations and street terror at the Journeyman Day of the
Catholic Kolping Association in June 1933 in Munich were officially still
judged a misunderstanding, and the response was episcopal calls for the
greatest possible restraint. Provocations during Corpus Christi processions,
increasing obstruction of the work of Catholic organizations, propaganda
against confessional schools and against crosses in schools, and the prohibition of Catholic publications — all this showed what Hitler's attempts at
ingratiating himself with the Catholic Church were really worth.

The Concordat between the German Reich and the Vatican, signed on
July 20, 1933, seemed to reward the stance of the Catholic Church. The
state solemnly guaranteed the free profession and public exercise of the
Catholic religion, the continuance and activities of Catholic organizations
and associations, provided they confined themselves to religious, cultural,
and charitable purposes, and the existence of Catholic schools and religious instruction. In return, newly installed bishops were required to
swear an oath of allegiance to the Reich government, and the Holy See
barred priests and members of religious orders from any involvement in
party politics. As an international treaty, the Concordat helped to stabi-

lize the new regime and gave its reputation a boost; it silenced political Catholicism, that is, the supporters of the recently disbanded Center Party and the BVP; and (for the time being) prevented stirrings of opposition. Later, resistance from within the ranks of the Catholic Church grew to the same degree to which the Concordat was subsequently ignored by the National Socialists.

The smashing of labor unions and the disbanding of political parties was the most spectacular chapter in the conquest of power by the National Socialists. But the process of Gleichschaltung in other spheres of society was no less effective. Agricultural organizations, some of which were already permeated with National Socialists by the late 1920s, were the quickest to fall. Richard Walther Darré, after 1930 the head of the party's Apparatus of Agrarian Policy and also (after 1931) of the Central Office for Race and Resettlement of the SS, was able to unite all farmers' associations and the Reich Land League in short order. Then, in April 1933, he gained control of the agricultural cooperatives, and finally he "coordinated" the Chambers of Agriculture. As Reich farmers' leader he reported directly to the chancellor. In institutional terms his power was established by his appointment as minister of food and agriculture in June (following Hugenberg's resignation), and by the creation of the Reich Food Estate in September 1933. Membership in the Reich Food Estate was compulsory for anyone engaged in the production, processing, or sale of agricultural products. Darré thus had two chains of authority at his command: as minister he controlled the state agencies of his ministry, and as farmers' leader the regional, district, and local farmers' leaders of the Food Estate. In the early years of the Nazi regime, Darré wielded considerable influence as a *völkish* ideologue who had coined the slogan "blood and soil." His career went into decline because of competition with Himmler's ideas, on the one hand, and Göring's plans, on the other. He fell out of favor because of his incompetence in managing the food supply under wartime conditions and was dismissed in 1942.

The organizations representing the interests of industry were "coordinated" in a much less dramatic manner. With help from an SA strike force, which occupied the offices of the Reich Association of German Industry on April 1, Gustav Krupp von Bohlen und Halbach was appointed chairman of the association, which was known as the Reich Estate of German Industry beginning in June 1933. But the independence of big industry remained essentially untouched, since Hitler needed the industrialists— as he did the Reichswehr—if he was hoping to re-arm Germany in order to wage war.

The middle class and its representative organizations were caught in the crosshairs of the National Socialist League of Struggle for the Commercial Middle Classes, which, beginning in March 1933, organized boycotts of department stores, consumer cooperatives, and corporations, and forced the heads of associations to step down, thus gaining control of the retail and trade sectors. Of course, measured against the party program of the NSDAP, real success, namely the strengthening of the middle class at the expense of big business, did not materialize after the NSDAP leadership halted actions against department stores, including Jewish ones, in July 1933 because they were putting jobs at risk. In August, the League of Struggle was made part of the National Socialist Organization of Crafts, Retail, and Trade; two years later it disappeared into the German Labor Front. One plank in the party program and ideology, which was important to many members of the NSDAP, had been quietly sacrificed to pragmatic necessities.

The Law for the Safeguarding of the Unity of Party and State, which was promulgated at the end of the first year of Hitler's government, encapsulated the dualism that would characterize National Socialist rule until its downfall. The intent of this law was to both postulate and contain the influence of the party on the administration of the state by means of a sort of official proclamation. Its immediate effect was that the deputy leader of the NSDAP, Rudolf Hess, and the chief of staff of the SA, Ernst Röhm, became ministers without portfolio. Shortly before, on November 12, 1933, Hitler had held Reichstag "elections": with a turnout of 95.2 percent of all eligible voters, 92.2 percent of the ballots were cast for the single ticket of the NSDAP (7.8 percent of the ballots were invalid). The "election" was combined with a plebiscite on Germany's decision to withdraw from the League of Nations and the Disarmament Conference, which Hitler had proclaimed with great fanfare on October 14, 1933. An overwhelming majority of voters, 95.2 percent, approved of Hitler's move. Evidently most Germans were in agreement with his leadership; all opposition had either been silenced, or, like the voices of Communist and Socialist opponents of the new order, reduced to futile and dangerous protests employing leaflets, wall slogans, and so on, whose sole purpose was to demonstrate that the opposition still existed underground, in a state of illegality.

3

CRISIS AND THE TRIUMPH
OF DICTATORSHIP

THE MOST CRITICAL YEAR of the new regime stretched from the summer of 1933 to the summer of 1934. Diplomatically Germany was sliding into ever greater isolation. Even Hitler's hero Mussolini kept his distance, viewing Italy's role more as that of a balancing element alongside the western powers than as Hitler's ally. Not least the gathering strength of the National Socialists in Austria reinforced the reserve of *il duce*. Within the ranks of the NSDAP, there was tension about the party's future course. In July 1933, after the disappearance of the Center Party, the NSDAP's last potential competitor, Hitler declared that "revolution" would give way to "evolution." The uncontrolled terror perpetrated by the SA and the SS ever since the party had come to power was to be toned down in order to calm the public. Beginning in August, Göring, minister-president of Prussia since April 1933, disbanded the Auxiliary Police and gradually closed down the "unauthorized" concentration camps and torture cellars of the SA. Like Hitler, he was opting for the path of legalizing and formalizing the party's power. One instrument to that end was the secret political police, which in Prussia and Bavaria, the two largest German states, had been removed from the authority of the internal administration. The Gestapo was under Göring's direct control as of April 1933. He turned it into a special executive force alongside the judiciary. In Bavaria the political police force was headed by Heinrich Himmler, SS leader and as such subordinate to the chief of staff of the SA. While Göring chose the quieter pace for implementing power, announced by Hitler for tactical reasons, Himmler, as head of the SS and a Nazi functionary still in

Festivities at the Feldherrenhalle, November 9, 1933. Gouache by Ernst Vollbehr. Münchner Stadtmuseum, Munich.

the second tier of power, was for the moment in the camp of Ernst Röhm, the head of the SA. With the help of his paramilitary group, Röhm was out to preserve and even intensify the dynamic character and revolutionary impulse of National Socialism.

Röhm—a career officer with a boorish personality, an early fellow traveler and intimate friend of Hitler's, contemptuous of all bourgeois respectability—saw himself as the champion of a political soldiery and regarded his SA as a future militia-based popular army in competition with the Reichswehr. The SA men, most of whom had been recruited from the army of the desperate unemployed by Hitler's promises of salvation, were eager to enjoy the fruits of victory without delay. The strategy of undermining and penetrating the state apparatus through administrative and legislative acts was not their idea of seizure of power and revolution. They were out for booty; they wanted to be taken care of with jobs and sinecures. Röhm was not content with the title of minister and that of state minister in Bavaria. Once the SA had absorbed all national militias and veterans' organizations, the last of which was the Stahlhelm, Röhm had four and a half million men under his command. His vision of fusing this revolutionary guard with the Reichswehr—the professional army that saw itself in the tradition of the imperial soldiery—into a popular militia was derived from activist and radical currents in the NSDAP, currents which had found expression in 1931 in the revolt of the East German SA under its leader, Walter Stennes.

Sullen rumbling from the ranks of the revolutionary vanguard, who felt they had been shortchanged when the party came to power, offered Ernst Röhm the backdrop for speeches and articles in which he called for a "second revolution." Hitler, meanwhile, had opted for an alliance with the Reichswehr and the traditional elites and against Röhm's militia ideas. Hitler needed both the Reichswehr and big industry for his expansionist goals. He was willing to make concessions, all the more so since his loyal minister Blomberg had, in October 1933, dismissed key officers in the Reichswehr who were critical of the new regime. These included the chief of the General Staff Department, General Wilhelm Adam, and the chief of the Command Staff, Kurt von Hammerstein.

The sympathy of the army for the National Socialist government was not automatic; instead, the Reichswehr's loyalty was mediated through the person of President Hindenburg. Hitler had to be aware of this, and of the growing rivalry between the SA and the Reichswehr. In forging his tactical compromise with the military, whose political ideals were embodied more in the Wilhelminian empire than in Hitler's egalitarian and plebeian state, he wagered that the military shared his nationalism and his ambition of returning Germany to the rank of a great power. While the military accepted Hitler for the sake of this shared ambition, the alliance created conflicts between Hitler and his followers.

The socio-revolutionary dynamism of the SA clashed with Hitler's tactic of "the slow completion of the total state," and Röhm made him increasingly aware of this. In April 1934 he criticized Hitler's "incomprehensible leniency" toward reactionaries and his failure to "have cleaned house ruthlessly." The SA chief proclaimed the "second revolution" and in so doing announced the movement's claim to the programmatic goals it had marched for during the "period of struggle." Hitler had on his side Röhm's rivals within the NSDAP, Göring and Goebbels, who were busy establishing their own spheres of power within the state and society, and Himmler, who was eager to get himself and his SS out from under the SA and who wanted to rise to the top echelon of Hitler's followers.

Both the Reichswehr's Office of Counterintelligence and the Security Service (SD), a secret service of the NSDAP organized within the framework of the SS by Himmler's helper Reinhard Heydrich, collected material against Röhm. Göring had a dossier prepared about the SA chief's

Uniform of an SA man, Group "Hochland," from
around 1933. Münchner Stadtmuseum, Munich.

homosexuality, which had long been public knowledge but had been a
taboo topic. Hitler hesitated, but then on June 4, 1934, he talked Röhm
into furloughing the entire SA for four weeks.

For the time being the revolution had been sent into retirement, but
Hitler was now coming under pressure from different quarters. It began
to dawn on the conservatives around Vice Chancellor Papen just how dis-
mally their plans had failed. Moreover, it was very clear that the presi-

dent's days were numbered. Hindenburg's health was rapidly deteriorating. The question of how to arrange the succession was of critical import within the conservatives' scheme. Would a successor be able to contain Hitler by means of a military dictatorship? Should Hindenburg make a testamentary recommendation that the monarchy be restored?

Papen continued to try to bring these ideas to the attention of the aged head of state. And slowly he was coming to dread the ghosts he had summoned: though he was Hitler's vice chancellor, he now stood at the center of a circle of conservative opposition that was trying to save what had already been lost. Edgar Jung, who had published a cult book of the conservative revolution, *Die Herrschaft der Minderwertigen* (The Rule of the Inferior), had joined forces with Papen out of concern for the way things were developing. He was the author of a speech that Papen delivered on June 17, 1934, at the University of Marburg. His diagnosis of the condition in which Germany found itself as a result of the regime's activism was quite accurate: "Creation is not possible with never-ending dynamism. Germany must not turn into a train heading off into the blue yonder, with no one knowing when it will stop."

These words appeared to be directed against the restless agitators pushing for a second wave of revolution, but in fact were an attempt to slow down the entire development through a public appeal. Of course it was too late for that, but Hitler read the signals from the conservative camp as a threat on a second front. The dissemination of the speech, which also contained a passage about the "NSDAP's unnatural claim to totality," was blocked. Jung was arrested on June 26. Hitler turned down Papen's offer of resignation, but at the same time he outmaneuvered him with Hindenburg (who had fallen into a state of apathy toward the political developments and had withdrawn to his estate Neudeck in East Prussia).

Hitler was now determined to act—to eliminate the revolutionary potential within his party and suppress conservative critics—and he scheduled a meeting of the SA leaders for June 30 in Bad Wiesensee in Upper Bavaria, where Röhm resided.

The liquidation of the top SA echelon followed a script of sheer villainy. The SD and the Gestapo released news about an imminent putsch by the SA. The rumor had no basis in reality: in spite of its discontent, the SA was loyal to the cause, and Röhm's grandiose posturing was not backed by any plans for a coup d'état. "Hitler is faithless and at the very least must step down temporarily. If Hitler is not with us, we will do it without him," Röhm had grumbled in February following a meeting at the Reichswehr ministry. At the meeting, Hitler had described the role of the SA as one of providing border security and pre-military training, and described the Reichswehr as the sole army, which was to be given offensive capability and formed into a modern *Volksheer* (army of the people). And the charge that Röhm was part of a plot involving General Kurt von Schleicher, Hitler's predecessor as chancellor, the French ambassador, André François-Poncet, and Gregor Strasser, the erstwhile Reich Organization Leader of the NSDAP, was a complete fabrication. On the eve of the bloody strike against Hitler's internal opposition (known as the Night of the Long Knives), this accusation of treason was used as a form of autosuggestion and to win over Goebbels, with whom Hitler was to meet in Bad Godesberg. The third man at the meeting was Sepp Dietrich, the commander of the SS Bodyguard Regiment Adolf Hitler. Dietrich flew ahead to Munich to set things in motion (the Reichswehr was on alert and provided logistical support). In Munich, about 3,000 SA men unwittingly played into the Führer and chancellor's hands by marching through the streets in a rowdy procession in the early morning hours. It would seem that Hitler now actually believed in Röhm's treachery. He and his entourage sped to Bad Wiesensee in three cars, pulled Röhm and his companions out of their beds at the Hotel Hanslbauer early in the morning, and had them taken to Stadelheim prison in Munich.

Hitler had worked himself into a frenzy of rage; he was probably convinced that Röhm was a traitor and vowed revenge, all with enthusiastic support from the faithful at party headquarters in Munich, the so-called Brown House. Two of his companions from the early years, Rudolf Hess and Max Amann, fought over the privilege of shooting Röhm. Hitler hesitated while SS commandos in Stadelheim and in the Dachau concentration camp were liquidating leading SA officials, announcing their fate with the words "You have been sentenced to death by the Führer! Heil Hitler!"

Göring supervised the action in Berlin and expanded it to include "reactionaries," meaning the group around Vice Chancellor Papen. Its spokesman, Herbert von Bose, was murdered, as was Edgar Jung. Other victims of the death squads included former chancellor General von Schleicher and his wife; Schleicher's confidante, Major General von Bredow; and the chairman of Catholic Action, Erich Klausener. It was a good opportunity to settle old scores. Gregor Strasser, who had played a central role in the NSDAP until December 1932 as the proponent of the Socialist wing of the party, fell victim to his former comrades' thirst for revenge. Gustav Ritter von Kahr, who had been a sort of antagonist to Hitler during the Munich putsch in 1923, was hacked to death.

Röhm, who refused to comply with an order that he commit suicide,

ADOLF HITLER (1889–1945) was born in Braunau am Inn, the son of an Austrian customs official. He left secondary school without a degree and in 1907 and 1908 applied for admission to the Viennese Academy of Fine Arts. After being turned down twice, he lived an aimless life in Vienna as a painter of postcards, eventually leaving for Munich in 1913. In 1914 he volunteered for the Bavarian army. He was wounded in action in France and discharged from the army at the end of November 1918 in Munich. The Reichswehr employed the corporal as an informant at political meetings. In 1919, in the course of his duties, he encountered the right-extremist splinter group the German Workers' Party. He joined (as member 55) and made himself invaluable as a speaker. On July 29, 1921, he was elected chairman of the party, now the National Socialist German Workers' Party, and given dictatorial powers. Sentenced to five years in prison for his part in the attempted putsch on November 9, 1923, he served only nine months in the Landesberg/Lech prison. During his incarceration he styled himself as a national martyr and dictated the first volume of his book *Mein Kampf,* which would become the programmatic work of the NSDAP, which he re-founded in 1925. While this splinter group at the extreme edge of the right wing slowly gained importance (winning seven Reichstag delegates in the 1927 elections), Hitler solidified his claim to absolute leadership within the party and quashed any discussion of its political program. The "Heil Hitler" greeting became obligatory in the NSDAP in 1926 (after 1933 it was widely used, without any legal prescription, as the "German greeting"; on July 20, 1944, it was introduced in the Reichswehr as a military salute). In February 1932, Hitler acquired German citizenship when he was appointed a *Regierungsrat* with the Berlin delegation from Brunswick. On January 30, 1933, Hitler achieved his goal when Hindenburg appointed him chancellor. In short order he and his followers succeeded in eliminating all the institutions of a constitutional state and sweeping aside every obstacle to unimpeded autocratic rule. The merger of the offices of president and chancellor in August 1934 cemented Hitler's absolute dictatorship. His ideological positions had been established by the time he arrived in Munich at age twenty-four: his weltanschauung, a mixture of social Darwinist, biologistic, extreme nationalistic, and *völkisch* elements, underwent no further development. Hitler's worldview, dominated by pan-German and imperialistic ideas, was shaped by the kind of fears of modernity that were widespread in the Hapsburg monarchy prior to the First World War and by a radical hatred of the Jews. In the crisis following the First World War, thanks to his gift as a speaker, his unscrupulous demagoguery, and his mono-causal explanation of the world, Hitler was able to present himself as a political savior, first to discontented members of the petty bourgeoisie and then to a German citizenry that had lost its orientation. His political luck in solving the unemployment problem, his foreign policy successes in the 1930s, and the initial victories in the Second World War created his aura as Führer; his role as a figure of national integration remained unchallenged through Germany's military defeats.

was shot on July 1, one of the last victims. On July 2, Hitler ordered an end to the "cleansing action," which cost the lives of about two hundred individuals throughout the Reich, some of them innocent victims of mistaken identity. Göring covered up the traces as best he could, Hitler assumed all responsibility, and the cabinet passed a law declaring that the measures taken "to put down the acts of high treason" had been legal in that they constituted "national self-defense" (*Staatsnotwehr*). A telegram arrived from the president expressing deep gratitude: Hitler, it said, had "saved the German people from a grave danger." (Whether Hindenburg actually knew of the wording of the telegram or understood it is another question.)

Minister of War von Blomberg, who had introduced the "national emblems of the NSDAP" in the Wehrmacht as early as February, as a sign of his devotion to the movement, published an Order of the Day on July 1, 1934, praising the "soldierly determination" with which the chancellor had crushed the "traitors and mutineers." The Wehrmacht expressed its gratitude to him with "devotion and loyalty." It was not until two weeks after the Night of the Long Knives, on July 13, 1934, that Hitler stepped before the nation. In a two-hour speech before the Reichstag, he justified the murderous action and his role as "chief judge" of the nation, one who stood above the law. It should be noted that there were plenty of armed SS in the assembly when Hitler, in a tense atmosphere, openly acknowledged the murders: "You break mutinies by the same eternal iron laws. If someone reproaches me and asks why we did not employ the ordinary courts to render judgment, I can answer only this: in that hour I was responsible for the fate of the German nation and I was thus the highest judge of the German *Volk*! . . . I gave the order to shoot the main culprits of this treason, and I further gave the order to burn out the ulcers of our poisoned wells at home and the poison of foreign nations down to the raw flesh."

These events were outrageous, not just because the majority of the

Hitler rehearsed his speaking poses with the help of his personal photographer, Heinrich Hoffmann. Photograph taken prior to 1933. DIZ, SV-Bilderdienst, Munich.

German people saw them as a saving act of strength by their head of government against a menacing band of mercenaries. The real abomination was that the sense of justice and political morality had atrophied so swiftly in the nationalistic daze of Germany's "renewal" that this throwback to a state of tyranny was not lamented but joyfully applauded. The Reichswehr, too, which had lost two highly respected generals in the massacre, victims of targeted murders, accepted what had happened. The churches likewise wrapped themselves in silence.

The last barrier that separated Hitler from total dictatorship was the president, less as a person than an institution whose rights had been explicitly left untouched by the Enabling Act. On August 1, 1934, Hitler went

Hitler and his entourage at a campaign event in Berlin, 1932. DIZ, SV-Bilderdienst, Munich.

to see Hindenburg one last time. Upon his return to Berlin he had a law passed naming him Hindenburg's successor: the office of president was abolished and Hitler was granted the position of Führer and chancellor. This took place immediately prior to Hindenburg's death. This action exceeded the powers granted by the Enabling Act, but by this time nobody seemed to take offense. Surprisingly, Minister of War von Blomberg declared that it was his intention, "immediately after the death of the president, to have the soldiers of the Reichswehr swear an oath to the Führer and Reich Chancellor Adolf Hitler." This oath of loyalty, administered a day later, was a voluntary act of devotion, the final surrender of the armed forces to National Socialism. Was it done out of gratitude for the SA's having been brought to heel? Was it a calculated act in order to bind Hitler to the military? Hitler, in any case, was now in unrivaled possession of absolute power.

The back of the SA had been broken. Victor Lutze, its new chief, removed the leaders who considered themselves "political soldiers" in the Röhmian sense. Within a year, membership in the SA dropped by 40 percent. Henceforth the function of this revolutionary troop was, with the exception of the Kristallnacht pogrom against the Jews, little more than that of a veterans' club that was used to line the streets on special occasions but ceased to have any political role. Himmler's SS, which had furnished the death squads on June 30, now rose to become the elite of the system as a separate part of the party structure directly under the Führer. Eventually, as the instrument of terror in the implementation of the National Socialist weltanschauung, the SS developed a life of its own, which allowed it to move beyond its role in the apparatus of repression and become a state within the state.

The revolutionary phase in the takeover of power had come to a dramatic and violent end. The constitutional state had been destroyed, to the cheers of the people and state elites. Germany had been transformed into a totalitarian state in which the "Führer principle" had been established as the fulfillment of all political yearnings and held sway in all spheres of life.

4

SOCIETY IN THE NAZI STATE

A MONOPOLY OVER THE SHAPING of public opinion and sovereignty over cultural life were pillars of Nazi power. By establishing a Ministry for Public Enlightenment and Propaganda (March 13, 1933), the regime revealed its intention of being the guiding force in these spheres and demonstrated, a few weeks after it had attained power, how seriously it was pursuing that goal. In September 1933, Goebbels—the man in charge of the new department and, in his capacity as propaganda chief of the NSDAP, in possession of the key posts—created another instrument for implementing a uniform and centrally controlled cultural life along the lines of National Socialist ideas. The Reich Chamber of Culture, established by law on September 22, 1933, had a corporate structure, and membership was compulsory for all "creators of culture." It was overseen by a bureaucracy that was supposed to attend to the social and economic concerns of its members, and which exercised authority in the person of its director, Goebbels. Subdivided into seven separate chambers for literature, press, radio (abolished in 1939), theater, film, music, and fine arts, the Chamber of Culture was used to organize, "coordinate," and oversee all cultural life. Ideological concerns played a smaller role than compulsory membership: a journalist, sculptor, actor, musician, or writer who was denied membership (because he or she was Jewish or discredited for being a democrat) was automatically barred from his or her profession.

The Chamber of Culture was part of Goebbels's propaganda monopoly and was also directed against competing claims, such as those put forth by Robert Ley as the head of the DAF, or by the ideologue Alfred Rosenberg, who ran the League of Struggle for German Culture. Rosenberg,

Cover of the catalogue for the exhibit "Entartete
Kunst" (Degenerate Art), 1937, showing Otto
Freundlich's *Der neue Mensch* (The New Human).
AKG-images, London.

as the "Führer's Delegate for the Entire Intellectual and Philosophical Education and Instruction of the National Socialist Party," was eager to play
a role in the shaping of cultural policy.

Radio was the most important mass medium in the Third Reich. A
state institution even before the takeover by the Nazis, it was "coordinated" into the Reich Radio Company, which was staffed exclusively by
conformist personnel, and its content and operations were overseen by
the Reich Ministry of Propaganda. The *Volksempfänger* (people's radio receiver) created by the Ministry of Propaganda turned radio into the everyday vehicle of entertainment and propaganda. The first 100,000 VE 301s
(the number symbolized the date the party took power) were sold, at a
price of 76 reichsmarks, the day the unit was presented at the Berlin Radio

Advertising poster, Vienna, 1938: "All of Germany hears the Führer with the People's Radio."

Show in August 1933. Later the sets became even cheaper, and the number of households that owned a radio rose from 25 percent in 1933 to 70 percent in 1939. Goebbels's goal of turning the radio into the most important "instrument for influencing the masses" was soon achieved, thanks to the people's receiver and the regime's institution of collective listening to public broadcasts in restaurants, businesses, schools, and government offices.

Radio, as the head of the Radio Department in Goebbels's ministry put it, was "the device for proclaiming the currency of the National Socialist worldview." By transmitting the regime's cultic and consecrative rituals it served the goal of mass suggestion, while nonpolitical entertainment promoted domestic pacification.

Getting the highly diverse German press to toe the Nazi line was a more difficult process. After 1933, the paper of the National Socialist movement, the *Völkischer Beobachter,* became the organ of the government, as it were (several editions appeared simultaneously in Berlin, northern Germany, Munich, and later also in Vienna). The director of the paper's publishing house was Max Amann, who had served with Hitler in the First World War and had been a party comrade back in the Munich days. After 1922 he became director of the party's publishing house, Franz Eher Verlag; in 1933 he was appointed the NSDAP's Reich leader for the press, president of the Reich Association of German Newspaper Publishers, and president of the Reich Press Chamber. A sergeant in the First World War, Amann, along with Hermann Esser, was one of the most boorish men of the Munich camarilla, whose influence on Hitler was based on the early days of the movement. Within a very short period he rose to become the head of a press empire that overshadowed Hugenberg's media conglomerate.

When the party came to power, the National Socialist press accounted for a vanishingly small portion of the 3,400 dailies that existed in the German Reich. Moreover, the publishing houses in the various *Gaue,* with their poorly made papers, were heavily in debt. Reorganization began in the spring and summer of 1933 with the confiscation of all 49 Communist and 135 Social Democratic newspapers. In early 1934, Amann, as the head of the NSDAP's central publishing house, was given control over the publishers in the *Gaue.* In April 1935, in his capacity as president of the Reich Press Chamber, he began the process of systematic concentration in the newspaper business by issuing three directives. These directives allowed for the "Aryanization, de-commercialization, de-subsidization, de-confessionalization, and de-corporatization" of the newspaper publishing industry, as Amann's chief of staff, Rolf Reinhardt, cynically com-

General meeting of the Kaiser Wilhelm Society for the Promotion of the Sciences in Gürzenich Hall in Cologne, June 22, 1937. The lord mayor of Cologne, Dr. Karl Georg Schmidt (wearing his chain of office), is in the center of the picture. The others are, from left to right, Nobel prize winners Max Planck and Carl Bosch, Gustav Krupp von Bohlen und Halbach, and the banker Kurt von Schröder, in whose house in 1932 the stage had been set for Hitler's assumption of power. DIZ, SV-Bilderdienst, Munich.

mented on the acquisition or shutdown of the bourgeois mainstream media that now followed.

Although there were still 2,200 privately owned papers in 1939 after this spurt of concentration, they accounted for only a third of the total print circulation. The NSDAP press, with about 200 papers, printed 13.2 million of the 19.8 million newspapers that came onto the market every day in Germany. One paper that remained untouched at this time was the *Frankfurter Zeitung,* not only because it was a renowned bourgeois-liberal paper that could be used as a showpiece abroad, but also in deference to its majority stockholder, the chemical company I. G. Farben. However, shortly before the war the *Frankfurter Zeitung* did come under Amman's control. It ceased publishing in August 1943, against Goebbels's wishes. Important to the journalistic reputation of the regime was the weekly *Das Reich,* which was launched in May 1940. It proved a journalistic and financial success, its circulation rising to 1.5 million by 1942–1943.

After the first wave of concentration, private publishers were left primarily with the small and tiny papers in the provinces. Shutdown actions in May 1941 eliminated 550 papers "for the duration of the war." Another 950 papers were affected in the spring of 1943; these had to be sold to the National Socialist Press Trust, leased for the duration of the war, or incorporated into joint publishing houses with the National Socialist *Gau* press. These actions eliminated whatever meaningful competition still existed. Additional shutdowns occurred in the late summer of 1944. What remained were 625 private papers with 17.5 percent of the total circulation, as against Amann's Press Trust with 82.5 percent.

Max Amann had attained publishing and economic control over the German press. Authority over the content of the publications lay with Goebbels in his capacity as minister of propaganda, propaganda chief of the NSDAP, and president of the Reich Chamber of Culture. The Editors' Law of October 1933, which elevated journalists to the position of quasi-public officeholders and promised to free them from the publishers' right to issue directives, but in the process placed them under the regime's yoke, allowed Goebbels to exert influence in matters of personnel as well. The possibility of working in one's profession depended on political conformity prescribed by law. The Editors' Law thus functioned similarly to the Law for the Restoration of the Professional Civil Service and the Law on the Legal Profession: disliked individuals and Jews were banned from their professions.

Amann, who disliked the Editors' Law, often acted in competition with Goebbels. And beginning in January 1938, at the latest, he had to share his influence on the press with yet another authority: the Reich press chief, a post to which Hitler appointed Otto Dietrich, press chief of the NSDAP since 1931. According to bureaucratic procedure, Dietrich was to represent all ministries to both the domestic and foreign press. It was his task to keep the papers informed through daily press conferences. Although Goebbels had been able to tie him to his own ministry as a *Staatssekretär* (state secretary), within the party hierarchy Dietrich held equal rank. Moreover, by virtue of his office, Dietrich spent nearly all of his time around Hitler, to whom he reported directly.

After 1933, the press conferences of the Reich government degenerated into little more than the issuing of slogans, an occasion when jour-

The chief advocate of this kind of art, Adolf Ziegler, president of the Reich Chamber of Fine Arts, acquired the derisive nickname "Master of German pubic hair." Bayerische Staatsgemäldesammlung, Munich.

nalists received orders on what was to be reported in what form and to what extent and what was off-limits. The language rules were extremely detailed and constituted the heart of Nazi control of the press.

National Socialism claimed sovereign authority to shape all areas of the nation's artistic and cultural life. Playing on petty bourgeois reservations about modernism in the arts, National Socialists, supported by radical right-wing outsiders in the cultural life of the 1920s, had long been up in arms over artistic trends that ran counter to the prosaic, romanticized ideal of beauty so aggressively promoted by the League of Struggle for German Culture. In Thuringia as early as 1930, Wilhelm Frick, the National Socialist minister in charge of education and the Interior Ministry, had launched an iconoclastic assault against abstract, cubist, expressionist, and other avant-garde works of art. Cheered on by those with provincial artistic taste, the Nazis proceeded to denounce as "degenerate" everything in art, music, and literature that did not conform to the aesthetic, political, or racial ideals of Nazi ideology. The word "degenerate," which was taken from the biologistic vocabulary of racial ideology, revealed the thrust of the attack.

Munich, more than any other place, was given the task of providing a forum for art in the National Socialist sense. In 1933, Hitler declared the city the Capital of German Art. (Programmatic titles were also used to honor other German cities: Hamburg and Bremen were the Capital Cities of German Shipping, Frankfurt am Main was consecrated to the trades, Stuttgart to Germans living abroad, Essen and Chemnitz were dedicated to German industry, and Munich was also given the honorary title Capital of the Movement in 1935; Linz, Nuremberg, Munich, Berlin, and Hamburg also became Führer Cities.) In October 1933, the Führer laid the cornerstone of a House of German Art, which was to be exemplary in its architecture and take on central importance as an exhibition space.

The opening of this "cathedral of German art" on July 18, 1937, was an elaborate affair that included a three-day celebration with musical offerings at many sites throughout the city, theatrical performances, the obligatory speeches by Hitler and Goebbels, a military parade of party members, and a festive parade with the theme "2000 Years of German Culture." In the following years, as well, until 1944, the House of German Art hosted the "Great German Art Exhibition." Hitler became personally involved in selecting the exhibits, which offered a cross-section of the subjects officially in demand: Teutonic kitsch, blood-and-soil paintings glorifying rural life, anatomically precise nudes, martial sculptures by Josef Thorak, landscapes by Sepp Meindl, and peasant paintings by Thomas Baumgartner. The exhibit items for the House of Art were assembled every year with professional advice from Heinrich Hoffmann, Hitler's official photographer and a member of his personal entourage since 1921. Hoffmann adorned himself with the title "Reich Photo Reporter" and was appointed professor in 1938; mostly he enjoyed a lucrative monopoly on the visual images of Hitler and his inner circle.

Coinciding with the opening of the House of German Art, an exhibit on "degenerate" art was shown nearby. Subsequently, this show went on a four-year tour through thirteen other cities. A confiscation committee headed by Adolf Ziegler had selected nearly 600 works by 120 artists ("Degenerate Art since 1910") to illustrate what the National Socialists meant by "degenerate" art. Van Gogh, Franz Marc, Kandinsky, Oskar Schlemmer, and Marc Chagall were represented in the show, along with Max Beckmann, Paul Klee, Käthe Kollwitz, Otto Dix, George Grosz, Erich Heckel, and Kurt Schwitters. There had been precursors to this exhibit after 1933 which had denounced un-German "cultural Bolshevism," and a companion show on "degenerate" music was organized in 1938 in Düsseldorf. The cleansing of the museums had begun with an authorization from the minister of propaganda: a decree from Göring in August 1937 exposed all art collections in Prussia to pillage, a Reich law in May of 1938

In the traveling exhibit "Entartete Kunst," Nazi cultural policy denounced modernity with racist slogans. The wall banner reads, "Like the niggerization of music and theater, the niggerization of the visual arts was intended to uproot the racial instinct of the *Volk* and help tear down the boundaries of blood!" DIZ, SV-Bilderdienst, Munich.

allowed for the "confiscation of products of degenerate art." The art lover Göring benefited personally from many of the artworks that were confiscated without compensation. The works shown in the exhibit "Degenerate Art" were constantly changing as important pieces were sold on the international art market to obtain foreign currency, as at the spectacular auction held on June 30, 1939, in Lucerne, where works by Picasso, Kokoschka, Gauguin, and others were put on the block.

All in all, more than 160,000 "degenerate" works of art were removed from German museums and collections. In March 1939, there were plans to burn about 1,000 confiscated oil paintings and nearly 4,000 prints because the building in which they were being stored was needed as a granary. It is not clear whether these plans were carried out. Another intervention in the cultural life of the nation occurred in the fall of 1939, when Goebbels outlawed art criticism. In its place he ordered "art appreciation," which was to be "less an evaluation than description and thus apprecia-

The cathedral of light over the Zeppelin Field, November 1938.

tion." The only writers worthy of engaging in such "appreciation" were those who "approached this task with purity of heart and the views and sentiments of a National Socialist."

The most important and visible means of expressing Nazi aesthetics was architecture, which Paul Ludwig Troost (who died in 1934) had established in his capacity as "First Architect of the Führer." His successor, Albert Speer, elevated his eclectic neoclassicism into a brutal architecture of representation and power. Hitler took an active interest in it, personally sketched designs, advised the architects, and felt quite the brilliant artist, with his builders obsequiously reinforcing his self-image. Speer, who enjoyed Hitler's utmost confidence and then his friendship, inflated the regime's architectural ideas into visions of mammoth dimensions. Initially the largest project was the grounds of the party rallies in Nuremberg. The entire complex—the Zeppelin Field, a staging ground for 300,000 people; the March Field, for mock maneuvers by the Wehrmacht in front of 115,000 spectators; the German Stadium, with 400,000 seats; and the Congress Hall, with a capacity of 50,000—had been conceived as an architecture of cult, power, and subjection, as the stony setting for

Leni Riefenstahl gives cameraman Guzzi Lantschner directions in the
Olympic stadium, Berlin, August 1936.

a uniformed mass of humanity. Although the complex was never completed, rallies took place there until 1938 (there were no more after the
outbreak of war): hours of show marching by the party's auxiliary units
and associated organizations (after 1934 also the Wehrmacht), followed
by nightly rallies under the "cathedral of light" created by anti-aircraft
searchlights. The crowds for the Hitler speeches, numbering into the hundreds of thousands, were replaced three to four times during such an event,
which could last from four to eight days.

The NSDAP rallies were immortalized by a young film director, Leni
Riefenstahl, who had already made a name for herself as a documentary
filmmaker. In 1933 Hitler commissioned her to document the rally "Victory of Faith." She did more than merely document the event, and her
second such film, in 1934, *Triumph des Willens* (Triumph of the Will), revealed her sensitivity and skill in shaping the apotheosis of National Socialism in the cult of the Führer. Films about the 1936 Olympics (*Fest der
Völker* [Festival of Nations] and *Fest der Schönheit* [Festival of Beauty])
consolidated her fame and Hitler's favor. After 1945, of course, Riefenstahl downplayed the latter, as she did her last film from the Nazi era,

To study sightlines and the degree of incline at the site for the Nuremberg party rallies, in 1938–1939 Speer had a wooden mock-up built on a scale of 1:1. This mock-up of the bleachers was erected on a slope in the Hirschbach valley (Oberpfalz). The stadium itself was never built. Projectbüro Reichsparteige-lände, Nuremberg.

Tiefland (Lowland, 1940–1941), for which she was said to have used con-scripted Sinti and Roma, who had allegedly been promised that they would be spared deportation to Auschwitz, a promise that was not kept. The films of the party rallies became icons of the Nazi cinematic aesthetic.

Up to the summer of 1938, when work began on fortifying a 630-kilometer strip of the border between Aachen and Basel, the site of the party rallies in Nuremberg was Germany's largest construction project. The frenzied building activity that began in 1934 was an expression of the regime's claim to power and its self-image during its stabilization phase. Speer, appointed inspector general of the capital, was also busy with plans for rebuilding Berlin on a megalomaniacal scale. Among other things, the plans called for the largest domed hall in the world, rising to a height of 726 feet and located at the center of a grid system; a triumphal arch; and monumental administrative and government buildings for a future world capital.

While Germany sank to a third-rate level in most areas of art and lit-

The rebuilding of Berlin into "Germania," capital of the new world power, was to culminate in the largest building in the world, a "Great Hall" for 180,000 people, and in a triumphal arch on the north-south axis. As inspector general of buildings for the Reich capital since 1937, Albert Speer was responsible for carrying out the planning "in accordance with the ideas of the Führer." Valuable historical structures were recklessly sacrificed to make way for the envisioned construction, whose originality lay entirely in its size. DIZ, SV-Bilderdienst, Munich.

erature as a result of Nazi cultural policies, musical activities remained notable. The regime's somewhat diffuse policy on music was aimed chiefly at excluding Jewish musicians, stylizing the operas of Richard Wagner into cultic events, and denouncing both jazz and atonal music. The aesthetic needs of the Nazi bosses were largely met by operettas, dance tunes, and light music; marches and all manner of utilitarian music were en vogue. Yet alongside these kinds of musical expression stood the cultivation of the classics, one venue being a wealth of festivals, which also offered party leaders an opportunity for impressive public appearances.

Outside of Germany, concerts by first-rate orchestras and soloists also served as an alibi that Germany was a cultured nation. Compared with the composers and musicians who remained in Germany as opportunists or "apolitical" persons, chief among them Wilhelm Furtwängler and Richard Strauss (who even held the post of president of the Reich Music Chamber from 1933–1935), those who emigrated were in the minority. Paul Hindemith and Arnold Schönberg, Alban Berg, Ernst Krenek, and Kurt Weill, pilloried at the exhibition of "Degenerate Music" on the occasion of the Reich Music Days in Düsseldorf in 1938, were hardly missed, given the presence of composers promoted and honored by the regime, which included the likes of Carl Orff, Hans Pfitzner, and Werner Egk. Similarly, in the theater world the much-honored Gustaf Gründgens seemed to make up for the departure of Erwin Piscator, Max Reinhardt, and Fritz Kortner. A quite remarkable opportunism was demonstrated by the young conductor Herbert von Karajan, who became a member of the NSDAP twice in 1933, once in April in the Austrian city of Salzburg, although there was no compelling need to do so since the National Socialists were not in power there, and then in May in Ulm, which was a more favorable career move.

The entertainment sector flourished. Operettas and pop songs were the most popular musical genres, especially since they were hardly politicized. Like the innocuous entertainment films, we can see them as part of the regime's social policy, which kept the "*Volk* community" in high spirits with melodies by Nico Dostal, Paul Linke, and Franz Lehar, pop tunes sung by Zarah Leander, Evelyn Künneke, Marika Rökk, and Hans Albers, and cinematic audience favorites like Heinz Rühmann, Johannes Heesters, Luise Ullrich, Viktor de Kowa, Willy Birgel, Brigitte Horney, and many others. The Reich radio and the state-run film industry (beginning in 1937, Ufa [Germany's largest film company], the Tobias Company, and the new Terra Filmkunst were controlled by the Ministry of Propaganda) were suitable and highly popular instruments of mass entertainment.

Nazi society was characterized by a cult of youth to which the officials paid homage at every opportunity. In return, the regime placed the younger generation under obligation and claimed total control over it. Beginning in December 1936, the Hitler Youth, originally only the junior branch of the NSDAP, became the state youth league; starting in March 1939, membership was made compulsory, the goal being to reach all young people from the age of ten. The operative principle in the uniformed Hitler

Wilhelm Furtwängler, head of the Berlin Philharmonic after 1922 and of the Gewandhaus Orches-
tra in Leipzig until 1928, and director of the Vienna
Philharmonic in 1928–1930 and 1939–1940, was
the most celebrated conductor of his day. In 1933
he still supported Jewish musicians such as Bruno
Walter and Otto Klemperer. When Paul Hindemith's opera *Mathis der Maler (Mathis the Painter)*
was banned, he even stepped down from his post,
but after a private discussion with Goebbels he
made his peace with the regime. His style of monu-
mentality and deeply probing interpretation of the
classical and romantic repertoire set standards very
much in keeping with the spirit of the times. DIZ,
SV-Bilderdienst, Munich.

After a stint in the theater and his breakthrough with *Die Drei von der Tankstelle* (The Three from the Gas Station, 1930), Heinz Rühmann became a well-paid popular star. During the Third Reich he appeared in thirty-seven films, in most of which he embodied the prototype of the little man. Because of his close association with the regime, he separated from his Jewish wife in 1938, and she emigrated to Sweden following their divorce. The biggest hits of the "state actor," to whom Goebbels also took a personal liking, were his propagandistically staged films about military training at the Rechlin air base, *Quax der Bruchpilot* (Quax the Crash Pilot, 1941) and *Die Feuerzangenbowle* (The *Feuerzange* Punch, 1944). DIZ, SV-Bilderdienst, Munich.

Youth was "youth is led by youth." Physical training and ideological indoctrination were the primary purposes of a program that came to embrace nearly nine million youths. From age ten to fourteen they served as *Pimpfe* (boys) or *Jungmädel* (girls), then as Hitler youths during scouting games on the road and at Heritage Evenings (*Heimatabende*). For young women, following their stint in the League of German Girls (*Bund Deutscher Mädel*), there was the BDM Organization Faith and Beauty (BDM Werk Glaube und Schönheit), where girls between the ages of seventeen and twenty-one were prepared for their roles as wife and mother in the Nazi state. At the head of the state youth organization, whose sphere of authority embraced the entire "physical, spiritual, and moral education

Gustaf Gründgens is regarded as one of the greatest theatrical geniuses of the twentieth century. The stations of his meteoric career include appointments as director of the Berliner Schauspielhaus (1934), Prussian state councillor (1936), director general of the Prussian State Theater (1937), and "state actor." In his roman à clef, *Mephisto,* Klaus Mann portrayed Gründgens as the incarnation of a characterless opportunist who seeks the protection of those in power to fulfill his artistic ambitions. Deutsches Theatermuseum, Munich.

of youth" outside of the school and the family (and increasingly in competition with them), stood the youth leader of the Reich, who was simultaneously the head of a top-level Reich office and a party functionary with the title "Reich Youth Leader of the NSDAP." Until 1940 that post was held by Baldur von Schirach, who also made a name for himself as a lyricist with youth-inspired poems. Following his appointment as gauleiter and governor of Vienna, he was succeeded by Arthur Axmann, whose dubious posthumous fame rests on the fact that he sent children to defend Berlin in the spring of 1945.

The schools remained fairly untouched during the first years of the Third Reich, aside from the Gleichschaltung of teachers and the closing of private schools. And with the exception of ideological guidelines for history books and racial science, classroom content was also reshaped much less dramatically than it might have appeared from new militaristic rituals such as the honoring of the flag and the "German greeting." More far-reaching interventions in the educational system occurred between 1937 and 1941, when the secondary school system was confined to upper schools for boys, upper schools for girls, and a few humanistic grammar schools (*Gymnasien*), and when teacher training was simplified. In keeping with National Socialist ideology, the educational content was changed to convey a heroic picture of history, emphasize Germany's greatness and claim to world power status, and justify the exclusion of everything "foreign" with the help of racial and genetic "science." The effectiveness of these changes was limited, however, and the schools were, in general, not the place where the systematic indoctrination of German youth took place.

The situation was very different at the elite schools with which the regime experimented. The National Political Training Institutes (*Nationalpolitische Erziehungsanstalten,* NAPOLA) were state-run boarding schools whose students graduated with the requirements for university matriculation. These schools were under the personal supervision of the minister of education, Bernhard Rust. Beginning in 1936, the SS exerted a growing influence on the selection of students and the educational guidelines. After 1937, the NAPOLA had competition from the Adolf Hitler Schools, which were jointly supervised by the organization leader of the NSDAP and the Reich youth leader. Virtually identical to the NAPOLA in structure and educational ideal (the emphasis was on physical and ideological training), the goal of the Adolf Hitler Schools was to prepare the future leaders of the NSDAP. A special place was occupied by the Reich School of the NSDAP in Feldafing: founded as a private school for the SA, it was under the authority of the deputy of the Führer after 1936 and remained independent from the other Nazi elite schools.

The Third Reich was a male society. The image of woman was shaped by the idealization of her roles as mother and keeper of the home, educator of her children, and a wife under her husband's authority. She could incur guilt through "refusal to procreate" or infertility. The upbringing and education of girls was oriented toward the ideal of future motherhood. Higher schooling for girls was impeded, coeducation rejected outright. Until the war, when women were drawn on as a reserve labor force in large numbers and in violation of the reigning ideology, the regime did everything it could to keep women out of the workplace.

The idealization of motherhood was promoted by Mother's Day, which

Frau Dr. Johanna Haarer

Die deutsche Mutter und ihr erstes Kind

In 1934, physician Johanna Haarer (1900–1988) published *Die deutsche Mutter und ihr erstes Kind* (The German Mother and Her First Child). This seemingly nonpolitical book of advice on infant care in fact propagated the norms of the Nazi state where early childhood education was concerned. In the absence of competing books, this catechism for young mothers had huge print runs. With a slightly modified title and content, it is still available today. In her book *Mutter erzähl von Adolf Hitler!* (Mother, Tell Stories about Adolf Hitler! 1939), Haarer showed herself to be a fanatical activist for Nazi propaganda in the children's room. Bildarchiv Preußischer Kulturbesitz, Berlin.

became a permanent holiday after 1934, and after 1938 by the Honor Cross of the German Mother, a medal of honor awarded in three classes: bronze for women who had four to six children, silver for those who had six to eight children, and gold for those with eight children or more (provided the mother was a Reich German and the children were "Aryan" and "ge-

The Nazi ideal of womanhood was propagated in the League of German Girls (*Bund Deutscher Mädel*). Österreichische Gesellschaft für Zeitgeschichte, Vienna.

netically healthy" [*erbgesund*]). By September 1941, 4.7 million mother crosses had been awarded. These kinds of gestures (an honorary payment for mothers with many children was sacrificed to financial considerations) were intended to compensate for women's lack of political rights and men's hostility toward their emancipation. Even the Reich women's leader, the fanatical National Socialist Gertrud Scholtz-Klink, was subordinate to men in her high offices. As the leader of the National Socialist Women's League she was under the authority of the chief of the National Socialist People's Welfare Organization, and as head of the Women's Labor Service, the Women's League of the Red Cross, and the women's bureau of the DAF, she always had male superiors.

Celebrations were part of everyday life under the Nazi regime and included events such as the production battles (*Erzeugungsschlachten*) of the Reich Food Estate, the Reich Professional Competition of the DAF, and the yearly Winter Relief of the People's Welfare Organization. The cycle of festivals began on January 30 with a speech by Goebbels to the pupils in the morning, followed by a speech by Hitler to the Reichstag. The evening saw a reenactment of the torch parade of January 30, 1933. February 24 was Foundation Day, a commemoration that brought to-

Injured veterans of the First World War in front of the honor stands at an SA parade in Nuremberg, 1934. DIZ, SV-Bilderdienst, Munich.

gether the "old fighters" in Munich. Heroes' Remembrance Day, in March, celebrated with Wehrmacht parades in Berlin, replaced the National Day of Mourning under the Weimar Republic. On the last Sunday in March, fourteen-year-olds were ceremoniously admitted into the Hitler Youth. On the eve of Hitler's birthday, ten-year-olds were mustered

Leo von Klenze's Königsplatz in Munich, an elegant space from the early nineteenth century, was redesigned as a party forum according to plans by Paul Ludwig Troost. It was expanded on the eastern side with the addition of the Führerbau, Hitler's office building (left), and the Administrative Building of the NSDAP. Behind, in immediate proximity, lay the old party headquarters, the Brown House. At the center of the forum were two honorary temples, to which the remains of the "casualties of the movement," those killed in the 1923 putsch, were transferred on November 9, 1935. The Königliche Platz, as it was called after 1937, was the chief cultic site of the NSDAP. Klenze's grass had to make way for flagstones in 1936. (The temples were dynamited in 1947, the lawn was restored in 1988.) Zentrum für Antisemitismusforschung, Berlin.

into the junior division. The Führer's birthday on April 20 was observed with pomp, military parades in all garrison cities, and a party celebration (usually in Munich, at the party forum in the Königsplatz). On this occasion new party functionaries were sworn in. May 1, National Labor Day, celebrated with heritage groups and folk dance troupes, was supposed to displace the traditional Socialist day of international labor solidarity from popular memory. It was followed on the second Sunday in May by Mother's Day—the Nazis did not invent this holiday either, but successfully appropriated it to their cause. It received official recognition by the first awarding of the Honor Cross to three million mothers in 1939.

Between 1937 and 1939, the summer solstice in June was observed with mass events in the Olympic stadium in Berlin. The annual cycle of festivals reached its high point in September with the mass spectacle of the party rally in Nuremberg. This was followed by Harvest Thanksgiving Day, celebrated by hundreds of thousands on the Bückeberg near Hameln. In 1937, the crowd numbered no less than 1.2 million: Hitler walked through its midst, on a "path through the *Volk*," to the harvest altar at the top of the mountain, where, in the name of the nation, he received the harvest crown from the Farmers' Estate. On the evening of November 8, the "old fighters" met in the Bürgerbräukeller in Munich to commemorate the attempted putsch of 1923. On November 9, the "martyrs of the movement" were remembered in a macabre ceremony. That same day those who had finished their stint in the Hitler Youth were admitted into the NSDAP; the festivities concluded with knightly oaths of loyalty by the new SS generation. The last two entries in the annual cycle of Nazi festivals did not meet with an enthusiastic reception: the Winter Solstice, introduced in 1935, and the Yule Festival, a Germanization of Christmas.

This is by no means an exhaustive catalog of festivals and rituals. There were all kinds of special occasions with marches by formations in uniform, speeches by party notables, and prescribed jubilation.

National celebrations, monumental self-presentations, an unending stream of suggestive speeches by the Führer, the entertainment, leisure time, and cultural activities of the Third Reich, which reached their heyday in the years before the war—all of this was, in the end, merely compensation for the strains and stresses of everyday life and competitive struggle in the Third Reich.

5

THE HITLER STATE

IT WAS NOT ONLY the majority of the bureaucratic, military, economic, and cultural elites who came to an arrangement with the National Socialists, either in voluntary and joyous submission or because they felt "compelled" to do so by opportunism. After the regime's first string of successes, the majority of the population was happy to accommodate itself to the new state of affairs. Constitutional theorists, both prominent and opportunistic representatives of the field, moved swiftly to furnish the theoretical underpinnings (in the form of new definitions) of National Socialism, and to provide it with a conception of the state that would match the ideological claim from its early years as a movement and reflect the situation following its assumption of power. Carl Schmitt, a professor of constitutional and international law in Berlin and a member of the NSDAP since May 1, 1933, was one of the first who brushed aside the entire catalogue of standards and norms of the liberal-democratic Weimar Constitution. In its stead he postulated a tripartite structure of "state, movement, *Volk*" (also the title of his 1933 pamphlet) as the new framework of the state, the organizational outline of a political entity.

The NSDAP, as the movement, outranked the two other elements (*Volk* and state) of the new constitutional trinity and was responsible for its overall unity, thus representing the "constitution of the political unity." Schmitt went on: "Every one of the three words, 'state,' 'movement,' 'people,' may be utilized for the whole of the political unit. But, simultaneously, each characterizes a specific side and element of the whole. Therefore, the state permits itself to be designated in a narrower sense as the politically static part, the movement as the politically dynamic element,

GERMANY
BERLIN·1936
1ˢᵗ-16ᵗʰ AUGUST

OLYMPIC GAMES
INFORMATION AND HANDBOOKS FROM ALL TOURIST AND TRAVEL AGENCIES

The 1936 Olympic Games in Berlin and Garmisch-Partenkirchen, staged as the"Festival of Nations," were used by the regime as an opportunity to display a "new Germany." Never before had a host nation invested so much money to take advantage of the games for self-promotion. The organization, the accompanying programs, but also the athletic achievements of the German team made the games a splendid propaganda success for the Third Reich. AKG-images, London.

and the people constitute the nonpolitical side which [realizes itself] under the protection and shadow of political decisions." The state in the narrower definition was, according to Schmitt, the executive, administrative, and judicial organization. The "state and *Volk*-bearing" NSDAP was an elite, an order, but also a movement that one could continue to call a party (since misunderstandings could now be ruled out). As such it was to pervade and lead the state and the *Volk*. The latter, finally, was defined as a sphere entrusted to self-government, one that encompassed the economic and social order based on professional groups as well as communal self-administration. Although the Schmittean model of the "tripartite structure of the political unity" is unequivocal in its jubilant condemnation of the liberal-democratic system, it replaces it with a vague terminology that is of no use whatsoever in either interpreting the reality of the National Socialist state or offering a constitutional-theoretical explanation for it.

The year 1933 also saw the publication of the book *Der Totale Staat* (The Total State) by Ernst Forsthoff, a promising young professor of constitutional and administrative law. In it Forsthoff distinguished a governing order (*Herrschaftsordnung*) from a national order (*Volksordnung*). The former rested on the distinction between leading and being led as the ordering principle of the state, a distinction that could only be metaphysically realized. In other words, while subjection to Adolf Hitler's personal claim to leadership was—according to Forsthoff—sufficient to establish the total state, it was not sufficient for the continuation of that state beyond Hitler's death. The principle of authority and the supra-personal "Führer principle" were to be combined in the authoritarian state. A comprehensive worldview was to provide the connecting link and stabilizing element in this equation. The so-called *Volksordnung* rested on a corporatist structure on the basis of a "racially similar" (*artgleiche*) community and shared convictions. In plain language that meant the exclusion of enemies, explicitly the Jews as members of a "foreign race," and the "binding nature of a single ideology." In the final analysis, Forsthoff's programmatic tract about the total state was nothing more than the opportunistic attempt to reconcile the ideology and the success of the NSDAP and its Führer in the "struggle period" with the actions taken in 1933 from a position of power. In essence Forsthoff was not talking about a total state but an authoritarian state that would require a twofold structure: a predictable and bureaucratic side and a commanding and hierarchical side organized in the form of personal rule. The early attempts by Schmitt, Forsthoff, and others to explain the Nazi state, to subject it to catego-

Illustrative material for classroom lessons on
racial studies and eugenics, 1938. The title reads,
"Spending for those with hereditary diseases—
social consequences." The caption reads, "Reform
school in E. with 130 mentally retarded—annual
expenses around 104,000 reichsmarks—for this
money one could build 17 single-family homes
for genetically healthy workers' families. Those
with hereditary diseases are a burden on the *Volk!*"
Zentrum für Antisemitismusforschung, Berlin.

rization and at the same time to participate in shaping it, missed the reality of the Third Reich, not least because they sought to distill a kind of National Socialist doctrine of the regime from Nazi ideology.

By contrast, later explanatory models, such as Ernst Fraenkel's theory of the "dual state" (Fraenkel published a work of the same title in 1940–1941 from exile in the United States) and Franz Neumann's *Behemoth* (published simultaneously in German and the United States in 1942), analyzed and systematized the actual structures of the Nazi state.

Fraenkel, drawing on compelling criteria, most of which he derived from the spheres of law and justice, highlighted the coexistence of the competing systems of a "normative state" and a "prerogative state" as the central feature of Nazi rule. Franz Neumann, on the other hand, diagnosed the fundamental problem in the antinomy between the state and the Nazi movement, with its tendency to dissolve all formal or functionally consistent forms of political power. In August 1944, when he was writing the preface to the second edition of his book, Neumann saw the development of the Nazi regime heading in a direction in which the dualism of state and party would be abolished, "the remnants of the rational and administrative state" completely obliterated. The party would replace the state with the "amorphous, shapeless movement, thus transforming the little that remains of the state into more or less organized anarchy." But Neumann was perhaps the first who also understood the Nazi system as a process of continual change. This sets his interpretation apart from many later attempts, especially those undertaken under the banner of a political theory of totalitarianism. These accounts proceeded from a variety of false premises: either they presumed, given the efficiency with which National Socialism engaged in evil, a monolithic structure of power and a corresponding, well thought-out technique of rule, or they overestimated the ideology of National Socialism and therefore came to see the state and the party as a consistent, rationally operating machine for the implementation of programmatic goals.

Like all Fascist movements that arose in Europe after the First World War, National Socialism had no intellectually self-contained program and no theoretical framework for the construction of state and society. Unlike Communist ideology, the Fascist movements and the regimes they erected were content with a few basic convictions that were constructed from various elements: nationalistic attitudes were always present; racist (especially anti-Semitic), *völkisch,* and xenophobic views were a usual part of the mix; anti-Communist components were a universal and anticapitalist elements a frequent ingredient. With the help of a panoply of antimodernist, antiliberal, and antidemocratic components, the regimes used these basic convictions to engage in demagoguery. The "Führer principle" went hand in hand with the exclusion and persecution of discriminated minorities, the propagation of the right of the stronger, the implementation of political goals through brutal force, the glorification of war, and contempt for any kind of weakness. A characteristic feature of all Fascist movements were paramilitary groups, whose function it was to fight opponents as well as integrate followers.

Once power had been attained, which was the primary and true goal, the declared claim of Fascist rule was to infuse state and society with the postulates of its ideology. In Italy, Benito Mussolini had staged the March on Rome in October 1922, which was not a seizure of power but the prelude to being given a mandate to govern in alliance with conservative elites. Hitler, in his second attempt, far surpassed *il duce,* whom he admired, by forcing through his claim to power against all competitors and reshaping the state and society. He was able to do so not because of the persuasive power of National Socialist ideology, but thanks to propaganda, political tactics, and help from conservative partners.

The party program of the NSDAP, proclaimed on February 20, 1920, in the beery haze of the Hofbräuhaus in Munich, was a hodgepodge of attractive phrases and popular demands that were summarized in the Twenty-Five Points and declared "unalterable" in 1926. Important points were the demand for a Greater Germany in which the boundaries of the *Volk* should coincide with the borders of the Reich; the revocation of the peace treaties of 1919; the expansion of German colonization; the exclusion of Jews from German citizenship; the restriction of citizenship to "*Volk* comrades," who were defined by racial criteria ("German blood"); and a halt to immigration. The vague demands that Roman law be replaced by German law and that national health standards be raised, the calls for "legal warfare against intentional political lies and their dissemination through the press," for "positive Christianity," and for a struggle against the "Jewish-materialistic spirit" answered the need for verbal radicalism. Early followers and voters probably took more seriously the party program points promising the "abolition of all income unearned by work and exertion" and the breaking "of interest slavery," the "confiscation of all war profits," the "nationalization of all corporations," the "creation of a healthy middle class," the "immediate socialization of the huge department stores and their lease, at low rates, to small tradesmen," land reform, and a "ruthless battle against . . . common criminals, usurers, and profiteers."

And promises is all they would remain. Ideology, where it did not concern racial and expansionary goals, was primarily decoration. Propaganda, as Hitler had made it very clear to his faithful followers early on, was more important than any discussion of the program, the last of which took place at a meeting of the NSDAP leadership in Bamberg in 1926; thereafter Hitler put a stop to any debate. All attempts to challenge Hitler's leadership by means of the party program had run their course prior to 1933 and were settled when the internal opposition either left the NSDAP (in the case of Straßer) or submitted to Hitler (in the case of Goebbels).

The party comrades had a need for an explanation of how the world worked, for a social and political vision, and for a self-contained edifice of ideas that encapsulated their longings and desires. Hitler met that need with the monologues he delivered for hours on end to a fascinated audience at his rallies, which were staged to perfection. Anybody who was so inclined could pick up *Mein Kampf* to find out what sort of worldview had triumphed with Hitler's leadership.

In contrast to the Fascist movement in Italy, the NSDAP was a party largely focused on and integrated by its leader. It was precisely its ideological deficit that made possible the Hitler party's remarkable unity. Italian Fascism, in comparison, had three basic currents—nationalists, agrarian Fascists, and syndicalists—with many additional differentiations. Wolfgang Schieder has described it as a "loose association of power groups centered around individuals and competing with one another for primacy within the movement." Instead of ideological differences, the NSDAP had rivalries and power struggles, with Hitler functioning to the very end as the undisputed authority to mediate and settle them. These internal party rivalries played a decisive part in preserving the dictator's power.

On January 30, 1933, the NSDAP had about 850,000 members, most—though by no means all—recruited from the lower middle class, the petty bourgeoisie. One-third of the NSDAP counted itself among the working class; about half of them were unemployed at the end of the Weimar Republic. There were relatively few women in the party, but substantially more young people than were found in the ranks of the bourgeois parties or the Social Democrats. A huge influx of new members began after January 30, 1933; by May 1, the number of party comrades had tripled. The ratio of "old fighters" to "March casualties" alone makes clear that it would be difficult for the NSDAP to maintain the claim that it was the elite formation in the National Socialist state.

Civil servants and teachers, in particular, were strongly represented among the new members in the spring of 1933. Although they drew the suspicious attention of the party leadership, they did promote the trend of the NSDAP toward becoming the state party, a trend that emerged inevitably after the takeover of power. On December 1, 1933, the government issued the Law for Securing the Unity of Party and State. This law was significant primarily for three provisions: the NSDAP was given the status of an institution of public law; the Führer's deputy and the chief of the SA became part of the government; and the party was granted jurisdiction over its members. More interesting than the language of the law are the official party attempts at defining the relationship between party and state that were made in its wake. An official party statement in 1936 declared that it was conceivable for "party and state to be one and the same," namely when all party comrades believed in the party's worldview and the laws of the state were the clear expression of that view. The ideal state would then consist of the community of like-minded individuals. Such illusions, however, were mere stylization for the benefit of the national comrades.

The dynamism of the movement—whether it actually still existed or whether it was merely invoked in memory of the "struggle period"—was to live on. To that end the party had to preserve at least the appearance of

Heinrich Hoffmann, a member of Hitler's inner circle since 1921, took on the title Reich Photojournalist and monopolized the photographic documentation of party life and Hitler's "court." In this 1933 photo he is shown taking a group picture of the Reich leaders and gauleiters with Hitler in the center. With the appointment of Reich governors (*Reichsstatthalter*), the states, which had been politically "coordinated" in 1933, lost their sovereign rights. By 1934 the federal system had been eliminated. Nearly all governors were also NSDAP gauleiter. DIZ, SV-Bilderdienst, Munich.

an elite minority, though naturally one that had the right "to continually infuse the apparatus of the state with the currents of its intellect and will. The party must preserve this function for itself, and it must be vigilant not to become excessively bound up in the state's bureaucratic machinery. Should it fail to do so, it runs the risk of being devoured by the bureaucracy of the state and rigidifying into a party bureaucracy itself." The compromise between the distant ideal and the actual state of affairs desired for now was put this way in party parlance: "If the *Volk* in all its parts has not yet been pervaded by the party and its worldview, party and state must remain separate. The party will then be an order in which a selection of the leader and the fighters takes place. These fighters disseminate the worldview among the *Volk*. The party should prepare the emotions and will of the people for legislative activity, so that the emotional state of the *Volk* will be in harmony with the actual laws of the state." This passage comes from the "Organisationsbuch der NSDAP" (Organizational Handbook of the NSDAP), the primer for party comrades and officials that was published in a new edition every year and contained definitions, organizational charts, and descriptions of the various hierarchies.

The party was thus responsible for educating and training the nation and for selecting leaders for positions of power within the state. The function of the NSDAP lay in making the people receptive to the government's measures and supporting the goals of the leadership of the state by means of propaganda. And this was the deeper meaning of the Law for Securing the Unity of Party and State, namely to separate the two spheres of power.

The law declared the NSDAP to be "the representative of the German state idea and indissolubly linked to the state." But it was not entirely clear what that meant. There was the nebulous plan (never implemented) for a future connection between the top echelons of party and state in the form of a Great Senate. This Senate, on the one hand a pure party institution, on the other hand the highest body of the state, was vaguely propagated as a kind of National Socialist college of cardinals that would choose a successor to Hitler when the day came.

The institutional interconnection of party and state occurred in a certain fashion on the level of the *Gau* leaders who simultaneously held state offices. In 1935, six of the total of thirty gauleiters in the territory of the Reich were also the supreme presidents (*Oberpräsidenten*) of Prussian provinces, ten were governors, two (Goebbels and Rust) were ministers. Of the six Bavarian gauleiters, two were also in charge of administrative districts, one was state minister, and one, Josef Bürckel, held the office of commissioner for the Saar region after 1935. However, with the exception of the supreme presidents, who had power and influence within the official Prussian channels, these state offices were not very significant: the governors, with authority that was not clearly defined, stood more alongside than above the mediatized state governments and had primarily decorative functions as representative and supervisory organs at the behest of the Reich government. But after the Gleichschaltung of the states, at the latest after the crushing of the SA, there was little left to supervise. It was only after the outbreak of war, when defense commissioners were appointed for every defense district, that a number of gauleiters were given administrative and political responsibilities that carried real power: they could call on the individual "*Volk* comrade" to render services or contributions in kind and could intervene in the organization and personnel policy of the general administration.

Yet the NSDAP was not content to provide functionaries for state positions as an elite and cadre party and otherwise exert a propaganda influence on the *Volk* through its own leadership corps and apparatus. Beyond its own party members, millions of people were marshaled in the various organizations—SA, SS, National Socialist Motor Corps, Hitler Youth, National Socialist German Students' League, and National Socialist Women's Organization. And the associated organizations, too, were instruments of rule with existential meaning for the individual person, regardless of his or her position toward National Socialism. Following the crushing of the SA, the SS developed its own small empire within the National Socialist state; at the same time, as the special executive power of the Nazi state, it was its most loyal organ.

The associated organizations of the NSDAP had grown out of the coordination campaign and the compulsory consolidation of professional and other associations: they included the National Socialist German Physicians' League, the National Socialist Lawyers' Association, the National Socialist People's Welfare Organization, the Reich Civil Service League, and more. The most important organization was the German Labor Front (DAF) with a membership five times that of the NSDAP. In 1938 the DAF counted 23 million members on its rolls, in 1942 about 25 million; they were commanded by a monstrous bureaucracy of 40,000 functionaries.

After the quashing of the unions, the DAF was the sole organization representing workers, white-collar employees, artisans, and tradespeople. But it had neither the right to negotiate wage contracts nor any way to influence the regulations governing work and vacation time. The task of the DAF was to "form a true *Volk* and achievement community of all Germans," as the relevant decree by the Führer put it. This meant political education of its members. But that task had also been assigned to the NSDAP itself, and competition between the party and the DAF was thus inevitable. The same is true for the series of conflicts that arose because the head of the DAF, Robert Ley, was simultaneously the Reich organization leader of the NSDAP and because the bureaucracy of the DAF, octopus-like, extended its reach everywhere.

The top organizational echelon of the NSDAP was anything but a homogenous party bureaucracy or a tight mechanism of control and guidance. It was not only the struggles over competence and the rivalries among the *Reichsleiter* of the NSDAP—some of whom had real power

At the Königsplatz in Munich: Deputy of the Führer Rudolf Hess, center, with his hand raised in the Hitler greeting; to his right, the head of the DAF, Robert Ley; to his left, Martin Bormann; at far left, Max Amann, president of the Reich Press Chamber and managing director of the party's publishing house and of the *Völkischer Beobachter*. DIZ, SV-Bilderdienst, Munich.

while others had none, although those things could change very rapidly—that prevented the center from sending steady and effective guidance down to the lower ranks. One of the most important structural features of the NSDAP was that power evolved on a personal level: a person's position was determined not so much by the office he held as by a catalogue of personal and systemic qualities and merits, such as subordination, ties to the Führer, toughness, the strength to prevail over competitors, and the merits he had earned in the "struggle period."

One of the reasons comparisons between the NSDAP and Communist parties miss the mark is because the National Socialist party center was institutionally weak and often unable to impose itself on the lower party structure. The real power centers of the party lay at the level of the gauleiters and below. The self-confident men at the middle level insisted on recognition of the old merits they had earned in the movement and had personal ties to Hitler. Moreover, after 1933 some of them were given special state powers and commissions (especially during the war, in the administration of the newly conquered territories), one feature of which was that those who exercised them were responsible solely to Hitler. But that was essentially an increase in power geared toward the individual, a reward for a vassal's loyalty, and it was only indirectly related to the structural weakness of the top NSDAP leadership.

The party apparatus had a tendency to evade control and intervention by the top party echelon, the Führer's deputy, and the departmental *Reichsleiter* of the NSDAP. In 1942, the gauleiter of Oldenburg, Carl Röver, noted that the authority of the NSDAP center had suffered considerably, in particular from the quarrels between the top functionaries. He went on to say that "a unified and uniformly led corps of higher party leaders no longer exists," every man "has more or less gone on out on his own." Martin Bormann, who, as head of the party chancellery, took over the duties of the Führer's deputy in greatly enhanced form (after Rudolf Hess had flown to England on a self-appointed peace mission), tried strenuously to contain the urge by top functionaries to make themselves independent, to restore the institutional homogeneity of the party, and to break the positions that were directly responsible to Hitler; he failed. However, following precisely the principle he was fighting, he derived considerable benefit for his own position from his activities. Beginning in 1943 he carried the additional title of secretary to the Führer, and as such he controlled access to Hitler by most other top functionaries, who first had to come to an arrangement with him (sometimes as the final authority). It was of no great importance any longer whether these functionaries were from the state or party apparatus. Over time the institutional differences between them were increasingly eroded. The relationship between state and party had early on been fixed in a kind of state of suspension.

Therein lies another difference from Italian Fascism. After the phase in which National Socialism deployed its power and imposed itself politically, in 1934 the dynamism of the movement was suspended, to the chagrin of the party's proponents of vigorous action. Having opted for a stabilization of the system, which until 1938 was sought above all in bringing the leadership of the state into harmony with the conservative elites in the bureaucracy, the military, and the judiciary, the NSDAP was consigned to secondary spheres of action. The dictum that "the party commands the state" was proclaimed, though its application was at best indirect. In Italy, the Fascist movement, following its takeover of power, was clearly subordinate to the state, which is why there was no possibility of revitalizing it. In contrast, the vague integration of the NSDAP under the postulate of the unity of party and state did allow for the revival and radicalization of the party after 1939, thereby making possible the regime's tremendous explosion of energy during the years of war and in its final phase.

The constitutional state had finally perished in June of 1934. What characterized the organization and exercise of Nazi rule was the erosion of the state as it had been understood until then, namely as the regular, uniformly organized exercise of public power. The normative state was replaced by a very different prerogative state. That state's crucial component was the power of the Führer, in which the official authority of the state and non-normative authority merged in a new form of personal absolutism. This absolutism was bound neither by the norms of positive law nor by a moral law that preceded the state; moreover, it claimed the right to suspend them both.

Legitimacy was derived from metaphysical formulas such as "the historical mission" or "the law of life of the German *Volk*." The Führer's claim to power imposed itself only gradually, through the accumulation of the highest state offices in the person of Hitler, in combination with the leadership of the party. The process took place on the basis of laws and decrees that were initially based on the Weimar Constitution, through the breakup of state power into a multitude of departmental polyocracies, and through the circumvention and erosion of state authorities.

In the end, the authority of the Führer, which imposed itself ever more clearly as the exclusive principle of government during the regime's war years and final phase, also suspended the duality of party and state. As it was, the functional division according to which the party was to articulate the political will of the people and the state was to execute that will bureaucratically had remained mere theory, because both the NSDAP and the state could be used, alternatively and complementarily, as instruments of the Führer's power.

While the uncoordinated coexistence and clash of state and party offices often undermined "the consistency and uniformity with which power was exercised," it stabilized "the ruling system as a whole and the absolutism of the Führer at the top," according to Martin Broszat. It mattered little to this mechanism that Hitler, transfigured by the myth that surrounded his person, had become far removed from the apparatus, or that the Führer's will was voiced only sporadically and contradictorily through intermediaries. On many occasions, Hitler's reluctance to settle conflicts, whether by calculation or some other reason, acted as a spur and an incentive to his underlings.

At the same time, however, because of the growing internal organizational chaos, the regime increasingly lost the character of state rule. Franz Neumann recognized this as early as 1941, when he wrote, "But if the National Socialist structure is not a state, what is it? I venture to suggest that we are confronted with a form of society in which the ruling groups control the rest of the population directly, without the mediation of that rational though coercive apparatus hitherto known as the state. This new social form is not yet fully realized, but the trend exists which defines the very essence of the regime."

6

ECONOMIC AND SOCIAL POLICY

ON FEBRUARY 1, 1933, HITLER mentioned two primary goals of the government that were to be achieved in four-year plans. Characteristically, he did not do this before the Reichstag but in a radio proclamation to the German *Volk* late in the evening. His speech was reprinted in the *Völkischer Beobachter,* published as a pamphlet, and posted on the advertising kiosks common in German towns and cities. Using the martial diction of National Socialism, Hitler announced the "rescue of the German farmer" in order to preserve the foundation of the nation's food supply and existence, and the "rescue of the German worker" through a massive and comprehensive "assault on unemployment." He emphasized the seriousness of his intent with the often-quoted line "Now, German *Volk,* give us four years' time, and then judge and pass sentence on us!"

Unemployment—a consequence of the crisis in the world economy after 1930 and the cause of political crises and the impoverishment of the population—was a crucial background factor for the rise of the NSDAP and its takeover of power. Hitler had been tireless in promising an end to the misery: his government would stand or fall on its success or failure to keep this promise, and quickly, for rule based solely on terror could not be sustained indefinitely.

The crisis had hit its high point in January 1932, when unemployment reached more than 6 million (although we must add to the official statistics the invisible army of part-time workers, emergency relief workers, and other hidden unemployed). In January 1933 the number was not much lower. But there were signs that the world economic crisis was subsiding, and the job creation programs put in place by Hitler's predecessors were

REICHSAUTOBAHNEN
in DEUTSCHLAND

Highways (*Autobahnen*) were of the highest prestige value for the Third Reich. As the "roads of
the Führer," their importance went far beyond
their role in traffic engineering. The company
Reichsautobahnen was established in June 1933,
after the Association for the Preparation of the
Roadway Hanseatic Cities–Frankfurt–Basel
(HAFRABA) had presented detailed highway
plans. The project was ideal for mass employment,
which could be put to good propaganda use. By
the middle of 1936, 125,000 people were working
on highway construction sites, providing everywhere a vivid demonstration that the regime
was conquering unemployment. However, the
new roadways, 3,000 kilometers of which had
been finished by December 1936, had no military
significance. Transporting troops and materiel
remained the task of the railroads. The cost of
the highways was exorbitant: by the time work
was halted in 1941–1942, about six billion reichsmarks had been spent, most of which came from
social security contributions. Deutsches Historisches Museum, Berlin.

Julius Streicher (foreground), gauleiter of Franconia and publisher of the anti-Semitic paper *Der Stürmer,* and Fritz Todt, inspector general of the German Road and Highway System, inaugurate a new stretch of highway near Nuremberg. DIZ, SV-Bilderdienst, Munich.

starting to take effect. The German economy recovered more quickly than those of neighboring countries, but credit for that did not yet belong to National Socialist policy, which built on the concepts and policies of the Weimar Republic. Subsequently, the German economy was favored by the international trend, and eventually—and most importantly—it displayed a new willingness to take risks in the financing of programs.

Hjalmar Schacht, appointed president of the Reichsbank in March 1933, pleaded successfully for the hitherto uncommon policy of deficit spending, which accepted massive borrowing to jump-start the economy. Two laws for reducing unemployment, passed in June and September 1933, provided financial tools in the form of loans to states and communities. These loans were used to create work and jobs that were favorable to the middle class during the first two years of National Socialist rule and paid homage to the ideology of the nobility of manual labor, an ideology intended to overcome class barriers. Public-interest labor service aimed at improving and cultivating the land avoided the use of machines as much as possible in order to employ the greatest number of workers, as did the highway project. Marriage loans—which simultaneously served a population policy that rewarded reproduction—were also measures to combat unemployment, since the interest-free loans required (until the fall of 1937) that the woman give up her job or refrain from entering the workforce in the first place. Finally, the introduction of compulsory military service in March 1935 and of a compulsory six-month stint in the Labor Service in June 1935 took pressure off the labor market. Of course, the numbers were also fudged to clearly highlight the regime's successes in the so-called labor battle, the fight against unemployment. Those employed in emergency work in the Labor Service, and young people given agricultural work for little pay as part of the job creation program no longer appeared in the unemployment statistics, even though they were not gainfully employed under normal conditions. The breakup of the unions and the new "Führer principle" within companies made it easier to control the labor market: workers' right to strike, right of association, and freedom of movement were no longer an issue, while wages and working conditions were dictated by the government's trustees of labor.

Nevertheless, the government's success was dramatic. In 1933 the number of unemployed still averaged just under 5 million. In 1934, the average for the year dropped to 2.71 million (with a high of 3.61 million); by 1935 there were 2.15 million unemployed (the year having begun with just under 3 million), and by 1936 full employment was reached in sectors such as construction and the metal industry. In 1937–1938, many companies were already complaining of a shortage of workers.

When it came to the loudly proclaimed efforts to "rescue the German farmer," the first thing farmers noted was the "coordination" of agrarian associations and agricultural organizations, followed by control of the production and distribution of agricultural products by the Reich Food Estate. Such vaunted achievements of the new regime as the removal of Jewish cattle traders soon showed their downsides: contrary to anti-Semitic propaganda, relationships of trust had often existed between farmers and Jewish traders; more important, Jewish dealers had advanced credit until the next harvest, whereas the functionaries of the Reich Food Estate acted as the ruthless agents of the new compulsory organization.

Following the 50 percent debt relief promulgated in June 1933, and the

Hjalmar Schacht was a crucial figure in the financial policies of the Third Reich. In December 1923 he was named president of the Reichsbank, but he resigned that position in 1930 following disagreements with the government over Germany's foreign debt. After that he joined the Harzburg Front (an alliance of rightist nationalists who opposed the government of Chancellor Heinrich Brüning). He played a role in Hitler's rise to power by recommending him to Hindenburg and to big industrialists. In March 1933, Hitler reappointed him president of the Reichsbank and made him minister of economics in August 1934. As plenipotentiary-general of the war economy after the end of 1935, he became entangled in turf battles with Göring, resigning his post as economics minister in November 1937 and his position as president of the Reichsbank in January 1939, though he remained in Hitler's government until 1943 as minister without portfolio. Later Schacht had loose contact with the opposition that was forming in response to the course the war was taking. He was arrested at the end of July 1944 and sent to the Ravensbrück concentration camp, then to the Flossenbürg camp. The international military tribunal in Nuremberg acquitted him in October 1946. A subsequent de-Nazification court deemed him a "major offender" and sentenced him to eight years in a labor camp. That sentence was thrown out on appeal in September 1948, clearing the way for Schacht's postwar career as a banker and financial adviser. DIZ, SV-Bilderdienst, Munich.

simultaneous and not very effective Law on the Re-formation of German Farmers, which was supposed to help young farmers without claim to an inheritance acquire landholdings, the Hereditary Farm Law of September 1933 seemed a trailblazing approach to meeting the interests and needs of the farmers. At least that is how the propaganda machine presented this pinnacle of National Socialist agrarian ideology. Henceforth, a hereditary farm (*Erbhof*) was any farm or forest holding large enough to support one family, but no more than 125 hectares. A hereditary farm passed to the principal heir intact; the rights of co-inheritors were limited to training in a profession, refuge (*Heimatzuflucht,* the right to return to the farm in dire circumstances), and dowry. In addition, hereditary farms could not be mortgaged. While this did place heavily indebted farms beyond the reach of creditors, it prevented the necessary investments because of a lack of capital, and the farmer's loss of freedom of movement and control over his property were also considered drawbacks.

The ideological guise did not make up for the downsides of the policy, and these soon revealed themselves in a rural exodus from the land and in the technological modernization of many hereditary farms, which was not supposed to be possible. The law paid solemn homage to farmers as the "blood source of the German *Volk.*" Only the owner of a hereditary farm, who was honorable, a German citizen, and "of German or kindred blood" (which had to be documented in a great proof of ancestry going back to 1800), was called a *Bauer* (peasant) under the new law. Large landholders and smallholders were not permitted to carry this lofty title — they were mere *Landwirte* (farmers).

The sort of land reform that would have been required to improve the agrarian structure was not undertaken, out of deference to the medium and large enterprises. Much like the ideology about the promotion of the middle class, the agrarian policy of the Third Reich was largely limited to declamations, while assigning agriculture a place among the regime's practical necessities. Despite the continuing and growing rural exodus, and the resultant decline in the number of agricultural workers, caused not least by competition in the labor market from the armament industry, the level of self-sufficiency rose to over 80 percent. Harvest service by the Hitler Youth, the compulsory year for women eighteen to twenty-five who wanted to take up a profession, and the Labor Service were not able to fill the gap in the demand for agricultural labor, nor were they able to smooth out social tensions and class differences, as the government tirelessly proclaimed. It was hardly possible to speak of happy farmers who were in agreement with the regime and repaid the propagandistic ego-

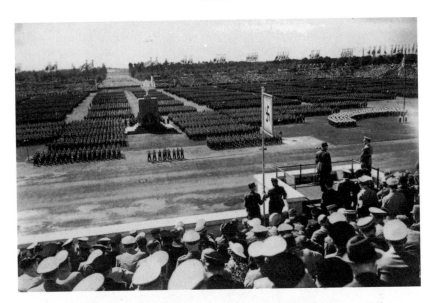

Great muster of the Reich Labor Service at the NSDAP rally in 1937. "The Reich Labor Service is a service of honor to the German *Volk*. All young Germans of both sexes are required to serve their *Volk* in the Labor Service. The Reich Labor Service is intended to educate the German youth in the spirit of National Socialism into a *Volk* community and to instill an honest attitude toward work, especially a proper respect for manual labor." To combat mass unemployment, the Brüning government, beginning in 1931, promoted voluntary labor service for the public good. By eliminating all competing institutions, Konstantin Hierl, a party member since 1929 and until 1932 Organization Leader II of the NSDAP, managed to "coordinate" the entire organization in 1933 into the NS Labor Service. Hierl, a retired colonel, reached his goal in June 1935, when service was made compulsory by law and the Reich Labor Service (*Reichsarbeitsdienst*) was established as a state organization: upon reaching the age of eighteen, all Germans were required to perform six months of labor service, which was organized in military fashion in camps. Österreichische Gesellschaft für Zeitgeschichte, Vienna.

stroking with devotion to National Socialism. Party statistics from 1935 reveal that only 12.6 percent of party comrades were farmers. And the Gestapo, in a situation report in 1936, reached the devastating conclusion that the farmer "was the person least reached by National Socialism." He was the most reticent during meetings, had the least attendance at party events, and press advertising was least successful with him.

The economy of the German Reich had recovered more quickly from the world economic crisis than the economies of other countries. In part this was the result of long-term economic cycles, but mostly it was due

After initially keeping his distance, industrial magnate Gustav Krupp von Bohlen und Halbach, shown here greeting Hitler at the entrance to his villa Hügel in Essen, became very close to the regime. In 1933 he appealed for donations to the Adolf Hitler Fund of the German Economy, and in 1934 he was made chairman of the Reich Association of German Industry (*Reichsverband der deutschen Industrie*). DIZ, SV-Bilderdienst, Munich.

to the effect of the government's path toward autarchy and rearmament, pursued and guided with the help of state contracts from 1934 on. The financing schemes were as ingenious as they were adventurous. As a way of creating credit, Schacht had come up with the system of "Mefo bills of exchange." For that purpose, a Metallurgische Forschungsgesellschaft (Metallurgical Research Society, Mefo for short) was set up in April 1933 as a fictitious company. Its capital of one million reichsmarks was raised from companies in heavy industry, Krupp, Siemens, Gutehoffnungshütte, and Rheinmetall. Interest-bearing bills eventually totaling 12 bil-

Berlin ißt heute sein Eintopfgericht

In the summer of 1933, under the umbrella of the National Socialist People's Welfare Organization (*Nationalsozialistische Volkswohlfahrt,* NSV), the Winter Relief Fund (*Winterhilfswerk,* WHW) was called into being as a sensational action to aid the needy. Donations from businesses and organizations, door-to-door and street collections, and wage deductions raised considerable sums of money. The goal of the WHW was not only to finance the activities of the NSV, but also to instill in the public a willingness to sacrifice and the spirit of *Volk* community. Public "one-pot Sundays," where the Nazi elite put in an appearance, demonstrated the goals of enforced frugality. The banner reads, "Today Berlin eats its one-pot meal." DIZ, SV-Bilderdienst, Munich.

lion reichsmarks were drawn on this company, with a maturity date beginning in 1938. Because the bills could not be paid, the money presses were started up and the financing of armaments and full employment was pursued with an inflationary monetary policy. The state, meanwhile, was hoping that it would be able to pay off its debt with future war booty. We can trace the development in the proportion of expenses for the military in the overall budget: in 1933 they amounted to 4 percent, in 1934 to 18 percent, in 1936 they were up to 39 percent, and by 1938 half of public expenditures were devoted to the military. Tax receipts could not cover the financial exertions of rearmament and preparation for war.

The middle-class ideology of the NSDAP program had long since been shelved. The department stores were neither "communalized" for the benefit of the middle class, as the 1920 NSDAP program had demanded,

Modellanlage
»KdF-Seebad Prora«

On the island of Rügen, the regime had plans for a Kraft durch Freude (Strength through Joy) barracks-style facility for 20,000 people (KdF Seaside Resort Prora); the cornerstone was laid in 1935. The rough structures (dormitories, restaurants, a theater, a train station, wharves) were completed by 1939. During the war Prora, instead of welcoming vacationers, provided temporary housing for injured soldiers, evacuees, and refugees. Zentrum für Antisemitismusforschung, Berlin.

nor were they expropriated. The anticapitalist noise of the "struggle period" had likewise fallen silent. Gottfried Feder, the financial theorist of the early NSDAP, who had coined the slogan "Break the Slavery of Interest," was dismissed from his post as undersecretary in the Ministry of Economic Affairs in August 1934 (after a brief interlude as commissioner for settlement matters, he was provided an appointment as professor at the Technische Hochschule in Berlin). Big business—which, contrary to popular belief, did not finance Hitler's rise to power, its monetary contributions, expressions of its favor, having flowed largely to the bourgeois parties of the right, chiefly the DNVP—quickly came to terms with National Socialism and was happy to do so. This was reflected in the Adolf Hitler Fund of the German Economy, which was initially used to finance the campaign in the spring of 1933. Thereafter, following an appeal by Gustav Krupp, a yearly donation amounting to 0.5 percent of wages paid out in all German companies was put at Hitler's disposal by the Reich Association

Leopold Schmutzler painted this scene, titled *Arbeitsmaiden, vom Feld heimkehrend* (Maids Returning from the Field). Propaganda phrases like the appeal for the "battle of production," the glorification of agriculture in the ideology of "blood and soil," and an agrarian romanticism in art and literature which mystified the nobility of farming life and German soil were expressions of the new era.

of German Industry (Reichsverband der deutschen Industrie) and the Union of German Employers Associations (Vereinigung der deutschen Arbeitgeberverbände) for the task of national reconstruction. Most of the total of 700 million reichsmarks raised this way was used for Hitler's art purchases and for gifts to functionaries of the NSDAP, ministers, and high military officers.

The first models for state intervention without nationalization of the economy were the "gasoline agreement" concluded at the end of 1933 with I. G. Farben for the construction of new plants that would produce synthetic gasoline, followed a year later, on December 1, 1934, by the Law on State Price and Purchase Guarantees for newly built plants producing synthetic gasoline, buna (instead of rubber), and rayon. The efforts at achieving autarchy were supported in the area of foreign trade by Schacht's New Plan (1934), which set in motion a bilateralization and control of foreign trade (especially with the countries of eastern and southeastern Europe) on the basis of commodity exchange programs designed to pro-

To sweeten its social policy, but also to accelerate the motorization of Germany, the regime and Hitler personally pushed Ferdinand Porsche's plans to produce a *Volkswagen* (people's car) at a price of 1,000 reichsmarks. Beginning in 1934, the German Labor Front supported the project of the Kraft durch Freude (Strength through Joy) car with fifty million reichsmarks. The Nazi organization Kraft durch Freude (Strength through Joy) promoted the purchase through a savings plan with prepayments ("Five marks a week you must set aside, if in your own car you wish to ride!"). Three hundred thirty-six thousand subscribers, 60,000 of whom had already paid off their purchase in full, were hoping to take delivery of a *Volkswagen*. None ever received it, since the factory was switched to military production and turned out only military vehicles for the Wehrmacht after 1939. Österreichische Gesellschaft für Zeitgeschichte, Vienna.

tect Germany's scarce foreign exchange reserves (industrial exports in return for agricultural and raw materials imports). The state's expenses for rearmament, which rose rapidly after 1934 (1934: 1.9 billion, 1938: 18.4 billion reichsmarks), formed the foundation for the massive boost to production aimed at building up the military and a self-sufficient economy. With the beginning of the Four-Year Plan (1936), this trend also found expression in the centralized concentration of the supervisory authorities, who were charged with rationing scarce economic resources (raw materials, foreign currency, labor) in accord with the state's priorities and supervising the state-ordered wage and price freeze.

While private property as the foundation of the entrepreneurial economy was not touched, and the principle of free market competition was not repealed, the state's interventionist techniques severely constrained entrepreneurial investment and production. And despite the participation of large companies in the state's production planning (and in spite of considerable profits), these techniques also reduced and fragmented the political influence of big business.

State intervention was even more pronounced in the area of labor law and the labor market. The Law on Working Conditions of January 20, 1934, transferred the setting of wage scales and the supervision of matters within companies to government authorities (trustees of labor), even though in practice, offices of the party and the DAF, which were represented on the trustees' consulting committees, participated in this process. The abolition of any collective representation of the workers prevented wages from rising in tandem with economic growth once full employment had been reached.

Moreover, the introduction of the Labor Book (*Arbeitsbuch*) in 1935 began the dismantling of workers' freedom of movement, a process that was substantially reinforced by the various decrees on obligatory service issued in 1938–1939. Despite the loss of the basic social rights of participation and freedom, the restoration of social security after years of extreme economic misery and massive unemployment was undoubtedly one reason why the initial animosity and reservations toward the NS regime waned among many workers, most of whom had grown up in a Socialist tradition of labor unions. One indication of this is the decline in illegal Social Democratic and Communist agitation during these years.

Compared to the enormous expenditures on rearmament, investments in social policy were very modest. For example, expenditures for the construction of housing averaged 0.25 billion reichsmarks between 1934 and 1938. What is more, the quality of the housing built by the Reich Home Office (*Reichsheimstättenamt*) of the DAF was far below the standards of the Weimar period. Social policy measures such as the promotion of marriages were counteracted by cuts in subsidies for housing construction.

The indebtedness of the German Reich rose from 12.9 billion reichsmarks in 1933 to 31.5 billion in 1938. In January 1939 the Reichsbank warned that the "economy of unrestrained public spending" was a threat to both monetary stability and domestic peace. Hitler responded to this criticism by accepting Schacht's resignation from the Reichsbank. The money presses were now turned on to finance state expenditures. It was clear what

Starting in 1934, an annual trade competition
was organized by the leadership of the Reich
youth and the German Labor Front, as a way
of monitoring the level of vocational training
and ideological knowledge among those about
to embark on their careers, and to provide an
incentive for hard work by offering winners the
prospect of state support. This picture shows
the hairdressers' competition on April 16, 1939,
the first round of which required a shampoo
and set. Österreichische Gesellschaft für Zeitgeschichte, Vienna.

the consequences of the economic policy pursued since 1936 would be:
bankruptcy or war. It is true that Schacht's efforts had been aimed at rearmament and autarchy, but they had remained more or less within the
bounds of economic reason. War as the method of imposing the rights
of the stronger, first to revise the Versailles treaty and then to conquer
living space, was the embodiment of National Socialist ideology. To that

3. Jahrgang Nr. 25
Einzelpreis: RM. 0.75

Berlin, den 5. Dezember 1939

Der
Vierjahresplan

ZEITSCHRIFT FÜR NATIONALSOZIALISTISCHE WIRTSCHAFTSPOLITIK

Amtliche Mitteilungen des Beauftragten für den Vierjahresplan Ministerpräsident Generalfeldmarschall Göring

Hochöfen der Hermann-Göring-Werke in Betrieb

The Joint Stock Corporation for Ore Mining and Smelting Works Hermann Göring was set up on July 15, 1937. Its initial purpose was the mining and smelting of low-grade acidic iron ore in the Salzgitter region. Göring personally chose the location of the smelting works and of Hermann Göring City, which was planned as a model National Socialist settlement. During the war the Hermann Göring National Works developed briefly into a huge European enterprise employing 600,000 workers. It absorbed the heavy industry and the coal and steel industries in Austria, Czechoslovakia, and Poland, spreading from France into the Soviet Union. After 1944, this industrial empire collapsed as quickly as it had grown. Shown here is the cover of "The Four-Year Plan: A Magazine for National Socialist Economic Policy." Bildarchiv, Stadt Salzgitter.

end the German economy had to be made ready for war in line with Hitler's ideas, which meant that it had to become self-sufficient and immune to a blockade in the production of goods that were important to the war effort.

In May 1936, Göring established a committee on raw materials and foreign currencies. Composed of industrialists and air force officers, it presented, in August of the same year, its calculations on the necessary industrial capacity, raw materials, and synthetic products such as gasoline and buna. In a secret memo, Hitler approved the breakneck pace of rearmament recommended by the report and appointed Göring the plenipotentiary in all economic matters relating to war preparations. This appointment gave rise to Göring's mammoth agency, the Plenipotentiary for the Four-Year Plan, which he ran, from his official seat as minister-president of Prussia, as a kind of super-ministry that cut across all layers of bureaucracy.

With Hitler's memo on the Four-Year Plan and its proclamation at the party rally in September 1936 the path to rearmament had been taken, and it was pursued without regard for cost-benefit relationships. Driven by the prospect of booty and victory in war, the government engaged in a predatory exploitation of the national economy, smelted inferior ores under state direction in the name of self-sufficiency in raw materials (at the Reich Work Hermann-Göring), and promoted expensive processes in the chemical industry (buna, hydrogenation of coal). The failure of wages to keep pace with rising prices, along with cutbacks in consumer goods, which the government had studiously avoided until then, created discontent within the population. The regime countered these undesirable stirrings of unhappiness with propaganda campaigns against "carpers, whiners, and grumblers"—and where these general preventive measures failed, it resorted to terror.

7

TERROR AND PERSECUTION

IT WAS INEVITABLE that a regime whose ideology was grounded in the right of the stronger, in a friend-foe mentality, and in the claim to absolute disposition over human beings would devote special attention to disciplining and shaping society. "Alignment," "ideological schooling," and "coordination" were the words used to describe this process. It went hand in hand with the exclusion, oppression, and persecution of "outsiders," of ideological opponents, of all those who must not and would not be part of the new order. Apart from those with different political views (although they could possibly be reeducated), this group included all those who for racial reasons had no place in the "*Volk* community": Jews, gypsies, and other "aliens" (*Artfremde*), among them the illegitimate children of black French occupation soldiers in the Rhineland, to a certain extent also Sorbs, Kashubians, Poles, and other ethnic groups living on the territory of the German Reich. They were joined by undesirables such as homosexuals and "asocial elements" as well as religious minorities who refused to toe the line. The disabled were discriminated against, persecuted, and murdered not because they were "alien" or socially stigmatized, but because they were unwanted on the grounds of "racial hygiene."

The Law on Hereditary Health, promulgated in July 1933, was one of the first preventive measures aimed at "genetically diseased offspring." On the basis of this law, about 400,000 individuals suffered compulsory sterilization by the end of the Third Reich: among others they included welfare recipients, the chronically unemployed, alcoholics, "asocial elements," the mentally ill, and the physically disabled. At the very least, the regime felt, these "deadweight people" (*Ballastexistenzen*) should not be allowed

Signpost in Dachau, 1936: the sign on the right points in the direction of the concentration camp, the sign on the left to the SS training camp. KZ-Gedenkstätte, Dachau.

to reproduce. Doctors, social workers, and teachers were required to report suspected cases to the health office. If the Hereditary Health Court (which was established at every district court [*Amtsgericht*]) gave its approval, the health office requested sterilization. This was merely the prelude to the "eradication" that began in 1939 against the backdrop of war, a government-initiated killing of undesirables, first within the German *Volk* itself and then among the "subhumans," people labeled as "lives not worth living" and "inferior."

The methods of exclusion and persecution varied, stretching from the prohibition against engaging in one's profession, to imprisonment, to physical and psychological abuse, all the way to physical destruction. The instruments of persecution were both the organs of the normative state — laws, the judiciary, the executive — and, to a rapidly rising degree, special institutions outside of the normative structures, such as concentration camps, the terror system of the SS, and the Gestapo. The police force, initially part of the regular executive power of the state, underwent a transformation: eventually it left the normative sphere, indeed the sphere of the state as such, and, having merged with the SS, became an organ of a special power derived from the person of the Führer.

The National Socialists made resolute use of the law and the judiciary to persecute and fight their opponents and "undesirables." The Reichstag Fire Decree of February 1933 tightened criminal law for political and other crimes, while the Decree for the Defense against Treasonous Attacks on the Government of the National Uprising, promulgated in March 1933 (and later replaced by the Treason Law of December 1934), allowed for the criminal prosecution of "malicious statements" about prominent Nazis and organizations of the Third Reich. Any criticism, any careless expression of discontent, any private judgment of the regime that did not conform to the official line could become a punishable offense. The door was opened wide for informers.

In March 1933, special courts were set up to prosecute "treason" cases. Not only were the rights of the accused severely curtailed in these courts, there was no appeal. Beginning in November 1938, any offense whatsoever could be prosecuted before a special court if the deed was deemed to have been especially "grave or reprehensible." Punishments meted out by the special courts were draconian and became more so as time went on. During the war these special courts were regarded, in the words of Roland Freisler, as the "courts-martial of the domestic front," and they lived up to that designation by imposing 11,000 death sentences.

In April 1934, the People's Court (*Volksgerichtshof*) was set up, initially

The People's Court, set up in 1934, was less an organ for administering justice than an instrument of terror. It imposed the majority of its 5,200 death sentences after 1942, under the chairmanship of Roland Freisler (shown here on the left). Bildarchiv Preußischer Kulturbesitz, Berlin.

as a special court. Two years later, in April 1936, it was transformed into a regular court with jurisdiction over cases of treason and high treason; subsequently its jurisdiction was extended to offenses involving major destruction of military property, aid and comfort to the enemy, espionage, and demoralization of the troops. The court passed sentence in two stages and there was no appeal.

In spite of the fact that the administration of justice showed a tendency to follow the official government line, in spite of the strong influence ("guidance") that the government exerted on the judiciary, based on the principle "the law is what helps the German *Volk*" and on the notion of the "common sense of the people," and in spite of the excessive penal practice that resulted from this (for example in "race defilement" cases), the courts and the manner in which sentences were carried out still offered some degree of legal security. All the accommodation to the Nazi state notwithstanding, the courts were not simply organs for carrying out political persecution.

Apart from the abuse of the law and the judicial system as instruments of persecution, the privatization of public force was characteristic of the Nazi state. A decree from the Führer and chancellor in June 1936 centralized the entire police force—previously a matter of the states—and placed it under Himmler's control. Himmler now bore the title Reich leader of the SS and chief of the German police in the Ministry of the Interior, where he held the rank of undersecretary. In his new capacity as chief of the police, he formally ranked just below the minister of the interior, although in fact he was his equal.

In and of itself, the subordination of the entire police force to the authority of the Ministry of the Interior was not an extranormative and therefore illegal act. In actuality, however, the police were not subordinated to the Ministry of the Interior at all, but were removed from its oversight and given to the Reich leader of the SS as the head of a subdivision of the NSDAP. The subtleties lay in the details: over the protest of Minister of the Interior Wilhelm Frick, the new post of police chief was not given to Himmler as the person who also happened to be the head of the SS party division, which would have simply been one of the many and customary personal unions in the Third Reich; instead, it went to Himmler explicitly in his capacity as the Reich leader of the SS. However, as chief of the SS Himmler was directly responsible only to Hitler. Naturally the personal and direct subordination of the police chief to the minister of the interior mattered little compared to Himmler's direct access to the Führer. The overriding loyalty was owed to the higher-ranking superior, Adolf Hitler, the charismatic incarnation of National Socialism, and not to the departmental head of the state apparatus, Wilhelm Frick.

When it came to official channels, the government department of the Ministry of the Interior and the minister at its head were simply circumvented. This development was therefore only superficially about the centralization of the police, which was merely a side effect. In actuality, it was the first stage in separating the police from the apparatus of the state and a step toward institutionalizing a special executive outside the normative structures. The office of Reich leader of the SS and chief of the German police—the formal addendum "in the Ministry of the Interior" that was attached to the title was something Frick personally had to insert into the draft of the decree—was a real union between an institution of the Führer's power, the SS, and a government department, the Ministry of the Interior, with the former clearly dominant. Himmler, one should note, never maintained an office as chief of the German police in the ministry. He exercised the relevant functions outside of the ministry with the help of his SS apparatus. Revealingly enough, he also declined clarification of his standing in civil service law with respect to his post as chief of the German police.

As early as 1937, Himmler began to merge the personnel of the SS and the Order Police (the *Schutzpolizei,* urban constabulary, and the *Gendarmerie,* rural constabulary). This process of disconnecting the police from the structure of the state reached its high point in September 1939, when the Security Service (technically the secret service attached to the party but in fact monopolized by Himmler's organization) and the Security Police (Gestapo and Kriminalpolizei, criminal police) were combined into the Reich Central Security Office (Reichssicherheitshauptamt, RSHA). The RSHA was firmly embedded within the SS system, and it was not entirely clear whether and when it was exercising functions within and outside of the normative structures.

One central area of the executive power—the police—had now ceased to be under state control and had become instead part of the SS, which derived its own legitimacy exclusively from the Führer of the NSDAP. We can put it differently: through a constant accumulation of power and the incorporation of spheres of authority, the SS, Hitler's bodyguard from the 1920s, developed into the most important instrument of rule in the Third Reich, and at the same time into a second and super state with unheard-of instruments of coercion and intervention (such as concentration camps), its own organs of enforcement, its own economic enterprises that exploited the labor of inmates, a separate army (the Weapons SS, with eventually around 600,000 soldiers in 38 divisions), and the authority to extinguish millions of human lives in special extermination camps and through mobile units. The classic state authorities were used to render auxiliary services in these myriad activities. Compared to this authority, the posts of minister of the interior and commander of the Reserve Army, which Himmler also assumed in 1944, the last year of the war, were mere secondary offices.

Concentration camps, places where political enemies were interned and tormented, had sprung up all over the German Reich in the spring of 1933 without any centralized planning. The Reichstag Fire Decree at the end of February 1933, with its suspension of basic personal liberties, provided the formal basis for arbitrary incarceration, commonly referred to as "protective custody." The official definition of "protective custody" in 1938 spoke of a "coercive measure by the Gestapo" against individuals "who, by their conduct, endanger the existence and safety of the *Volk* and the state." In 1933–1934, functionaries of the NSDAP, the SA, and the SS could also request "protective custody" at will, which was implemented in sev-

Concentration camp inmates march through Dachau, secretly photographed by a resident in 1933 or 1934. KZ-Gedenkstätte, Dachau.

enty concentration camps, in special sections of penal institutions and prisons, in approximately sixty detention sites of the SA and the SS, and in many other torture chambers in barracks, abandoned factories, and tavern basements. Legal appeals did not exist for those in protective custody. According to documents from the Ministry of the Interior, there were about 27,000 political prisoners in concentration camps in July 1933. Between 500 and 600 individuals had died in the camps by October 1933. In the beginning prisoners were guarded by police and SA men, rarely by the SS. Revenge on political enemies and retribution against proponents of a democratic system characterized the climate in the camps in these early days. Inmates were subjected to the degradation of endless roll calls and military drills, physical abuse to the point of death, and the humiliation of meaningless labor.

Within a year and a half the badly organized terror calmed down and most of the camps disappeared. One camp, located at Dachau near Munich, the "capital of the movement," took on central importance and became the model for the rationally planned and organized system of terror that was set up later and has come to be associated with the term "concentration camp." On March 20, 1933, Himmler, Reich leader of the SS and at the time the provisional police chief of Munich, had announced the establishment of a concentration camp for political enemies of National Socialism. The next day the first individuals in "protective custody" arrived on the grounds of the former munitions factory in Dachau. Initially guard duty was in the hands of the *Schutzpolizei*, the regular constabulary. In April, Himmler put the camp under the authority of the SS, thus laying the cornerstone for an empire of terror. In June 1933, Theodor Eicke, an SS officer with a dubious past, was named commander of the Dachau camp. It was Eicke who developed the camp regimen, the physical infrastructure with guard towers and electrified fences, and the administrative guidelines that were subsequently used in all concentration camps to the end of the Third Reich.

The early, "unauthorized" concentration camps gave the German language a metaphor for killing and murder, for violent despotism and desperate powerlessness, for the extreme humiliation of the victims. In many places—Wuppertal-Kemna or Eutin, Oranienburg near Berlin, Hohnstein in Saxony, Fuhlsbüttel in Hamburg, Sonnenburg east of the Oder River, Oberer Kuhlberg in Ulm, on the military training grounds of Heuberg in Württemberg—the camps gave a visible display of the force of the national revolution. After the gradual shutdown of these early camps, a new order of terror developed centered on Dachau. The infrastructure of persecution included the concentration camps of the second generation, newly established by the SS Inspectorate of Concentration Camps and well-thought-out for their purpose: Sachsenhausen near Oranienburg (July 1936), Buchenwald near Weimar (July 1937), Flossenbürg in the Upper Palatinate (May 1938), and the women's camp at Ravensbrück north of Berlin (May 1939), which took the place of Lichtenburg near Torgau. Neuengamme near Hamburg had been opened in the fall of 1939; following the *Anschluß* of Austria, a camp with particularly harsh conditions of incarceration was set up in August 1938 in Mauthausen near Linz.

Terror was exercised in the Third Reich with the help of a well-devised system. "Protective custody," for its victims a construct of lawlessness and arbitrariness, followed administrative rules, was systematized as an instrument of coercion, centralized, and institutionalized alongside the regular power of the state defined by laws and other norms. But it was not until the war that the SS, run by Himmler and continuously perfected, would unleash all its power and unchecked terror.

8

DISCONTENT AND OPPOSITION

NEEDLESS TO SAY, not all Germans made their peace with the National Socialist state, whose manifestation in the summer of 1934 as a dictatorship with a totalitarian claim on everyone and everything could not escape the notice of even the most ardent and naïve patriots. The referendum of August 19, 1934, which had approved Hitler's omnipotence as "Führer of the German Reich and *Volk*" by combining the offices of president and chancellor with a voter turnout of 95.7 percent, still produced 10.1 percent "no" votes and 2 percent invalid ballots.

At the work council elections in March 1933, the National Socialist Shop Cell Organization (NSBO) had won only a quarter of the votes. And the trend continued. The Law on the Ordering of National Labor, issued on January 20, 1934, which placed economic enterprises under the "Führer principle" and defined the business community as a relationship of allegiance and loyalty (*Gefolgschaft*), called for "councils of trust" to be established alongside a company's managing directors, with elections set for April 1935. The outcome for the NSBO's single list was so disastrous that such elections were never held again, on Hitler's personal order. The official announcement stated that the NSBO had received 83 percent of the votes; the real figures remained a secret.

Discontent gradually grew in the countryside. The measures in favor of farmers from the early days, such as the raising of agrarian protective tariffs and the option of a government-supported conversion of debt, were overshadowed in popular sentiment by the negative effects of the Reich Food Estate's regimentation and bureaucracy, as well as by the rural exodus, which was encouraged by the regime's labor policy and flew in the

August Landmesser (indicated by the arrow, with arms crossed), a worker at the Blohm and Voss shipyard in Hamburg, refuses to perform the Hitler greeting at the launch of a warship in 1938. He had been found guilty of "dishonor to the race" and had therefore, although a party member since 1931, come to oppose the regime. DIZ, SV-Bilderdienst, Munich.

face of Nazi ideology. What is more, clashes between representatives and organs of the party and the clergy also caused grumbling among the churchgoing rural population.

Shortages of food, created after 1935 by the precedence given to the armaments industry (guns instead of butter), created another source of discontent. The propaganda campaign against "grumblers and carpers" made clear that enthusiasm for the Führer state had its limits in everyday life.

Only a few weeks following the assumption of power there was already little sign of the ideological enemies of National Socialism, chiefly members of the workers' movement. On February 7, 1933, at a secret session of the Central Committee of the KPD in Ziegenhals near Berlin, Ernst Thälmann, leader of the party, had called upon party functionaries to engage in "the most vigorous action" in order to expose "the regime of Fascist terror, capitalist starvation, and imperialist war as a government of capitalists and big landowners." In the face of concerted terror exercised by the new rulers, mass resistance by the KPD's 360,000 members through strikes and demonstrations was as much wishful thinking as the hope of taking advantage, before long, of the discontent and "revolutionary" situation engendered by the Nazi regime. The illusions of this kind of resistance also included the KPD's opposition to the SPD: unmindful of their common enemy, Communist propaganda denounced SPD members as "social Fascists." Above all else, Communist opposition, which was carried on with illegally produced leaflets and pamphlets brought in from abroad, was an exercise in self-affirmation at the price of enormous casualties.

The KPD used spectacular actions to call attention to the fact that it still existed: red banners hoisted on top of factory smokestacks, slogans chanted from courtyards in Berlin, and the like. These actions were as ineffective as they were risky and costly. While the Nazi regime was consolidating itself, the ranks of the Communists were rapidly thinning, with their widely distributed pamphlets neither harming National Socialism nor winning the Communists allies from other oppositional circles. The prisons and concentration camps were filling up, and leadership positions in the (illegal) KPD turned over with ever-increasing frequency.

The balance sheet of Communist resistance during the first two years of the Third Reich is characterized more by large losses than successes. Actions were largely limited to demonstrations, which cost the party's functionaries and activists their freedom and their lives. A new course was charted in the summer of 1935. Instead of using propaganda leaflets, the work of persuading discontented workers to join the resistance was to be carried out one-on-one in the workplace. This is what the Communist International in Moscow had decided at a meeting with the German comrades, a meeting with the conspiratorial name Brussels Conference. The stifling bureaucratic oversight of the party basis in the German underground that had been exercised by the KPD's organization abroad was loosened. The German Communists were to fight the Nazi regime with greater independence than before, and if possible now also in alliance with the Social Democrats and other enemies of the regime. Needless to say, this new strategy of a popular front could not overcome the skepticism toward the doctrinaire Stalinist Communists that existed among those enemies of the regime. It was only during the war that members from various camps, not only the KPD and the SPD, cooperated in individual resistance groups.

A great many members of the Social Democratic workers' movement had withdrawn to private life after their party had been outlawed. But within the environment of workers' settlements they cultivated a Social Democratic milieu. This milieu, taking the form of neighborhood, sociability, camaraderie, and mutual help, created a sphere in which Nazi ideology had no influence and Nazi propaganda no effect. The basic attitude was that of quiet refusal and resistance. It manifested itself in listening to forbidden foreign radio broadcasts, in the exchange of critical views of the regime within small circles, in shops and taverns that were run by Social Democrats and functioned as news exchanges and places to find solace among like-minded individuals.

This was not resistance, nor did the Nazi regime consider it threatening. The oppositional stance weakened considerably with the Hitler government's successes in social policy and its diplomatic and military triumphs. The Socialist groups who were most active in the resistance during the first years of Nazi rule were not organizationally part of the SPD. There were three main organizations that had broken away from the Social Democrats prior to 1933, stood left of the SPD politically, and only gradually—at the end of the war by way of emigration—found their way back into the SPD fold.

The largest group in terms of membership was the Socialist Workers' Party of Germany (Sozialistische Arbeiterpartei Deutschlands, SAPD), which was represented in Berlin and central Germany, but also in other large cities and industrial areas. The SAPD, whose most prominent member would be postwar Chancellor Willy Brandt, had its foreign headquarters in Paris and an illegal leadership in Germany. About 5,000 SAPD members worked in the resistance in 1935 and 1936. By 1937, however, most had fallen into the clutches of the Gestapo. A few managed to hold on beyond 1939.

Another group took is name—Begin Anew (Neu beginnen)—from the programmatic tract it published in Prague in the fall of 1933. In this tract the group justified its own claim to leadership of a reformed workers' movement with sharp criticism of the policies of the SPD and KPD in the Weimar Republic. In the fall of 1935 and spring of 1936, raids by the Gestapo led to the arrest of a large number of its members. Among those who escaped was Fritz Erler, who was able to continue the resistance from the underground. However, with the exception of a few remnants in southern Germany, Begin Anew had been smashed by the fall of 1938.

The International Socialist Struggle League (Internationale Sozialistische Kampfbund, ISK) operated in a way very similar to the other two groups. This small organization maintained local bases through the German Reich and headquarters-in-exile in Paris. The ISK engaged in anti-Nazi propaganda by distributing leaflets and painting slogans on streets and walls. Its most important instrument for informing the German public were the "New Political Letters" published monthly between October 1933 and the end of 1937. Five vegetarian restaurants and a bread shop, all run by ISK members, were an important source of income and the economic backbone of the resistance organization.

One of these vegetarian restaurants was in Frankfurt am Main. Twenty-eight-year-old Ludwig Gehm worked there as a cook. He was also a courier for the resistance movement, using his shopping trips to the vegetable market as an opportunity to distribute leaflets. On weekends he rode his motorcycle to secret meetings with like-minded individuals, took endangered persons out of the country, and transported illegal propaganda literature from Paris to Frankfurt. For four years, until their arrest in 1937, Ludwig Gehm and his friends were wily and tireless enemies of the National Socialists.

The most spectacular action was undertaken by the ISK resistance fighters in Frankfurt on May 19, 1935, the Sunday Hitler was scheduled to preside over the ceremonial opening of the first segment of the highway between Frankfurt and Darmstadt. During the preceding night the resisters had painted slogans such as "Hitler = War" or "Down with Hitler" on the pavement and bridges and had disabled loudspeakers. Of course the slogans were discovered prior to the festivities. On the bridges they were covered up with swastika flags, on the pavement they were covered with sand. Rainfall washed away the sand and exposed the writing again.

The resistance of the workers' movement—as varied and diverse as the organizations and groups engaged in it—was not limited to propaganda actions. The struggle against the regime also included public insistence on democratic and constitutional ideals. At the beginning of the Hitler period many Social Democrats and members of leftist Socialist organizations ended up in prisons and concentration camps for taking such a stance, as did the Communists, whose ideals were opposed to those of the Nazis, but also to those of the Social Democrats. Maintaining a personal stance in the face of spreading enthusiasm for National Socialism was an attitude of refusal, one that frequently—especially during the war—led to opposition and resistance.

The day-to-day interference in church life, the Nazis' fight against religious orders (staged as a storming of the monasteries), and the "priest trials" against members of the regular clergy for alleged foreign-currency smuggling and sexual offenses, which the Nazis used to attack the

Catholic Church between July 1935 and the end of 1937, startled church leaders. The papal encyclical "Mit brennender Sorge" (With Deep Anxiety), issued in March 1937 and written in consultation with German cardinals and bishops, criticized the situation in Germany and distanced itself from National Socialist ideology: "It is with deep anxiety and growing surprise that We have long been following the painful trials of the Church and the increasing vexations which afflict those who have remained loyal in heart and action in the midst of a people that once received from St. Boniface the bright message and the Gospel of Christ and God's Kingdom." The pope reminded the Hitler government of the Concordat, which had been signed "to spare the faithful of Germany, as far as it was humanly possible, the trials and difficulties they would have had to face." Pius XI also criticized the racial policies of the National Socialists, though without mentioning the Jews directly. This encyclical was read in all churches. The circulation of the text under the eyes of the Gestapo was a great organizational feat. But in the years that followed, the majority of Catholic bishops remained unwilling to confront the Hitler regime.

Cardinal Bertram of Breslau, chairman of the Bishops' Conference, was inclined toward compromises with the regime, even as he protested against state interference in the rights of the church. Instead of a vigorous engagement with the methods and goals of National Socialist policies, which some bishops repeatedly called for, Bertram was content with petitions formulated in restrained language. Most prelates argued that one must not endanger the life of the church and make its day-to-day operations even more difficult. Bishops such as Konrad Graf von Preysing in Berlin and Clemens August Graf von Galen in Münster, who persistently pushed for a more determined stance by the Bishops' Conference, remained in the minority.

In contrast to the Catholic Church, the Protestants were split: the German Christians, led by Bishop Ludwig Müller, were proponents of the wing loyal to the regime. Müller, elected in September 1933, wanted to form the twenty-eight state churches into a single German national church in the spirit of National Socialism. The German Christians' declaration of December 1937 stated, "As he has with every nation, the eternal God has made a unique [*arteigen*] law part of the fabric of our *Volk*. It took form in the Führer Adolf Hitler and in the National Socialist state he has shaped." The Confessional Church opposed the German Christians and became the gathering place of the oppositional Protestant faithful. The Second Confessional Synod of Dahlem in October 1934 had already postulated an "ecclesiastical emergency law" against the totalitarian

The theologian Dietrich Bonhoeffer was a proponent
of the Confessional Church and ran its illegal seminary.
In 1940 he was prohibited from teaching, speaking, or
publishing. Until his arrest in March 1943, he was an
important figure of the political resistance. DIZ, SV-
Bilderdienst, Munich.

state; the rift within the Protestant church was becoming increasingly
unbridgeable. The establishment of a Reich Ministry for Ecclesiastical
Affairs in 1935, headed by longtime National Socialist Hanns Kerrl, did
not in any way dampen the *Kirchenkampf,* the struggle between church
and state. In fact, it peaked in 1937 with the arrest of about eight hundred
pastors of the Confessional Church.

In the evangelical camp, individual pulpit proclamations in 1935 were
directed against the "racial-*völkisch* worldview." One memorandum by the
"radical wing" of the Confessional Church to Hitler condemned state-
ordered anti-Semitism, the existence of concentration camps, the arbitrary despotism of the Gestapo, and other manifestations of the Nazi state.

Pastor Martin Niemöller, a U-boat commander in
the First World War and then an opponent of the
Weimar Republic, resisted the Nazi "coordination"
of the church. In 1937 he was convicted of "abusing
the pulpit" and was detained in concentration camps
until 1945 as a "personal prisoner of the Führer."
DIZ, SV-Bilderdienst, Munich.

But the memorandum was secret, and a public pulpit proclamation admonished the faithful to show obedience toward secular authority. The
churches as public institutions did not close ranks to protest emphatically
against the deprivation of the rights of German Jews by the Nuremberg
Laws in September 1935, or against the November pogrom in 1938. Public resistance motivated by Christian faith was offered only by individuals, both clergy and committed laity, who spoke up to call injustice by its
name: men like the Catholic priest Max Josef Metzger, who was arrested
several times and executed in April 1944; the Protestant pastor Julius von

Jan, who publicly denounced the November pogrom of 1938; the Catholic dean of the Cathedral of Berlin, Bernhard Lichtenberg; or the Protestant Heinrich Grüber, who publicly stood up for the Jews and was persecuted for his efforts. Resistance out of Christian conviction was offered by pastor Dietrich Bonhoeffer, who was murdered in the Flossenbürg concentration camp in 1945; by the Jesuit fathers Augustin Rösch, Alfred Delp, and Lothar König, and by others. These individuals constituted a minority within the two large Christian churches. They alone had to bear the consequences of their protest, a risk they knowingly accepted. All in all, during the period of Nazi rule, about nine hundred Protestant Christians — clergy and laity — were arrested and punished for offering resistance that was inspired by their faith. They were sent to prisons or concentration camps; twelve of them were executed.

Opinion among Protestants diverged when it came to the "Aryan paragraph." A statement by the theological school at Marburg had concluded that this kind of discrimination was irreconcilable with Christian teachings. The theologians at the University of Erlangen, on the other hand, summed up their position as follows: "More than ever before, the German *Volk* today regards the Jews in its midst as a foreign nation [*Volkstum*]. It has recognized the threat that an emancipated Jewry poses to its own life and is defending itself against this danger with exceptional legal regulations." The faculty thus explicitly approved the racial policy of the secular authorities.

By virtue of his statements critical of the regime and his brave protest in sermons and church services, Pastor Martin Niemöller became the leading figure of the Protestant resistance. In the fall of 1933, when discrimination against the Jews was introduced into the churches, he founded the Pastors' Emergency League (*Pfarrernotbund*), which six thousand pastors joined by the end of the year. Many Christians of the Confessional Church took their cues from him. He was arrested in July 1937 and remained incarcerated in a concentration camp until the end of the Nazi regime.

Jehovah's Witnesses (known at the time as International Bible Students or *Ernste Bibelforscher*) were the only community of faith that resisted the National Socialist state unconditionally. The Germany community, about 25,000 strong, was outlawed in 1933. Roughly half of the members continued their "preaching service" (*Verkündigungsdienst*) in the underground. Jehovah's Witnesses refused to perform the Hitler greeting and above all refused to serve in the military. The Nazi regime responded with implacable persecution, arresting nearly 10,000 of them. About 1,200 paid with their lives for the resistance in this community of believers, which after 1936/1937 also used leafleting actions in an effort to enlighten the population about the criminal character of the Nazi state. In so doing it took committed action against the Nazi regime that went beyond trying to defend its own interests.

9

THE PERSECUTION
OF THE JEWS

ANTI-SEMITISM SERVED the National Socialists as an explanatory model for all the national, social, and economic misfortune the Germans had suffered since their defeat in the First World War, and it was the spur that Hitler used to goad his followers into action. The ideas put down in Hitler's *Mein Kampf,* which were preached by the leader of the NSDAP and his subcommanders and culminated in the call for a "solution to the Jewish question," went back to "insights" and claims advanced by the sectarians and fanatics who propagated modern race-based anti-Semitism in the last third of the nineteenth century. Without a trace of originality, the Nazis adopted the ideology of hatred for the Jews wholesale from the manifestos and pamphlets that had been circulating in large numbers since the 1880s, and which narrow-minded zealots had used to impress uneducated minds with simplistic explanations of the world. One social level higher, the educated middle class was profoundly influenced by Richard Wagner's essays (*Das Judentum in der Musik* [The Jews in German Music]) and by the weighty cultural history written by his son-in-law, Houston Stewart Chamberlain, *Die Grundlagen des 19. Jahrhunderts* (The Foundations of the Nineteenth Century). No less effective was the solemn mixture of national pathos and hostility toward the Jews promulgated in numerous lectures, essays, and books by the Prussian historian Heinrich von Treitschke, another idol of patriots in the Wilhelminian empire.

One of the most influential publications over the long run was Eugen Dühring's book *Die Judenfrage* (The Jewish Question), which first appeared in 1880. Following the principle that "exceptional conduct and ex-

Poster for the anti-Semitic exhibit "The Eternal
Jew," which was shown in a number of large cities
in 1937–1938. Münchner Stadtmuseum, Munich.

ceptional laws" were necessary against an "exceptional tribe," Dühring
called for radical exclusion: ineligibility of Jews for civil service, especially
the judiciary, the "de-Jewification" of the press, social ostracism of "mixed
marriages," "mediatization of the Jewish financial dynasties," and so on.
Decades later his demands reappeared in the program of the NSDAP. Demands he had framed in the language of the educated bourgeoisie were
put into practice starting in 1933, beginning with the rollback of Jewish
emancipation and leading to the Jews being stripped of their rights and
plundered of their wealth.

Even more effective and more widely read than Dühring's tract was
the *Handbuch der Judenfrage* (Handbook of the Jewish Question), first
published under this title in 1907 (it had been published earlier, under a
pseudonym, as "Antisemiten Katechismus" [Catechism of Anti-Semites]).

Die Judenfrage

als Frage des Rassencharakters
und seiner Schädlichkeiten
für Existenz und Kultur der Völker

*

Mit einer gemeinverständlichen
und denkerisch freiheitlichen Antwort

von

Dr. Eugen Dühring

*

Sechste, vermehrte Auflage,
in Frau Beta Dührings Auftrage
herausgegeben von H. Reinhardt

LEIPZIG
O. R. REISLAND
1930

The programmatic text of modern anti-Semitism,
first published in 1880: title page to Eugen Düh-
ring's *Die Judenfrage als Frage des Rassencharakters*
(The Jewish Question as a Question of Racial
Character and Its Harmfulness to the Life and
Culture of Nations).

Its final printing in 1944 brought the total number of copies to 330,000.
Its author, Theodor Fritsch, was an obsessed and professional anti-
Semite, like Dühring. Both Fritsch and Dühring used racist stereotypes
as their arguments; Dühring in fact boasted of having been the first to
frame "the Jewish question" as a racial and not a religious problem. Together with many less well-known fellow polemicists, they provided a second generation of anti-Semites, including the Nazi Julius Streicher and
even Hitler himself, with slogans against the Jews.

The phrase "the Jewish question," which had come into common use

Title page to "Die Protokolle der Weisen von Zion" (The Protocols of the Elders of Zion: The Jews' Program for World Conquest). Although easily recognizable as a crude forgery, this pamphlet, written in Russian shortly before 1900, appeared in numerous editions and translations and became the most widely disseminated anti-Semitic text, one intended to prove the "Jewish world conspiracy."

in Germany in the 1840s, had anti-emancipatory connotations. Beginning in 1889, the rapidly proliferating anti-Semitic organizations and political parties, which elevated enmity of the Jews to a program, used the phrase in their political fight against the Jews. The goal was to prevent—subsequently, to revise and undo—the legal equality of the Jews. The agitators employed fears of foreign infiltration that were grounded in traditional religious reservations and premised on the racist construct that the Jews were constitutionally alien. As a counterimage to the Jews they held up an "Aryan race" embodied in the Germanic peoples. The demands they put forth as part of their "solution to the Jewish question" included the deprivation of rights by way of alien laws, a prohibition against immigration of eastern European Jews, and the expulsion of those who had been living in Germany for centuries. Fantasies of destruction also appear in anti-Semitic texts, concealed behind words and phrases such as "rendering harmless," "de-Jewification," "removal," "eradication," and other connotations and associations. Here is one example from Dühring: "Something like an isolated [*internierter*] Jewish state therefore means the extermination of the Jews by the Jews." Elsewhere he writes, "The only way to remove the state of Jewification [*Judenhaftigkeit*], however, is to remove it along with the Jews."

One author described the Jews as an "alien element" in the "German body" and called for their "eradication." Ottomar Beta put it more bluntly in 1875: he wanted to "exterminate the spongers [*Schmarotzer*], or at least prevent them from engaging in usury," for this would "dispel the dismal darkness in which the sponger flourishes and in which the spirit of the German *Volk* withers away." It was this very metaphor of spongers and parasites that Adolf Hitler picked up. In *Mein Kampf* he wrote that the Jew was "only and always a *parasite* in the body of other peoples," always seeking "a new feeding ground for his race." The Jew "is and remains the typical parasite, a sponger who like a noxious bacillus keeps spreading." The result, Hitler prognosticated, was that "wherever he appears, the host people dies out after a shorter or longer period."

The metaphor of the "freeloader" or "sponger," which played a significant role in National Socialist propaganda, was as fashionable among Germanophile anti-Semites of the nineteenth century as many of the later language regulations were among the National Socialists. One anti-Semitic pamphleteer wrote in 1891, "The simplest and most practical solution, however, would be that of turning the tables on the Jews and inflicting on the Jews what they teach against us and what they in fact undertake against us to the extent they can do so without getting punished. One would then do with them as the English have done with the thugs in East India, kill them all without regard for age and sex. Needless to say, this kind of solution is out of the question, at least for us Germans."

What is remarkable in this passage is the line of argumentation, which accuses Jews of wanting to harm non-Jews, especially the Germans. This reversal of reality is found again in the alleged "declaration of war by the Jews," which the *Völkischer Beobachter* invented in March 1933 to justify

The methods of *Der Stürmer* included the denunciation
of "friends of the Jews" and their public pillory, as well
as crude and obscene caricatures that influenced simple
minds. In 1933 the paper had a circulation of 20,000,
which by 1944 had risen to nearly 440,000. The impact
of the paper was also based on the so-called *Stürmer*
boxes displaying the latest edition at busy locales all
over Germany. The headline shown here declares
"Master of the Lie." The picture shows an emigrated
Jew broadcasting propaganda until the hand of the
Nazis reaches out to crush him.

the outrages against the Jews and as a reaction to foreign press reports
about excesses in Germany.

Even a very superficial examination of the recipes of the older anti-
Semitic writers, which were then picked up by the National Socialists a
generation later, does not justify Daniel Goldhagen's recent conclusion

that an "eliminationist anti-Semitism" was unique to Germany and fundamentally different from the resentment against Jews in other nations. At first the consequence of National Socialism was merely that Adolf Hitler's political sect, favored by the political and economic circumstances of the 1920s and eventually taking power with the help of allies from the nationalistically minded middle class, helped itself shamelessly and unscrupulously to the existing arsenal of phrases and defamations and put whatever it found to use for its own purposes.

The pathological ideas in Hitler's worldview culminated in his malignant caricature of the Jews and in fantasies of a Jewish world conspiracy (linking it with what many perceived as the life-threatening danger of Bolshevism). Once the seeds of anti-Semitism that had remained dormant prior to the First World War began to sprout, his ideas touched on widespread fears among his audiences, fears that were stoked with rhetoric and with every kind of propaganda. The vilest practitioner of this propaganda was Julius Streicher, who resided in Nuremberg and was the NSDAP's gauleiter of Franconia. An elementary school teacher whose real profession after 1918 was that of *völkisch* demagogue and anti-Semitic agitator, Streicher, one of Hitler's earliest supporters, had founded the weekly *Der Stürmer* in Nuremberg in April 1923. The publication was the forum for an anti-Semitism that appealed to the basest instincts. Beginning in 1927, the paper's motto, which appeared weekly as the bottom rail on the front page, was a quote from the German historian Treitschke: "The Jews are our misfortune."

Because of his brutal manner and other character defects, Streicher was a highly controversial figure even within the NSDAP. Following charges of corruption he lost his political power in 1940. He remained editor and publisher of *Der Stürmer,* where he continued to propagate (until 1945) his extremely obtuse version of anti-Semitism, which held the Jews responsible for all the evil in the world. Of course Streicher was merely unusually crude and strident in his demagoguery. The tenor of the hatred of the Jews was the same in Hess, Göring, Goebbels, and Himmler. Robert Ley, the head of the DAF and organization leader of the NSDAP, was not far behind Streicher in his speech and writings. After all, anti-Semitism also formed the fulcrum of Hitler's thinking, and by extension the core of the programs and practices of National Socialist policy.

In 1933, the German Reich had a little over half a million citizens (0.75 percent of the population) who were the target of this hatred, citizens who professed Judaism as a religious minority. A statistically undetermined number of other Germans were of Jewish descent, meaning that their parents or grandparents or distant ancestors had been members of

Veit Harlan (right) and Heinrich George. In 1940 Harlan, one of the most successful film directors of the Nazi period, made the film *Jud Süß*, which effectively captured anti-Semitic stereotypes on the screen. Harlan was put on trial
on several occasions after 1945. After his scandalous acquittal, he attempted a
postwar career, which was accompanied by protests and calls for a boycott of
his films. DIZ, SV-Bilderdienst, Munich.

the Jewish community, but they themselves had been assimilated into majority society, sometimes by converting to Christianity. National Socialists and other proponents of racial anti-Semitism ignored this fact and insisted on the supposedly Jewish characteristics of this group. Since 1871,
the Jews in Germany had enjoyed the same legal status as any other German citizen, though that did not necessarily entail social recognition, as
was shown time and again in practice. Repealing emancipation, something the anti-Semites of imperial Germany had been unable to achieve,
was one of the primary goals of the National Socialists.

The majority of Germans did not view the excesses and verbal abuses
committed after January 30, 1933, mostly by the SA, as the beginning of
a systematic persecution of the Jews. The noise and the acts of violence
against individual Jews in the spring of 1933 were seen as the intoxication
of victory and a national exuberance that would soon subside. But it be-

came clear very quickly just how serious the anti-Semitism of the National Socialists actually was. And soon it also became clear that the sympathies of the majority of the Germans were not necessarily with the Jews, even if they did not like the anti-Jewish violence carried out by Hitler's followers. That a "Jewish question" existed and had to be resolved, namely by prohibiting Jews from exercising their professions in areas in which they were overrepresented, by pushing them out of economic life, and by removing the influence the Jews allegedly exerted in public life, in culture, and in the financial world—that was a belief many Germans shared with the new rulers.

Jewish judges and lawyers were a particularly frequent target of terrorist attacks. The worst came in Breslau: on March 11, 1933, SA men stormed the court buildings and drove all judges and lawyers they believed to be Jews out of their chambers and offices and into the streets under a hail of blows and insults. Although non-Jewish colleagues expressed solidarity with the victims of the attack, the violent action found imitators, for example, two and a half weeks later in Görlitz.

Press reports abroad about excesses against Jews in Germany were presented as "atrocity propaganda" instigated by international Jewry and were used as the pretext for an action ordered by the NSDAP on March 28, 1933. This action called for a boycott of Jewish doctors, lawyers, and stores on April 1. The Central Committee for the Defense against Jewish Atrocity and Boycott Agitation, under the leadership of Julius Streicher, had declared it a defensive action. The Jew had "dared to declare war on the German *Volk*. All over the world he is using the press in his control for a large-scale campaign of lies against a Germany that has become national again"—these words could be read on a public notice for a mass rally in the Königsplatz in Munich, which was going to be held as a prelude to the boycott on the eve of the action.

The boycott was a failure, in part because (alongside acts of looting and physical attacks) there were individual displays of solidarity with the Jews, but chiefly because of the threatened impact on the German economy in the wake of sharp reactions abroad. The action was cut short: it marked the end of spontaneous violence against individual members of the Jewish minority and the beginning of organized persecution, the first step of which combined legal acts to deprive the Jews of their rights with discriminatory propaganda.

Official actions and legal acts aimed against Jews had been occurring on many levels since March 1933. On March 15, the Reich Ministry of the Interior sent a circular to the governments of the states, informing them

Reichsgeſetzblatt

Teil I

| 1933 | Ausgegeben zu Berlin, den 7. April 1933 | Nr. 34 |

Inhalt: Geſetz zur Wiederherſtellung des Berufsbeamtentums. Vom 7. April 1933.................... S. 175

Geſetz zur Wiederherſtellung des Berufsbeamtentums.
Vom 7. April 1933.

Die Reichsregierung hat das folgende Geſetz beſchloſſen, das hiermit verkündet wird:

§ 1

(1) Zur Wiederherſtellung eines nationalen Berufsbeamtentums und zur Vereinfachung der Verwaltung können Beamte nach Maßgabe der folgenden Beſtimmungen aus dem Amt entlaſſen werden, auch wenn ſie nach dem geltenden Recht hierfür erforderlichen Vorausſetzungen nicht vorliegen.

(2) Als Beamte im Sinne dieſes Geſetzes gelten unmittelbare und mittelbare Beamte des Reichs,

des jeweiligen Grundgehalts der von ihnen zuletzt bekleideten Stelle bewilligt werden; eine Nachverſicherung nach Maßgabe der reichsgeſetzlichen Sozialverſicherung findet nicht ſtatt.

(4) Die Vorſchriften der Abſ. 2 und 3 finden auf Perſonen der im Abſ. 1 bezeichneten Art, die bereits vor dem Inkrafttreten dieſes Geſetzes in den Ruheſtand getreten ſind, entſprechende Anwendung.

§ 3

(1) Beamte, die nicht ariſcher Abſtammung ſind, ſind in den Ruheſtand (§§ 8 ff.) zu verſetzen; ſoweit es ſich um Ehrenbeamte handelt, ſind ſie aus dem Amtsverhältnis zu entlaſſen.

Front page of the *Reichsgesetzblatt* (Reich Law Gazette) of April 7, 1933, announcing the Law for the Restoration of the Professional Civil Service. The "Aryan paragraph" contained in this law was used to exclude Jews from all spheres of life. Beginning in September 1933, the German Automobile Club no longer admitted Jews; as of January 1934, the voluntary fire department in Prussia was not allowed to have Jewish members; in February Jews were excluded from the Wehrmacht. Worse still were the prohibitions against pursuing various professions. As early as September 1933, the General Synod of the Prussian Union of Protestant Churches prohibited "non-Aryans" from being appointed as clergy and officials in church administration. The same held true for husbands of "non-Aryan" women. "Aryan" civil servants who married a person of "non-Aryan descent" would also be dismissed from church employment. The Editors' Law of October 1933 drove Jews out of editorial offices, another decree from the Prussian Minister of the Interior was aimed at Jewish gentleman riders and jockeys, and in March 1935 a stage ban deprived Jewish actors of their livelihood.

that the immigration of eastern Jews must be blocked henceforth. Three days later, the Berlin city administration announced that Jewish lawyers and notaries could no longer work for the capital. In Saxony, the kosher slaughtering of animals was outlawed, and on the same day, March 22, Thuringia repealed the sibling discount on school fees for Jewish students. On March 27, Cologne prohibited Jewish companies from being considered for public contracts; a guideline for the press appeared in Hesse, declaring it a "matter of honor" that "racially foreign, international Jew-

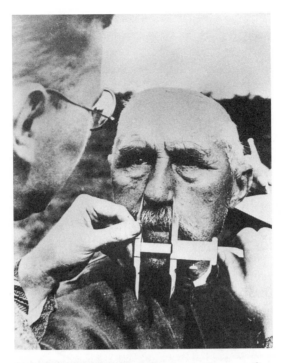

Anthropological "research" under the banner of
racial madness: the search for the "Jewish nose."
AKG-images, London.

ish influences" be purged from the news, entertainment, and advertising
sections of the papers. Berlin terminated the service of Jewish public welfare doctors on March 31; that same day, the Bavarian Ministry of the Interior ordered that all school doctors "of the Jewish race" be fired. In
Cologne, Jewish athletes were prohibited from using municipal sports
facilities. Frankfurt ordered a review of the German passports of all persons of "Semitic descent," while Düsseldorf prohibited the issuing of passports to Jews. In Munich, as of April 4, Jewish doctors in hospitals were
permitted to treat only Jewish patients. That same day, the German Box-
ing Association let it be known that Jewish fighters would henceforth be
excluded from any competition.

It took only a little over two months after the Hitler government had
assumed power for the first discrimination against the Jews to be enacted
by a Reich law. By virtue of the Law for the Restoration of the Professional Civil Service, promulgated on April 7, 1933, Jews lost their public

sector jobs. This was a first practical consequence of the NSDAP's party program. Initially the law allowed exemptions for those who had been civil servants prior to August 2, 1914, who had been frontline soldiers in the First World War, and who had lost a father or a son in the war. To the chagrin of the National Socialists, who were tireless in spreading the cliché of Jewish cowardice, this circle of exempted individuals turned out to be quite sizeable. The same thing happened with another piece of exclusionary legislation promulgated the same day, the Law Regulating Admission to the Bar. Lawyers of "non-Aryan descent," a phrase that henceforth brought disaster upon many lives, could have their admission to the bar revoked by September 30.

The exemption clause for combat veterans was a concession to Hindenburg, who had intervened with Hitler after Jewish war veterans had petitioned him for help. The president told Hitler that "if they were worthy of fighting for and bleeding for Germany, they should be regarded as worthy of continuing to serve their fatherland in their professions." How inconvenient the combat veteran exemption was to the government's intentions can be seen from the fact that of the 3,370 Jewish lawyers in Prussia, 2,609 were allowed to continue their work. The Central Office for Jewish Economic Assistance estimated that in 1933 about 2,000 higher civil servants lost their jobs and profession, while an additional 700 professors were fired by their universities.

Also in April 1933, the Law Against the Overcrowding of German Schools limited the number of Jewish students in educational institutions. This was the preliminary step toward complete exclusion, which was implemented in 1938. A similar method is reflected in the decree on the Restoration of Honesty in Cattle Trading that was published in Baden. It outlawed the "use of the Jewish language (Yiddish)" at livestock markets, a move that was based on the erroneous notion that German cattle traders would use the language of eastern Jews. This was followed by the exclusion of Jews from the Reich Association of the National Cattle Trade, and, in January 1937, by a law prohibiting livestock dealers who were not of German descent from engaging in their profession.

At the Reich Party Day of Freedom in September 1935, the government issued the Nuremberg Laws, which demoted German Jews to citizens with lesser rights. The Reich Citizenship Law established a distinction between "Aryan" citizens with full political and civil rights and "non-Aryan" subjects without those rights. The Law for the Protection of German Blood and German Honor prohibited marriages between Jews and non-Jews and made sexual relations between "persons of German blood" and Jews subject to draconian punishment under the newly introduced crime of "defilement of the race" (*Rassenschande*). The Nuremberg Laws undid the emancipation of the Jews and paved the way for the physical destruction of this minority. To be sure, the murderous consequences were not yet apparent, even to those affected, who were now treated solely according to racist categories, regardless of whether they regarded themselves as Jews, were members of a Jewish religious community, or even knew about their Jewish descent. Complicated definitions as to who was a Jew under the new laws, who was rated a *Mischling* (mixed breed) of the first or second degree, who was declared to be a *Geltungsjude* (a professed Jew), who bore the stigma of having "Jewish family ties," and who was protected from persecution (though not discrimination) by virtue of being in a "privileged mixed marriage" dominated the day-to-day lives of the minority, while the majority could avoid the dire consequences of the "Aryan paragraph" by providing "certificates of descent."

Beginning in March 1936, large Jewish families with many children no longer received government support. In October of that year, Jewish teachers were prohibited from tutoring non-Jews. In most cases this deprived those affected of the last source of income they had after being excluded from state employ. As of April 1937, Jews could no longer earn a medical degree; in September all Jewish doctors lost their hospital privileges; in July 1938 their medical licenses were revoked. Shortly thereafter, the same fate befell the few remaining Jewish lawyers and other professional and occupational groups.

At the end of 1938, all Jews were compelled to declare their assets if they exceeded 5,000 reichsmarks. In May, Jews were excluded from the awarding of public contracts; beginning in July, Jewish businesses had to be identified as such on the outside; that same month a new personal identity card was introduced for Jews. August saw a decree from the Führer forcing Jews to carry the additional names Sara or Israel; from the beginning of October, a red "J" was stamped into Jewish passports; that same month, at a conference about the goals of rearmament, Göring announced the elimination of Jews from the economy; from the middle of November, Jewish children were prohibited from attending German schools. This is only a sample of the measures that were taken. To them we must add the discrimination that local authorities devised: park benches with the words "Only for Aryans" painted on them, prohibitions against the use of municipal pools, signs posted at the entrances to towns and villages that read "Jews of all countries, unite, but not in Birken-

„Hier, Kleiner, haft du etwas ganz Süßes! Aber dafür müßt ihr beide mit mir gehen..."

In 1938, the publishing house that brought out *Der Stürmer* also published the widely read children's book *Der Giftpilz* (The Poisonous Toadstool), which used pictures and stories to train children to hate Jews. The text reads, "Here, kid, here is something sweet for you! But in return the two of you have to come with me . . ." Zentrum für Antisemitismus-forschung, Berlin.

werder," or "Wandlitz is not a Jewish paradise," or "The air in Buckow is unhealthy for Jews," or, the most common sign found at the entrances to restaurants, hotels, and stores, "Jews not welcome here."

November 9, 1938, marks the date when government action changed from legal and administrative discrimination of the Jewish minority to raw violence. The pretext for this event was the attempt by seventeen-year-old Herschel Grünspan to assassinate Ernst vom Rath, an official in the German embassy in Paris, on November 7. Young Herschel had intended this as an act of protest against the brutal deportation of 17,000 Jews of Polish citizenship from Germany in October 1938. The German diplomat succumbed to his injuries on November 9. At that time, Nazi grandees were

assembled in the Alte Rathaus in Munich for their traditional annual celebration of the attempted putsch in 1923. This was the right moment to
stage a pogrom, which came to be popularly referred to as Kristallnacht
(Crystal Night, a reference to the broken glass that littered the streets).
The popular mood had long since been stoked by a press campaign. In
Northern Hesse and Anhalt there had been attacks on synagogues and Jewish stores the previous day on local initiative. In Munich Goebbels was
preaching revenge and "retaliation." On the evening of November 9, the
party leaders in Munich picked up the phones and passed on the word—
now in the form of an order—to the propaganda offices in the *Gaue,*
whence it spread to the district and local group leadership and the SA staff
throughout the Reich. This had been agreed upon with Hitler.

Nazis all over Germany understood the order: a few hours later, synagogues were in flames, Jews were publicly mistreated, Jewish property
was stolen and destroyed. The party's call for a pogrom fulfilled in many
party comrades a need for action that had been dormant since the "struggle period" of the movement. But the organized vandalism against the
Jewish minority also spread to those not directly involved. There was no
small number of individuals for whom the pogrom was evidently an outlet for their lust for murder and destruction, which could now be publicly indulged since it was officially sanctioned. Glee and satisfaction over
the fate of the Jews were frequently observed reactions, expressed in plundering, blackmail, and denunciations and aimed especially at enriching
oneself at the expense of the outlawed Jews: targets of this desire were
businesses, apartments, offices, doctors' practices, and so on, all of which
were to be "Aryanized."

This night of terror unfolded in much the same way across the entire
Reich, of which Austria had been a part since March 1938. SA men and
members of other party organizations, usually dressed in civilian clothes
and embodying the "spontaneously surging anger of the *Volk,*" appeared
in front of Jewish community buildings and outside the stores and resi-
dences of well-known Jews. They heckled and broke windows. Synagogues
were favored targets: the riotous mobs broke down doors, demolished
interiors, and eventually set fire to the buildings. Fire departments had
explicit orders not to put out burning synagogues, only to protect neighboring houses if the flames threatened to spread. All across the land, the
mob—led by the SA and party notables (who were often simultaneously
mayors)—took delight in breaking into Jewish apartments and houses,
destroying furnishings, and abusing and humiliating terrified Jews—
merchants, lawyers, rabbis, and other respected citizens.

Kristallnacht. The burned-out synagogue in Nuremberg, where the November pogrom claimed more victims than in other German cities: nine Jews were murdered by the SA, ten committed suicide. Stadtarchiv, Nuremberg.

Some who were initially uninvolved got pulled in by the maelstrom of the pogrom; curious onlookers joined the raging fanatics to form a marauding, howling, violent mob. An urge to see what was happening drove people into the street, where the force of the events turned neighbors into plundering intruders, citizens into cogs in a collective frenzy. The perpetrators included fanatical Nazis, those seduced by the events, and some who simply happened upon the scene of a crime. They also included women and children and youths, as for example in the small town of Assenheim in Hesse (which had 1,216 inhabitants at the time, of which 21 were Jews). Here a seventeen-year-old journeyman bricklayer, who had no previous criminal record, was considered a nice young man, was not a Nazi, and was just home on leave from the Siegfried Line (also known as the Western Wall, which stretched from Kleve in the north along Germany's western border to Basel in Switzerland), joined the crowd that had gathered in town in broad daylight. Soon this young man was one of the worst offenders: he broke into the house of an elderly Jewish resident, beat him severely, drove him outside with kicks and down the street until the old man fell, whereupon he assaulted him on the ground until a man came to the victim's aid. In Büdingen, a journeyman butcher who was regarded as hard-working and able and who was not a member of either the Hitler Youth or the party drove a sixty-year-old Jewish woman, who had never done him any harm, three hundred meters through town under a hail of kicks and blows, threatening to throw her into the water.

In the small town of Treuchtlingen in Middle Franconia, 56 residents of the town (which had 4,227 inhabitants in 1933) were put on trial between 1946 and 1947 for their participation in the pogrom. The defendants included eight women. Their part in the pogrom allows us to draw some inferences about the participation of women, which usually took the form of derisive laughter, gawking, or plundering, stealing, and carting off goods and property. In Treuchtlingen we find women as participants in this breach of the public peace. Their active role is beyond doubt: they entered the picture not simply as agitators and inciters, but also engaged in acts of violence and destruction. For example, Sofie O. not only participated by shouting encouragement ("The Jewish swine hasn't had enough yet"), she personally smashed windows in the house of a Jewish doctor. Nora A. prevailed upon the SA to return to an already devastated Jewish residence and demanded further destruction by calling out, "It's not enough what's been smashed at Gutmann's." In another house she slashed open bedding and upholstered furniture, when fire was set to the synagogue she carried the gasoline, and she trampled the goods displayed in the window of a Jewish store.

Pogroms provide participants with an opportunity to live out sadistic and infantile-sexual aggressions. This applies also to Kristallnacht. What is remarkable is that the release of these urges did not require the shield of anonymity, that is, a different town or a large city. Instead, individuals perpetrated these excesses in their home communities, in their neighborhoods, where victim and perpetrator knew each other as neighbors and fellow citizens.

Newspaper ad in Vienna announced the reopening
of an "Aryan clothing store" under the new management of a member of the party. During the process
of the "Aryanization" of Jewish stores and businesses,
assets passed into non-Jewish hands for a fraction
of their worth. Österreichische Gresellschaft für
Zeitgeschichte, Vienna.

Moreover, the fact that adults involved children and youths in the
pogrom is an indication that in small rural communities there was little
distance to the regime's intentions toward the Jewish minority. In two
adjoining villages, on the morning of November 10, a growing crowd,
led by the local NSDAP chief and the mayor, moved through the streets
and perpetrated acts of violence against Jews. At the request of the mayor,
about two hundred school children were sent to the demonstration under the supervision of their teachers. They roamed about and complied
with the order to smash the windows of Jewish houses with rocks, eventually getting completely out of control.

There is evidence that many Germans felt ashamed in November 1938 and were shocked by what they considered a relapse into barbarism: the public humiliation, maltreatment, and robbing of members of a minority long since deprived of their rights, whom the Nuremberg Laws in the fall of 1935 had demoted from full citizens to residents with lesser rights. A few individuals took action: SA men had appeared at the Neue Synagoge on Oranienburger Straße in central Berlin and had set fire to the foyer. This synagogue, dedicated in 1866, with seating for 3,000 worshippers and splendid furnishings, was one of the most magnificent Jewish religious buildings in Germany. On the outside, the elaborate façade and the golden dome visible from afar also reflected the structure's eminence. None of that concerned the arsonists, but they were prevented from engaging in further destruction by Willhelm Krützfeld, the officer in charge of police station 16 at the Hackescher Markt, who hurried to the scene of the crime. He appeared at the synagogue accompanied by several police officers and with a document stating that the building was classified as a historical monument, drove out the SA men, and called the fire department, which did in fact show up and put out the blaze. Although the station chief was called before the chief of police to explain his actions, nothing happened to him.

Outside of Germany, this violation of basic German virtues such as respect for private property, thrift, respect for religious sites, and neighborly conduct were noted with disgust—everyday norms of social interaction seemed to have been suspended during the November pogrom. The German Reich had demonstrated to all the world that it was no longer a civilized nation. Civic conventions were still valid, just not for Jews in Germany—or other minorities, at the regime's discretion.

The pogrom had been staged as a ritualized degradation of the Jewish minority. That goal was pursued not only with the destruction of property and the humiliation and physical abuse of human beings during the night of November 9 and on the following day. The order for the incarceration of nearly 30,000 Jewish men in the concentration camps at Dachau, Buchenwald, and Sachsenhausen was partly intended to create pressure for emigration. This explains why well-off Jews were targeted; they were released once their families were able to present visas and tickets. But another goal of the action was to harm the unfortunate detainees in body and spirit by having them stand at attention and by beating them, demanding meaningless physical labor, making them fear for their lives and dishonoring them. The latter was easily accomplished by removing the cover of privacy from any manifestation of life under camp conditions, by degrading sanitary conditions, and by the sadism of the guards.

HERMANN GÖRING (1893–1946), a highly decorated fighter pilot in the First World War, was esteemed both inside and outside the NSDAP, which he joined in 1922. After the Hitler putsch he fled abroad. His political rise began after he reconnected with Hitler in 1927. He became President of the Reichstag in 1932, minister-president of Prussia in 1933, then minister of aviation. Because he was considered liberal and good-natured, Göring enjoyed special popularity as the second man in the state. In actuality the corrupt and vain holder of numerous offices (in 1934 he was named chief of forestry and hunting, in 1935 president of the Academy of Aviation Research, in 1936 commissioner of raw materials and foreign currency and plenipotentiary for the implementation of the Four-Year Plan, in 1940 marshal of the Greater German Reich), Göring was one of the harshest and most power-hungry representatives of the Third Reich. Thanks to his ruthlessness and his connections to the national-conservative upper middle class, the aristocracy, and big business, he played an important role in helping the NSDAP win power and stabilize its rule. Designated Hitler's successor in 1939, he lost prestige and authority during the war because of the poor performance of the air force, but also because of his laziness and drug addiction. Unlike Hitler he was less the fanatical proponent of *völkisch* ideology and more the revolutionary nationalist and symbol of the fateful alliance between National Socialism and German-national conservatives. Göring was the highest-ranking defendant at the Nuremberg trials. Sentenced to death after a self-confident defense, he escaped execution by committing suicide.

Jewish men experienced the prelude to the concentration camps in gymnasiums, schools, and auditoriums, where they were tormented and insulted for days on end.

On November 12, at the Ministry of Aviation, Göring presided over a meeting of all Reich ministers and representatives of the insurance industry to discuss the aftermath of the pogrom. The expropriation of the Jews was a foregone conclusion by this time; Hitler had already decided on a complete "Aryanization" of the German economy. The tally of property damage, compiled by Reinhard Heydrich for Göring, showed that 7,500 Jewish shops had been destroyed, that the "wrath of the *Volk*" and the "just outrage" of the Germans had claimed windows valued at ten million reichsmarks, and that vandalism and looting had caused damage of several hundred million marks. Nearly all synagogues and houses of prayer had been demolished or burned and ransacked. Added to this were hun-

Chief of the Luftwaffe Hermann Göring reviews soldiers
of the Condor Legion at the Moorweide in Hamburg. DIZ,
SV-Bilderdienst, Munich.

dreds of dead, victims of murder, deadly abuse, or suicide committed out
of despair or horror.

The ministers and officials at the meeting agreed that the Jews themselves should be liable for the damages caused by the pogrom (confiscation of the insurance benefits ensured that the Jews remained the ones
harmed). In addition, an "atonement fine" of more than a billion reichsmarks was imposed on the Jewish community in the form of a special tax.
The meeting then moved on to an exchange of ideas on how to remove
the Jews from German society once and for all under the most humiliating circumstances possible. Suggestions ranged from a prohibition against
entering German forests to the identification of Jews by means of special

Hitler and Göring (and behind them Baldur von
Schirach) in October 1936 at Obersalzberg.
Bundesarchiv, Koblenz.

dress or a badge as in the Middle Ages, a prohibition against using the
trains, and the banishment of Jews from entire city neighborhoods. In a
speech that Göring delivered on December 6, 1938, to gauleiters, *Oberpräsidenten* (heads of provinces in Prussia), and governors about "the Jewish question," he made it clear that on Hitler's explicit order, the exclusion of the Jews should proceed henceforth more discreetly and less
conspicuously than it had in November 1938. From now on, state organization should take precedence over wild action. The process of thoroughly
plundering the Jews and depriving them of all rights was now swiftly
implemented.

In the autumn of 1938, at the time of the November pogrom, of the

As here in Berlin on January 22, 1939, long lines formed at travel agencies as Jews sought to flee from the growing terror in the German Reich. DIZ, SV-Bilderdienst, Munich.

approximately 100,000 Jewish enterprises that had once existed, about 40,000 were still in the hands of their rightful owners. "Aryanization" had taken its heaviest toll in the retail sector: out of 50,000 Jewish shops, only 9,000 were left. The number of unemployed Jews had risen steadily; prohibitions against engaging in one's profession and forced sales of businesses had impoverished many. The Decree on the Elimination of the Jews from German Economic Life, promulgated on November 12, 1938, destroyed what livelihoods remained. As of January 1, 1939, Jews were barred from operating retail stores, offering wares and commercial services at markets and festivals, and running artisans' shops. Existing businesses were transferred to non-Jewish owners ("Aryanized"), usually for a fraction of what they were worth, or closed down. In either case it meant ruin for Jewish owners, since they could not dispose of the proceeds of a forced sale; these funds were paid into blocked accounts and were later confiscated for the benefit of the German Reich. Jews were forced to sell jewelry, precious stones, and antiques at prices substantially below their true value. In addition, Jews were no longer permitted to own stocks or bonds, which had to be surrendered into compulsory custody accounts.

Jewish real estate was also subject to forced "Aryanization." Jewish workers were fired, nearly all self-employed were barred from working. Of 3,152 doctors, only 709 still had the revocable permission to care exclusively for Jewish patients as so-called therapists (*Krankenbehandler*).

With the banning of Jewish papers and organizations after the November pogrom, Jewish public life was shut down. Plundered and impoverished, Jews were left to their private existence under increasingly dismal circumstances, faced with ever new harassment. The Law Regarding the Rental Conditions of the Jews of April 30, 1939, initiated preparations for aggregating Jewish families into "Jewish houses." Jews were to be crowded into apartments to facilitate supervision (and later deportations). "Aryans," so the official justification, could not be expected to live in the same houses with Jews.

10

THE ROAD TO WAR

THE FIRST WORLD WAR, Germany's first attempt to reach for world power, ended with a traumatizing defeat, the collapse of the monarchical-constitutional order, considerable loss of territory, financial disaster, and national humiliation. The symbol of defeat, disgrace, and misery was the Treaty of Versailles, which the Allies forced Germany to sign in June 1919. Germany lost Alsace-Lorraine to France and the Prussian provinces of Posen and West Prussia to Poland; it lost the Memel region and all of its colonies; Danzig became a free city under the mandate of the League of Nations and stood under Polish influence. In other areas, such as Upper Silesia and the Saar region, future plebiscites would determine their affiliation with the German Reich.

Austria, the German-speaking remnant of the Danubian monarchy, was barred from uniting with Germany. All told, Germany lost about 27,000 square miles of territory with 6.5 million inhabitants. The left bank of the Rhine came under Allied occupation for fifteen years, with Germany shouldering the expense. Germany was demilitarized, which meant that it had to hand over or destroy military hardware; it was permitted to keep an army of 100,000 men with no heavy weapons, tanks, or airplanes. To the oppressive burden of reparations payments were added offensive stipulations regarding Germany's war guilt and the demand that the emperor and leading military officers be handed over as war criminals.

The majority of Germans rebelled against the Treaty of Versailles, which in the eyes of many also tainted the democratic system of the Weimar Republic from the outset with the stigma of something imposed from the outside. From the beginning, the revision of the Versailles treaty was

Hitler's visit to Vienna and the Reichstag elections with the plebiscite on Austria's *Anschluss* was accompanied by the slogan "One *Volk,* one Reich, one Führer," which could be read everywhere on posters and decorations. Stiftung Dokumentationsarchiv des österreichischen Widerstandes, Vienna.

among the demands not only of the parties on the right. Of course, Hitler and the NSDAP were particularly successful with their demagoguery, combining the call for revision with radical blame directed at "the Jews" or "the Left," and denouncing the idea and practice of democracy as part of an international conspiracy against Germany. Breaking the chains of the "treaty of shame," overthrowing the Versailles order in Europe, recovering national greatness—this was the popular political desire that played a substantial role in bringing the Nazis to power.

The political attitude in the country and the expectations placed in the Hitler regime therefore included a certain kind of foreign policy. It was not only the military elites—who supported Hitler for this specific reason—who were hoping for the restoration of military sovereignty, a revision of the "bleeding borders" with Poland, the admission of Austria to the German Reich, and the recovery of the country's political and economic preeminence in central Europe and vis-à-vis southeastern Europe. These goals required little discussion between the conservative bourgeoisie and the nationalist extremists of the Hitler party. It also seemed as though there was agreement that these goals should not be pursued too impetuously, with all the risks that would entail. To the outside world Hitler therefore showed himself as peace-loving, so as to create the impression of continuity in the policy of revision, while behind the scenes he was preparing his true goal, the conquest of "living space" in conjunction with an aggressive race policy. It is worth noting that as early as February 3, 1933, Hitler indicated to the top echelons of the Reichswehr that new "living space in the east" had to be conquered and ruthlessly "Germanized" against the Slavic population. He had laid out his program in his declaratory work *Mein Kampf*: war against Russia in the form of an ideological war against Bolshevism, a race war against "Jewry," and a war of conquest to gain "living space" for the master race of the Germans. Yet few had taken these pronouncements seriously. To Hitler, foreign policy as a means of attaining these goals was a matter for the Führer: the weak conservative Foreign Minister Konstant von Neurath, and after February 1938 his successor, the compliant National Socialist Joachim von Ribbentropp, were allowed to play little more than supporting roles.

If the Communist Soviet Union was the chief enemy in Hitler's thinking, Great Britain was the partner of choice in the quest for world power. London, which was somewhat sympathetic toward the German demand for a revision of the Versailles treaty, was wooed by Hitler. But the regime in Berlin did not recognize the deeper conflict of interests that existed: Great Britain was not looking for an alliance with Germany against others, but was eager to integrate the Third Reich into a European peace by means of treaties.

The extension of the Berlin Treaty with the Soviet Union in May 1933 and the signing of the Concordat with the Vatican in July of the same year enhanced the standing of the German Reich with respect to international law. In October, however, Germany withdrew from the disarmament conference and the League of Nations. The nonaggression treaty with Poland in January 1934 seemed a reversal of a previous principle of

German policy, namely to ally with Russia against Poland, and it caused as much of a stir as the Hitler-Stalin pact did in 1939. In both cases, however, the true intentions did not match the letter of the treaties. In 1933–1934 the goal was to break open Germany's isolation, to thwart encirclement by the French-Polish alliance, and to gain time and a free hand in the pursuit of rearmament. For a long time, neither the conservative elites in Germany nor the foreign governments that entered into pacts with Germany realized that Hitler's foreign policy was aimed at concealing the regime's true goals.

Relations with neighboring Austria deteriorated once the National Socialists ruled Germany. Following the elimination of the parliament in March 1933, Austrian Chancellor Engelbert Dollfuß, with backing from Fascist Italy, sought to institute an authoritarian Christian-Catholic corporate state (Austrofascism). A special German tax for trips to Austria was intended as an unfriendly act on the part of Berlin and noted as such in Vienna. In June 1933, after a series of terrorist attacks, the NSDAP was outlawed in Austria. But the Nazi party carried on from the underground, while Dollfuß and his successors tried to preserve their small country's independence with the Austrofascist collective movement of the Fatherland Front. Rival parties were eliminated in a bloody civil war in February 1934. On July 25, 1934, SS Regiment 89 attempted a coup in Vienna. The uprising was crushed, but Dollfuß was shot and killed. After the failed coup, Germany's role in the July uprising was revealed, putting a severe strain on the Third Reich's relations with both Vienna and Rome. Berlin dissociated itself from the events in Vienna in order to contain the damage, but Germany's diplomatic isolation was obvious.

Mussolini had dispatched a division to the Brenner Pass to affirm Italy's role as Austria's protecting power and highlight the divergent interests of Rome and Berlin. This was all the more painful for Hitler as he had been trying for years, without much success, to win the favor of his idol, *il duce*. The two dictators had met for the first time in Venice in June 1933. At that time the atmosphere was marked by Mussolini's condescending attitude and was a far cry from the affirmations of friendship and the organized jubilation that greeted Mussolini on his return visit to Germany in the autumn of 1937.

Despite their affinity and outward commonalities, the agreement between Italian Fascism and National Socialism should not be overestimated. Ideologically the two systems were separated not only by German social Darwinist racism, but also by the fact that influential powers in Italy (the military, the church, the king) had not been "coordinated," brought under the heel of the regime. One thing they shared, of course, was expansionism. This was the basis of their alliance, propagated as the Berlin-Rome Axis from the autumn of 1936, and upgraded in May 1939 to a military alliance called the Pact of Steel. When relations between Berlin and Vienna were normalized in July 1936 with the signing of the Agreement on the Restoration of Friendly Relations, Mussolini had signaled ahead of time that he would henceforth tolerate German influence in the Alpine republic. One diplomatic observer subsequently coined the saying that the Axis was the spit on which "Austria would be roasted brown" (the Nazis were often referred to as the Brownshirts, after the color of their uniform). This had been preceded by Italy's attack on Ethiopia (then called Abyssinia), where Hitler had given political support to his diplomatically ostracized ally while secretly supplying weapons to emperor Haile Selassie.

The revision of the Versailles treaty was to be merely one stage of Nazi foreign policy, whose program was one of expansion and hegemony. As for the near-term goals of the regime, 1935 was already an extremely successful year. In January, 90.8 percent of the inhabitants of the Saar region voted for a return to the German Reich, an outcome that was celebrated as a great prestige-enhancing victory for the Hitler regime. In March, Hitler decided—alone and, surprisingly, without consulting the military or the Foreign Ministry—to reintroduce universal compulsory military service. Contrary to the expectations of the leadership of the Reichswehr, which thought that the timing was dangerous, the governments of Great Britain, France, and Italy expressed only restrained protest. The coup became a triumph for Hitler when the population responded enthusiastically. His protestations of peace formed the obligatory background music to these kinds of actions and had their intended effect, even during the risky coup de main on March 7, 1936, when German troops reoccupied the demilitarized zone of the Rhineland. This was an open breach of the Versailles treaty, which France accepted out of a feeling of powerlessness and Great Britain out of disinterest. Three weeks later, on March 29, 1936, in so-called elections for the Reichstag, 99 percent of the German citizens acclaimed Hitler's policy in the evident belief that they were on the path to new national greatness.

The years 1936 and 1937 were described by contemporaries, and later by historians, as quiet and—from the perspective of the regime—as splendid years leading up to the diplomatic triumphs of 1938. With all the attention on the Olympic Games, few noticed that the regime was setting up the Condor League to intervene in the Spanish Civil War. The Anti-Comintern Pact of November 1936, by which Germany and Japan ratified

Germany participated in the Spanish Civil War on the side of the rebellious general Franco with the Condor Legion, composed of about 5,500 Wehrmacht soldiers. On April 26, 1937, the Basque town of Guernica was leveled in a bombing raid by the Luftwaffe. The Republican government commissioned Pablo Picasso to paint *Guernica* for the Spanish pavilion at the World's Fair in Paris. The painting became the symbol of the horrors of modern war and the suffering of the civilian population. Museo Nacional Centro de Arte Reina Sofia, Madrid.

their anti-Soviet policy (Italy joined two years later), was of no special interest to the German citizen on the street, who was struggling day to day with a lack of fat and with all kinds of substitutes for consumer goods, the result of a foreign trade and currency crisis in the wake of the government's policy of autarchy. And he could not know about the secret directive by Minister of Defense Blomberg declaring neighboring Czechoslovakia a possible target of attack.

On November 5, 1937, Hitler met with the commanders in chief of the army, the air force, and the navy. Also present at the meeting were the minister of defense, the foreign minister, and Hitler's Wehrmacht adjutant, Colonel Hoßbach. With a certain solemnity, Hitler explained his expansionary goals to the top echelons of the Wehrmacht. In a first stage, possibly as early as 1938 given favorable circumstances, Austria and Czechoslovakia would be absorbed into the German Reich. This should make Germany ready for the escalation of its expansionist policy, ready for the struggle for world power. That conflict, Hitler noted, would have to come between 1943 and 1945, at the latest.

The memorandum that Colonel Hoßbach wrote a few days later was used after the end of the Third Reich as evidence that Hitler had planned a war of aggression. At the same time, however, it reveals disagreement

Male friendship among dictators: Hitler greets
Mussolini at the Kufstein train station on Septem-
ber 24, 1938, for the Munich conference. DIZ, SV-
Bilderdienst, Munich.

between the dictator and the military leadership: Minister of Defense
Blomberg and the commander in chief of the army objected to the speed
and timing of the planned actions and pointed to the diplomatic and military risks. Before long the dictator would have no more problems with
hesitant military men. Werner von Blomberg—minister of defense since
January 30, 1933, appointed to the new posts of minister of war and commander in chief of the Wehrmacht in May 1935, awarded the title of general field marshal in 1936 and the NSDAP's golden party emblem in 1937—
was dismissed at the end of January 1938 because he married a woman
who turned out to be a former prostitute. At the same time, the commander in chief of the army, Werner Freiherr von Fritsch, who, in spite
of his loyalty to National Socialism, had become inconvenient as an officer
with a Prussian-conservative mindset, became the victim of an intrigue

engineered by Göring and Himmler. The charge of homosexuality that was concocted with the help of a male prostitute did not stand up to the inquiry by a military court of honor. After his formal acquittal in March 1938, he was appointed colonel in chief of an artillery regiment, but he was not reinstated in his former post.

The scandal offered Hitler a chance to rebuild the structure of the military leadership. Henceforth he would be his own commander, which would also keep Göring and Himmler at arm's length. He placed the Wehrmacht under his direct authority, and the post of minister of war was dropped. Its place was taken in February of 1938 by the newly established High Command of the Armed Forces (Oberkommando der Wehrmacht, OKW) headed by the compliant General Keitel. As the head of the army Hitler installed the weak and colorless General Walter von Brauchitsch. Despite the acquittal and rehabilitation of Fritsch, which was intended to calm the critical voices in the military, the first stirrings of resistance appeared in the armed forces with plans for a putsch, not against the Führer but against Himmler's formations, the SS and the Gestapo, which the military eyed with suspicion.

Austria had been diplomatically isolated by the rapprochement between Rome and Berlin, and domestically the Austrofascist regime was feeling the heat over its opposition to both the workers' movement and the NSDAP. On February 12, 1938, Hitler summoned Austrian Chancellor Schuschnigg to his residence near Berchtesgaden, where he was pressured into accepting the Nazis into the government in Vienna. His attempt to salvage the sovereignty of the Republic of Austria through a plebiscite was thwarted by German threats. On the eve of March 10, Hitler gave his Eighth Army the operational order ("Special Case Otto") against Austria. The following morning the German ultimatum demanding that the plebiscite be called off was delivered in Vienna. That afternoon, Göring telephoned and demanded Schuschnigg's resignation; a few hours later, the SA having surrounded the chancellery, Schuschnigg complied. The path was clear for the National Socialist government. As demanded by Berlin, Arthur Seyss-Inquart took over. Seyss-Inquart, a Viennese lawyer who had already become minister of the interior on February 16 in response to German pressure, officiated as chancellor on March 11 and 12 and also assumed the powers of president on March 13. Austria's *Anschluss* to the German Reich was implemented under his government.

Following the ultimatum, German troops marched into Austria on March 12 to the thunderous applause of the Austrians. Improvisation took the place of detailed operational plans and nonexistent logistics; the left-

Left to right: Blomberg, Fritsch, and Grand Admiral Erich Raeder at the 1936 NSDAP rally in Nuremberg. DIZ, SV-Bilderdienst, Munich.

hand traffic in Austria at that time caused problems, as did the lack of gasoline depots, in the absence of which civilian gas stations were used. The previous day, when the Wehrmacht was beginning to cross the border, Heinrich Himmler, accompanied by a staff of police officers and SS leaders, had arrived in Vienna by airplane to begin the "coordination" of the Austrian police.

On the evening of March 12, Hitler met Seyss-Inquart in his hometown of Linz; discarding earlier plans, the two men decided to carry out the annexation immediately, without a transitional phase. On March 13, a Sunday, Seyss-Inquart declared the *Anschluss* and with it the establishment of the Greater German Reich. That same day the federal constitution law on the reunification of Austria with the German Reich was passed in Vienna, simultaneous with the Berlin law on the annexation of Austria to the German Reich.

This was the constitutional end of the Republic of Austria, whose territory, with 6.5 million citizens, formed the Eastern March (*Ostmark*) of Greater Germany for the next seven years. The cheers of 250,000 Austrians on March 15 for the Führer—who in a euphoric mood delivered the

"Work for the Jews, finally, work for the Jews!" the crowds jeered when Jews in Vienna, following the *Anschluss,* were forced to clean the streets in so-called scrubbing parties. Österreichische Gesellschaft für Zeitgeschichte, Vienna.

"greatest report of orders carried out" in his life ("I now report to German history the entry of my homeland into the German Reich")—stood in stark contrast to the terror and excesses of violence that accompanied the *Anschluss.* Seventy thousand opponents of the new order were briefly arrested, political enemies from the ranks of the workers' movement and conservatives were deported to Dachau.

A plebiscite on April 10 approved the emergence of Greater Germany with a 99.73 percent vote. In 1940, the Eastern March was divided into *Gaue*. The majority of the population was content with the situation. It was only after the collapse of Nazi Germany that many Austrians saw themselves as victims of National Socialism, the first to be attacked by the Third Reich.

In the meantime, Hitler concluded from indications by the British government that his participation in the European peace, which London was pursuing by means of its appeasement policy, would be rewarded with concessions in the matter of German territorial demands. He therefore began a campaign against Czechoslovakia immediately following the an-

Ballot for the plebiscite of April 16, 1938.
Österreichische Gesellschaft für Zeitgeschichte, Vienna.

nexation of Austria. Czechoslovakia emerged after the First World War
as an independent state from the breakup of the Hapsburg Empire, and
it was home to a German-speaking minority some 3.2 million strong. As
early as March 1938, Hitler encouraged the leader of the Sudeten Germans, Konrad Henlein, who was increasingly directed and financed by
Berlin, to raise autonomy demands that were impossible for the Prague
government to meet. The campaign "Home into the Reich" was used to
systematically intensify the "Sudeten Crisis" and expand it into an international conflict. Hitler, long since determined to smash Czechoslovakia, drove the escalation forward until the autumn with his demand—in

Signing of the Munich Accord. Left to right: Chamberlain, Mussolini, Hitler, Daladier, Ribbentrop. DIZ, SV-Bilderdienst, Munich.

the form of an ultimatum—that the Sudeten region be ceded to the German Reich. The area in question covered 11,000 square miles and accounted for 20 percent of the territory of Czechoslovakia.

The threat of war compelled oppositional officers around Ludwig Beck, the chief of staff of the armed forces, to try to change Hitler's course by submitting petitions and memoranda; another group went so far as to make plans for an attempt on the dictator's life. The resistance movement that was taking shape had also informed the British government. But Hitler moved more quickly than his opponents and won. At the height of the crisis, British Prime Minister Neville Chamberlain traveled to Berchtesgaden to try to influence Hitler. After strong-arming Prague into yielding to Germany's blackmail, Chamberlain offered Hitler the cession of the Sudeten region at a second conference at Bad Godesberg. This was meant to deprive Hitler of his pretext for military action. Immediately following the conference, in a speech at the Sportpalast in Berlin on September 26, Hitler demanded the Sudeten region by October 1, "one way or another," while at the same time declaring that this was the last territorial claim of the German Reich.

Three days later, the leaders of France (Daladier) and Great Britain

The citizens of Prague greeted the German troops with gestures of opposition and anger on March 15, 1939. DIZ, SV-Bilderdienst, Munich.

(Chamberlain) met with Hitler. The role of the mediator was played by Mussolini, who pushed proposals prearranged with Berlin. Eventually, Daladier and Chamberlain agreed to these proposals in the belief that this would pacify Germany. Acceptance of the Munich Agreement was dictated to the Prague government on September 30, 1938. The following day the Wehrmacht marched into the future "Reich Gau Sudetenland."

However, this annexation was only one stage in the destruction of the neighbor state. On March 15, 1939, the president and foreign minister of Czechoslovakia were summoned to Berlin. In the New Chancellery, just recently dedicated, they were forced to acquiesce in the destruction of their state, which began the very same day. Under the code name "Case Green" the Wehrmacht had been ready since October 1938 to attack rump Czechoslovakia. With the help of blackmail, Slovak politicians had been compelled to declare Slovakia an independent state and to call on Germany for protection and aid. By means of a "protective treaty," Slovakia became the first satellite of the German Reich. The Czech lands, whose industrial potential was of great importance to Germany's expansionist plans, were

This unflattering "gas protection for mother and child" was promoted in April 1939. AKG-images, London.

placed directly under German rule as a colonial entity, the Protectorate of Bohemia and Moravia.

Britain's appeasement policy had failed. On March 21, 1939, Hitler, undeterred by the stigma of being a liar, demanded the return of Danzig from Poland and concessions in the corridor set up in 1919. Two days later, on March 23, he sent troops into the Lithuanian Memel region and had the territory absorbed into the German Reich.

After the demands directed at Poland the world could have no more doubts about Germany's intentions. Hitler's directive to prepare for war dates from April 3, 1939. At the end of the month he cancelled the non-aggression pact with Poland and the naval agreement with Great Britain. Despite the gain in prestige from the Munich agreement in the autumn of 1938, Hitler had seen the agreement as a defeat rather than a victory,

British caricature on the Hitler-Stalin Pact of August 23, 1939. Hitler: "The scum of humanity, am I right?" Stalin: "The bloody murderer of the working class, I presume?" DIZ, SV-Bilderdienst, Munich.

because France and England had used it to underscore their claim to exert a shaping influence in Central Europe. At the same time, he despised the governments of the western powers as weak and unwarlike. By April 1939, the German dictator, unchecked by any opposition and surrounded only by obedient military men, was determined to attack Poland. The purpose, as he explained to the leaders of the Wehrmacht on May 23, was to win "living space in the east." The previous success of his threats and blackmail encouraged Hitler. Germany's still insufficient rearmament was something he intended to make up for—in a calculated war with France and Great Britain, and possibly also the United States—with speed, which he would use to create facts on the ground. Moreover, he was hoping that intervention by the western powers as a result of their treaty obligations toward Poland would be only formal in character, since neither Paris nor London was ready for war.

The Pact of Steel with Italy that was celebrated with the usual theatrical pomp in May 1939 was of little value, since Mussolini made it clear that he was still too weak as a partner in a European war. By contrast, news about the German-Soviet Non-aggression Pact, which was signed on August 23, 1939, was a diplomatic sensation. This pact, which threw Communists in the resistance to the Nazi regime and political refugees from Germany into despair and incomprehension, had been planned in Berlin as a large-scale deception and an alliance of convenience and temporary duration. Its aim was to isolate Poland, make it ready for destruction, and eventually divide it up. The goal had changed very little, as Hitler explained in August to a high-ranking visitor, the League of Nations commissioner for Danzig, Carl Jacob Burckhardt. Everything he was doing was directed against Russia. In Burckhardt's account of the meeting, Hitler told him that if the west was "too stupid and too blind" to understand this, he would be forced to come to terms with the Russians, defeat the west, and then "turn against the Soviet Union with all his combined powers." He probably would have preferred to ally with Great Britain to destroy Poland, but in his eyes the end justified the means, and so he would simply form an alliance with Stalin to reach his goal. Hitler probably did not state it in these words and possibly also not with the bluntness reported by the Swiss historian, but the account accurately summarizes the intentions behind his policies.

The immediate run-up to the attack on Poland consisted of ultimatums, deception, and blackmail. Following one last postponement of the assault planned for August 26, a fictitious Polish attack on the Gleiwitz radio station was staged on the morning of September 1 (executed concentration camp inmates in Polish uniforms simulated the presence of Polish soldiers on German territory). This created the pretext for launching the war. On the morning of September 1, 1939, Hitler proclaimed in the Reichstag that German soldiers had been "returning fire" since 5:45 that morning. The Second World War had begun.

11

DAILY LIFE IN WARTIME GERMANY AND THE RADICALIZATION OF THE REGIME

ON THE MORNING OF SEPTEMBER 1, 1939, when the population was informed by radio broadcast that the Wehrmacht had been given the order to launch a "counterattack" against Poland, the mood in the streets of Berlin was as gloomy as the overcast, gray sky. The situation was much the same in the countryside. The concerns of the farmers were perhaps more concrete than those of the city dwellers: they resented the siphoning off of workers and horses and the rationing of gasoline. Over the course of the month of September, reports of victory from Poland gave way to dejection; moreover, the regulations that severely constrained daily life provided the occasion for tension-releasing grumbling and griping. It had started with food ration cards and coupons, which would regulate consumption for a decade, long into the postwar period. Rationing had been prepared for since 1937 and was implemented on August 28, 1939. Henceforth people reckoned in "allotment periods" and distinguished between "normal consumers," heavy workers and other recipients of special bonuses, and those especially disadvantaged, like the Jews and forced laborers.

The war levy in the form of a special tax on alcohol and tobacco gave many regulars in taverns a reason to complain, and ill feelings existed in the first weeks of the war because it seemed that the older men and those who had fought in the First World War were drafted right away, while younger conscripts could be seen everywhere at home. Even more irk-

The grotesque ridiculousness of the tyrant was easier
to see from a distance: Charlie Chaplin in *The Great
Dictator* (1940). DIZ, SV-Bilderdienst, Munich.

some was the fact that most of the functionaries of the NSDAP were considered indispensable and were not called up by the Wehrmacht. Many
would have gladly seen the "old fighters," the "golden pheasants," at the
front line, where, as the solemn wish put it, they would have a real chance
to fight. But complaints were also heard from members of the NSDAP,
who, in spite of twelve- and fourteen-hour work days in armament factories, still had to perform party work (distributing propaganda, collect-
ing scrap material, etc.). The desire for exemption from party service for
the duration of the war was so widespread that it was explicitly mentioned
in the Reports from the Reich, secret situation reports prepared for the
regime by the SD, the party's internal information service.

On September 3, France and Great Britain, as Poland's allies, declared
war on Germany. The Commonwealth (Australia, New Zealand, Canada,
South Africa, and India) followed suit, and the American president,

Franklin D. Roosevelt, made no secret of his sympathies for the cause of the democratic states. Of course, Germany's concern over facing the superior force of the enemy subsided with the success of the Wehrmacht in its blitzkrieg against Poland. The fact that France was not ready for a modern war and believed itself secure behind the fortified Maginot Line, and that Great Britain—although it dispatched 200,000 troops to the continent—regarded a blockade of Germany as the most important weapon, reinforced Hitler's false assessment of the balance of power.

Germany's perception of Great Britain continued to be dominated by illusions. This was true for Hitler and the military leadership as well as for the German people. On October 10, 1939, a rumor spread like wildfire through the German Reich: the British government had resigned and the king had abdicated after London had concluded an armistice with Berlin. In some factories work stopped as employees and workers discussed the news. At the University of Berlin there was a surge of enthusiasm. A special report on the radio put an end to the euphoria around noon. Goebbels noted in his diary that the rumor had caused "genuine devastation." The reaction to the rumor reveals how far the mood of the Germans was from the war euphoria of August 1914.

In the west the military grew bored in a sitzkrieg, the armies facing each other in a standoff until the spring of 1940 while the brave Polish defense collapsed within a few weeks under the assault of two German army groups. Following bombings from the air, Warsaw capitulated on September 27; the war against Poland was over on October 6. A few days later the Polish state ceased to exist. The western Polish territories were annexed as the *Gaue* of Danzig–West Prussia and Posen (after January 1940 renamed Wartheland); eastern Poland, as agreed upon in the Hitler-Stalin pact, was occupied by the Red Army in September. After October 12, the central Polish region became the Generalgouvernement, a colonial entity under absolute German rule, governed by Hans Frank from Cracow. But Governor-General Frank, the prototype of the corrupt party bigwig, was soon no more than a figurehead, while real power was exercised by the SS. Heinrich Himmler, through "higher SS and police chiefs" with the rank of general on a district level, held the executive authority in his hands. Since October 7, 1939, Himmler, as Reich Commissioner for the Strengthening of Germandom, was also responsible for population policy in the conquered territories. In practice that meant the expulsion of Poles and Jews and the forced "Aryanization" of the annexed territories by settling and resettling "ethnic Germans" (*Volksdeutsche*), who were transplanted to the new fringes of the German Reich

This picture, made by a propaganda company in September 1939, was offered for reproduction with the following text: "These are real Polish caftan Jews, whose activities until now consisted of agitating in the most revolting and devious way against *Volk*-conscious Germandom. Their typically Jewish activities are now over. They are being assigned to a kind of work to which they may be unaccustomed, but which is far more useful than what they have been engaged in until now." Österreichische Gesellschaft für Zeitgeschichte, Vienna.

from their historical settlement areas in Bukovina (in northern Rumania), Bessarabia (in the southwest of Russia), the Baltic region, and so on. The systematic elimination of the Polish intelligentsia through the murder of teachers, doctors, and clergy was part of what the Germans understood by occupation and population policy.

After the Polish campaign there was another kind of booty, namely human labor. In the Generalgouvernement, Jews were the first to be forced into compulsory labor, initially in a completely random and unplanned way: the German authorities grabbed as many people from the streets as they happened to need. Eventually, after several waves of recruitment, one and a half million civilian workers and half a million prisoners of war from Poland were put to work in Germany in agriculture and the armaments industry.

The war was also the necessary backdrop for the intensification of the regime's ideological goals domestically. After the occupation of Poland,

This propaganda photo by the War Reporting Department (July 3, 1940) bears the official text: "Men from an SS police division enter a hotly contested village after destroying the enemy." Österreichische Gesellschaft für Zeitgeschichte, Vienna.

the social Darwinist population policy that had been propagated since 1933 against the disabled, who were called "burdensome lives," "defectives," "empty human shells," was practiced on inmates of Polish care homes who were unable to work. A mobile "special commando" did the killing with carbon monoxide from steel tanks. In Posen, mentally ill were murdered in a gas chamber. In a Polish forest, an SS unit shot patients from Pomerania and West Prussia.

Within the territory of the Reich, the murders began at the end of October 1939 in strict secrecy and under the euphemistic cover name "euthanasia." At first the formal basis was an oral authorization from Hitler, which was then put in writing on letterhead from the private chancellery of the Führer and back-dated to September 1, 1939. Karl Brandt, Hitler's personal physician, and Philipp Bouhler, the chief of the Führer's chancellery, were authorized to grant a "mercy death" to patients considered incurable "according to the best available human judgment of their state of health." Compulsory registration for newborns with deformities was in force beginning in August 1939. Registration forms and medical experts ensured an orderly procedure to the mass murder that now began

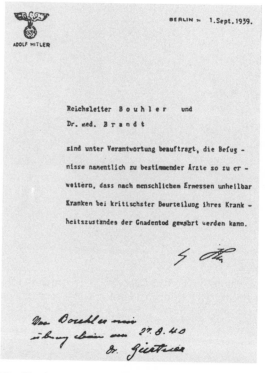

The "Action Mercy Killing" was merely a prelude to a population policy pursued through systematic mass murder. A little later, in 1942, the experiences gained from and the personnel involved in "Action T4" were put to direct use in the extermination camps in Poland during the Final Solution. The text of the Hitler decree concerning euthanasia reads, "Reich Leader Bouhler and Dr. Brandt are charged with the responsibility for expanding the authority of physicians, to be designated by name, such that patients considered incurable according to the best available human judgment of their state of health can be granted a mercy death."

and was carried out in facilities at Bernburg, Brandenburg, Grafeneck, Hadamar, Hartheim, and Sonnenstein. A nearly flawless organization was at work under the cover designation "Action T4," with headquarters at Tiergartenstraße 4 in Berlin.

A few registry offices issued death certificates, bodies were immedi-

Protective measures against air raids were rehearsed long before the war. At the end of April 1933 the government established the Reich Air Raid Protection League (*Reichsluftschutzbund*), which was responsible for training air raid wardens. A 1935 law regulated blackouts, air raid alarms, and the building and furnishing of bunkers. In Berlin in 1941, camouflage nets were strung across the street in front of the Brandenburg Gate. The air raid protection measures were largely ineffective. Once Göring's pronouncement that no enemy plane would reach German air space had been exposed as a lie in 1942, the propaganda of holding out remained the only weapon in the air war. Landesarchiv Berlin.

ately cremated. Recognizably false statements as to the cause of death often aroused the suspicion of families when they were notified, and the constant operation of the crematoria at the euthanasia facilities attracted the attention of neighbors.

It was not until the summer of 1940 that the judicial authorities learned of the events as a result of tips it received from citizens. Minister of Justice Franz Gürtner, troubled by the events themselves and by the lack of any legal basis for them, urged an immediate halt to the clandestine killing of the mentally ill. Gürtner died in 1941. His interim successor, Schlegelberger, personified the reactionary bureaucrat but was certainly no Nazi activist. Still, he emphatically solicited understanding and support for the "euthanasia" program from the subordinate offices in his department. Protests from the population were taken up by the churches. The bishop of Münster, Clemens August Graf von Galen, made the killing of the sick the topic of his sermon on August 3, 1941. In response, the killing of the adult disabled was stopped. The "euthanasia" of children with inconspicuous methods, such as injections or starvation, continued, as did the systematic killing of sick concentration camp inmates by means of poison gas in the "Action 14 f 13" (so called after its file number). By the time of the official halt of "euthanasia" in the summer of 1941, 70,000 had been killed, and after that another 50,000 would be killed.

Claiming absolute power over human lives, Nazi researchers carried out human experiments—justified as important to the war—in the concentration camps under a blanket of strict secrecy. Hitler had decided in May 1942 "that human experimentation is permissible in principle if the welfare of the state is at stake." The victims of these experiments were primarily Jews and gypsies, and also Soviet prisoners of war. The perpetrators were doctors who worked for the SS or were closely affiliated with it. Himmler, patron and sponsor in his capacity as the head of the concentration camp system, also took a personal interest in the experiments, making suggestions as an omnipotent dilettante which the doctors obligingly picked up.

In May 1942 there had been a crisis of confidence among the fighting troops because of poor medical care. In response, Professor Paul Gebhardt, the consulting surgeon of the Waffen SS, was given the opportunity to carry out experiments in the Ravensbrück concentration camp beginning in July 1942. To study the effects of sulfonamide compounds (sulfa drugs), infections were induced in inmates. The results were reported by SS doctors at professional meetings of the Wehrmacht.

Ravensbrück was also the site of experiments with bone transplantation. In the Sachsenhausen and Natzweiler concentration camps, experiments involving mustard gas and phosgene were conducted throughout the Second World War. At the Reich University of Straßburg, Professor August Hirt maintained a "collection of Jewish skeletons," for which he selected living victims at the nearby Natzweiler camp. Claus Schilling, a doctor of tropical medicine, was following an obsession of his own, rather than any serious scientific interests, when he ran an experimental malaria station at Dachau between February 1942 and March 1945. Between 1942 and 1944, Carl Clauberg, a professor of obstetrics and gynecology, experimented in Auschwitz on a method of sterilization without anesthesia. He injected caustic substances into the cervix of his test subjects (Jewish and gypsy women), which caused excruciating pain and lasting injuries, sometimes death.

As abominable as these experiments were, there was one category that—in intent alone—surpassed them all. The physician Dr. Sigmund Rascher, a Himmler protégé, was given the opportunity at Dachau to conduct low-pressure and cooling experiments that were aimed from the outset at the death of the experimental subjects. The pressure tests, carried out in a low-pressure chamber with support from the air force on the scientific rationale that it would help in "rescue from high altitudes," killed between seventy and eighty of the two hundred inmates involved, deaths that Dr. Rascher brought about deliberately from a sheer lust for murder. More dubious still were Rascher's cooling experiments that began in August of 1942: in order to study "the possibilities of water rescue," he submerged inmates in ice water and subsequently rewarmed them. Himmler took an especially active interest in these experiments. A few days before Dachau was liberated, Rascher was shot on Himmler's orders, and the traces of his activities were covered up.

From December 1946 to July 1947, the crimes of German doctors were brought before the bar of justice at the Nuremberg Doctors' Trial. This trial also proved that the incomprehensibly cruel experiments had been scientifically useless. They produced no results of any relevance to the conduct of the war, or, as some believe, to subsequent aviation and space travel.

The war also changed daily life in the Third Reich. Food rations got progressively smaller, the quality of the bread deteriorated rapidly, the shortage of fat was chronic. Work hours, which had stood at forty-eight hours a week before the war, climbed to fifty hours and more. In one area of labor market policy the regime tried to maintain its ideological standards. The role of the woman was not to change—as it had during the First World War—by having women take the place in the labor force of the men serving in the field. Needless to say, in spite of massive recruitment, foreign workers were not sufficient to fill the need for labor. Still, the number of gainfully employed women, which stood at 7 million in 1935 and had risen to 14.6 million by May 1939, did not change significantly during the war. In September 1944, 14.9 million female workers were registered. Concern for the stability of the home front kept the regime from introducing a general compulsory service for women, as Great Britain did in 1941, for example. For the same reason, for a long time the production of consumer goods was not slowed to the degree that the war economy would have demanded.

The longer the war went on, the more the regime took advantage of Germany's youth. Beginning in 1939, military training camps served to militarize school-age youth. The courses, which lasted several weeks and were run by the Hitler Youth, gave fourteen- to eighteen-year-olds military and tactical knowledge, ideological and physical training, and weapons training. The everyday life of children and teenagers during the war was determined less and less by school. They had to fill the gaps that the action at the front left among the men. Children and youths were employed as replacement workers in agriculture, the bureaucracy, the armaments industry, and social services. For school scrap material collection programs, children regularly had to bring in old paper, rags, iron, bones, bottles, and other raw materials. Students were also enlisted for aid and propaganda actions by the NSDAP, the NSV, and other organizations. They were sent out in class units to pick potato beetles and help bring in the harvest, look for medicinal herbs, and raise silkworms (to make parachute silk).

The *Kinderlandverschickung* (KLV), originally a social program in which children from big cities were sent to the country, removed young people from the influence of their family environment. Entire school classes were evacuated from areas threatened by the air war and housed in private homes, youth hostels, camps, hotels, and the like, at first in southern and eastern Germany, later in Bohemia, Moravia, and Hungary. The organization of the program lay in the hands of the leadership of the Hitler Youth, which was able to implement its educational ideas undisturbed in these settings, and against the influence of home and school.

By 1944, when the KLV organization collapsed, about 3 million children and teenagers were distributed among 5,000 KLV camps. About a third were not sent home in time and—often abandoned by their caretakers— they were overrun by the retreating front. Long after the war was over, the missing persons service of the Red Cross continued to search for students who had gone missing in the KLV program.

But as the war dragged on, students were also increasingly enlisted for military purposes. The air raid protection service was one of the more harmless jobs. Beginning in 1943, students between fifteen and seventeen— frequently an entire class at a time and housed in barracks, sometimes with their "emergency diploma" in their pockets—became anti-aircraft helpers and replaced anti-aircraft gunners who were dispatched to the front lines. From August 1943, when compulsory military service was expanded, boys under the age of eighteen were also drafted into the Wehrmacht, often directly out of the military training camps. By 1944 the regime needed fifteen-year-olds, and in the end the Nazis even put boys of twelve and thirteen into Wehrmacht uniforms.

Beginning in the winter of 1942–1943, the figure of the coal thief (*Kohlenklau*) was a ubiquitous presence on posters, matchboxes, at the movies, and on the radio. The appeal against wasting energy was popular, but oftentimes the public's response was critical of the lavish lifestyle of Nazi functionaries. Österreichische Gesellschaft für Zeitgeschichte, Vienna.

Three severely wounded young anti-aircraft
helpers, decorated with the "War Cross with
Swords," were guests of honor at the party
celebration in Munich on November 9, 1943.
DIZ, SV-Bilderdienst, Munich.

The war occasioned measures that the population understood to be
and accepted as necessary for the war, such as punishments for wartime
economic crimes and listening to foreign radio broadcasts, or the suspension of workers' freedom of movement. Institutional innovations included the Ministerial Council for the Defense of the Reich, headed by
Göring, who, after August 30, 1939, was empowered to issue decrees that
had the force of law, and the merger of the government offices of the security police (Gestapo and criminal police) with the party's Security Service (SD) of the SS into the Reichssicherheitshauptamt (RSHA, Reich
Central Security Office) as the headquarters of terror in Berlin. In early
September, Reinhard Heydrich, the head of RSHA, in a secret decree on
"principles of internal state security during the war," had ordered that "en-

emies and saboteurs" could be summarily executed by the Gestapo. Subordinate branches of this agency, which blended functions of the NSDAP and government tasks into an indistinguishable mix, included "inspectors of the security police and the SD" and state police (central) offices in Reich territory, "commanders of the security police and the SD" in the occupied territories, *Einsatzgruppen* (task forces) in the operational areas of the Wehrmacht, and SS and police attachés in the diplomatic missions in allied states. The executive of the Third Reich thus had at its disposal a seamless network which made it possible to lay hands on anybody anywhere and at any time. The Reich Central Security Office was also in charge of the more than one hundred "work education camps" that were set up in May 1941. Primarily foreign forced laborers were interned here under concentration camp–like conditions when that was deemed a necessary disciplinary measure because of "refusal to work" or for other reasons.

After the outbreak of war, the apparatus of terror and persecution was also expanded and intensified geographically. Near Danzig, camp Stutthof was set up in September 1939; originally intended for Polish civilian prisoners, it served officially as a concentration camp after 1942. Beginning in May 1940, Polish citizens were interned near Auschwitz in artillery barracks dating from the Austrian era; this installation would grow into the largest place of persecution and extermination within the Nazi sphere of power. In Silesia, the outer camp of Sachsenhausen, established in August 1940, developed into the separate concentration camp Groß-Rosen with numerous satellite camps. Near Hamburg the concentration camp Neuengamme was expanded beginning in the spring of 1940. In the Alsace, inmates were interned in the concentration camp Natzweiler-Struthof from May 1941. Beginning in October 1941, an SS prisoner of war camp was turned into the concentration and extermination camp Lublin-Maidanek, with functions similar to those of Auschwitz.

The regime also wanted to use the instruments of terror and coercion to offset the military and economic problems that had been masked by the successes of the blitzkrieg. Limited resources in terms of materiel and manpower forced the German military leadership time and again into surprise coups and maneuvers whose success fed illusions about Germany's military capabilities. The real balance of power became obvious at the end of 1941, after two years of war, and it was repeatedly driven home to the German population in the military catastrophes during the final two years of the war, right up to the capitulation of the Nazi regime.

The attack on Norway and Denmark on April 9, 1940, brought these two states under German rule and was the prelude to the offensive in the

Propaganda campaign to encourage vigilance against foreign spies. The text reads, "Pst! The enemy is listening." DIZ, SV-Bilderdienst, Munich.

west ("Case Yellow"). That offensive began on May 10, 1940, in violation of the laws of neutrality, with the occupation of the Netherlands, Luxembourg, and Belgium in preparation for the invasion of France. With the help of massive panzer divisions and motorized units, supported by the air force, the French campaign turned into another blitzkrieg. After ten days the panzer spearheads stood at the channel coast at Dunkirk. The British expeditionary corps and a part of the French troops barely managed to escape to England. Paris was occupied on June 14; eight days later Philippe Pétain, a marshal in the First World War and head of the French government since June 17, signed the armistice. The ceremonial signing took place at the same site where the Treaty of Versailles had been concluded, the forest of Compiègne, and in the very same railway car, which the Germans retrieved from a museum for the occasion. Hitler thoroughly enjoyed the situation when he announced to the French on June 21, 1940, that their country north of the Loire would be occupied and the French army demobilized. The southern, unoccupied part of

Hitler dances with joy after receiving the French request for an armistice at the headquarters in Bruly-le-Pèche in the summer of 1940. To his right is Martin Bormann.

France was administered by an authoritarian collaborationist regime headquartered in Vichy. Alsace and Lorraine were placed under the control of civilian authorities who were directly answerable to Hitler; governance was taken over by the neighboring NSDAP *Gau* chiefs and Reich governors Robert Wagner (Baden) for Alsace and Josef Bürckel (Saar-Palatinate) for Lorraine. Much like the treatment of Luxembourg, where the *Gau* chief of Koblenz-Trier, Gustav Simon, became the head of the Civilian Administration, this amounted to a de facto annexation.

In the summer of 1940, the Führer stood at the height of his popularity in Germany. During the French campaign he had for the first time personally intervened in military decisions, forcing through General Manstein's unconventional operational plan ("Sickle Cut") over the opposition of the high command of the army; in recognition of this act, Hitler's puppet Keitel, chief of the High Command of the Armed Forces, paid homage to the Führer by calling him the "greatest general of all times." At the end of June, on his visit to Paris, which he celebrated as a subdued triumph, accompanied by his architects Speer and Giesler and the sculptor Arno Breker, and in early July, when he publicly celebrated—to the ringing of church bells and the cheers of the crowds—the lifting of the humiliation of Versailles by the victory over France, even many of those who knew better were unsettled by the myth of Hitler's infallibility.

Great Britain, of course, was neither defeated nor willing to come to a political arrangement. Charles de Gaulle proclaimed it the duty of the French troops in the North African colonial territory to liberate the fatherland, and all plans to bring England to its knees soon proved to be fantasies. A direct assault with the goal of landing on the island ("Operation Sea Lion") had to be abandoned by the middle of September 1940: in the costly Battle of Britain, Göring's planes were unable to cripple the British defenses, destroy the English armaments industry, or attain the air superiority necessary for an invasion. The German navy was also too weak. Conditions were not conducive to the pursuit of other strategies, such as a continental blockade that included the Soviet Union, a plan favored by Foreign Minister Ribbentropp, or "warfare at the periphery," which Erich Raeder, commander in chief of the navy, recommended as a way of destroying Britain's position as a world power.

What is more, in the autumn of 1940, the Wehrmacht was forced to become engaged in secondary theaters of war. At the end of October, Mussolini attacked Greece; to prevent an Italian defeat, German units were dispatched to Greece and Yugoslavia at the beginning of April 1941. Again for reasons of prestige, to avert an Italian defeat, the German Africa Corps was assembled in early 1941 under the leadership of General Erwin Rommel. At the end of March the German units recaptured Cyrenaica, but over the course of the year the British drove them back to their original positions. The successes of 1940 seemed to repeat themselves in the Balkan war. On April 10, 1941, the independent state of Croatia established itself as a German satellite under the Fascist leader Ante Pavelic; Serbia came under German military administration on April 22; shortly thereafter, Greece was occupied. Only in Crete were British troops able to offer resistance for some time yet. These military operations, occupation, and the onset of partisan warfare tied up considerable German forces in a region that Hitler would have preferred to see quiet. Instead, Great Britain was engaged in the Balkans and the Rumanian oil fields had to be protected as an important supplier of fuel to Germany. This was all the more urgent since the Hitler regime had decided on war against the Soviet Union, and for this undertaking the southern flank of Europe had to be secured.

At the end of July 1940, Hitler had internally announced his "irrevocable" decision to conquer the Soviet Union. In December the Wehrmacht was given the directive for "Operation Barbarossa," an order to defeat the USSR in a quick campaign. Preparations were to be completed by the middle of May 1941. The principle of the battle in the east, Hitler explained to high officers in March 1941, was a "war of annihilation" that was to be conducted with savage hardness. By the beginning of June, the execution directives had been worked out in the form of the Commissar Decree, which was a violation of international law. The commanders in chief received the decree in writing and passed it on orally: civilian commissars "of every type and position," meaning Communist functionaries, were not to be taken captive but "eliminated" on the spot.

While preparations for the eastern campaign—including troop movements in Poland that did not escape the notice of the population—were under way, the puzzling political solo act of a prominent Nazi caused a sensation. Rudolf Hess, once Hitler's blindly obedient secretary, then deputy leader of the party, had climbed into a plane in Augsburg and flown it to Scotland, where he bailed out. His mission was to present the British government with a message of peace that he had dreamed up all on his own. Among Hess's delusions was the conviction that he was the messenger of Hitler, who, needless to say, declared him to be insane once his departure had been detected. The British government did not take the psychopath seriously. He was interned until the end of the war and then sentenced to life in prison at the Nuremberg trial of major war criminals, a sentence he served at the Berlin-Spandau prison until his death in 1987 as the last prisoner of the Allies. Had Hess not become the idol of neo-Nazis, who styled him into a martyr, the only thing notable about his "peace mission" would have been that he cleared the way for Martin Bormann. As the head of the party chancellery, Bormann now rose to become one of Hitler's most important confidantes, and during the following years he increasingly isolated him from contact with the outside world, including even high-ranking Nazi functionaries.

At dawn on June 22, 1941, the German Wehrmacht invaded the territory of the Soviet Union, its ally, with 153 divisions in three army groups—3 million men with 600,000 motor vehicles, 500,000 horses, 3,350 armored vehicles, and 7,200 pieces of ordinance. The goal was to crush the Red Army (5 million men) in four months, at the latest, and to conquer the industrial centers and agricultural surplus regions. Allies in this attack were Rumania, with a majority of its troops, and Italy, with an expeditionary force. Slovakia and Hungary joined Germany; Finland fought on the German side with the special status of comrade in arms. On June 29, 1941, Stalin, unprepared for a war with Germany, proclaimed the "Great fatherland war of the Soviet Union" and readied the population for a long period of privation.

Franz Halder, chief of the German army general staff, was convinced he could win the campaign in fourteen days. Hitler was dreaming about leveling Moscow and Leningrad, and in the middle of July he outlined the future division and exploitation of Soviet territory to top functionaries of the regime. On July 17, 1941, Hitler appointed the eccentric party ideologue Alfred Rosenberg, who since October 1940 had been in charge of a unit (the Rosenberg Task Force) that was plundering artworks from the occupied territories, minister for the occupied eastern territories.

The Wehrmacht's advance was unstoppable. Following the encirclement battles of Bialystok, Minsk, Smolensk, Kiev, and others, about three million Red Army soldiers were taken prisoner by October. Leningrad was encircled and cut off on September 8, and by the middle of October the German forces believed that Moscow was about to fall. Yet the numerical superiority of the Red Army had not been broken in spite of the losses. The Eastern War ground to a halt outside of Moscow. "Operation Barbarossa" had failed, the German forces were exhausted, unequipped and unprepared for a winter campaign. On December 5, the Russians launched their counteroffensive.

Six days later, on December 11, Hitler declared war on the United States after the Japanese allies had launched the Pacific War with their attack on Pearl Harbor on December 7. The Axis powers Germany, Japan, and Italy were now confronted with an anti-Hitler coalition that could draw on the economic and military resources of the United States, the Soviet Union's will to survive, Great Britain's determination and willingness to make sacrifices, and the resistance in the territories occupied by the Germans. From December 1941, Hitler no longer had the initiative. Shortly before Christmas he dismissed the commander in chief of the army, Walther von Brauchitsch, and assumed command himself. The result of the eastern campaign was catastrophic: with 831,000 killed, missing, and wounded, the Wehrmacht had lost a quarter of its forces. By the spring of 1942, another 900,000 men were lost. The war had already been decided with the defeat outside of Moscow, even if it would take another year for this to become obvious.

12

TOTAL WAR

TO IMPLEMENT THE IDEOLOGY of the master race during the annexation of the conquered territories in the east, Heinrich Himmler, as "Reich Commissioner for the Strengthening of Germandom," issued orders for an all-encompassing population policy that was discussed from the middle of 1941 under the name "General Plan East." This document was the blueprint for the dream of German rule between the Oder River and the Ural Mountains. In the settlement marches of Ingermanland (around Petersburg), Gotengau (Crimea and the Kherson region), in the territory of Memel-Narev (district of Bialystok and western Lithuania), and in thirty-six settlement centers, four million "Germans" (*Germanen*) were to exercise hegemony over the remnants of the indigenous population, who had been degraded to the level of slaves. In the discussions among the departments and offices involved, there was unabashed talk of deportations to Siberia or of how the "racially undesired elements of the population could be scrapped."

The course of the war prevented the implementation of the outrageous fantasies of Germanization. Still, three years of occupational rule in the east were terrible enough. A system of exploitation and terror, despotism and destruction operated in the two territories that had been under the control of the minister for the occupied eastern territories, Alfred Rosenberg, since summer 1941. In the commissariat Ostland, Heinrich Lohse, an "old fighter" and since 1925 gauleiter of Schleswig-Holstein, ruled over the four general commissariats of White Russia, Lithuania, Latvia, and Estonia. The Reich commissariat Ukraine was given to Erich Koch, gauleiter of East Prussia and a follower of Hitler since 1922 who was in-

Poster dating from the Allied air offensive of 1943.
The text reads, "The enemy sees your light! Black
it out!" AKG-images, London.

famous for his harshness. Koch transformed the initial willingness to col-
laborate on the part of many Ukrainians, who had welcomed the Wehrmacht as the liberator from Stalin's Communist yoke, into bitter hatred
for the occupation regime. The first attacks by partisans on the occupiers
were not long in coming.

In contrast to occupied western and northern Europe, where German
rule could draw support from the participation of indigenous Fascist
movements (Norway and the Netherlands) or from authoritarian collaborationist regimes (France), the only principles that applied in the occupied territories of Poland and the Soviet Union were subjection, oppression, and destruction.

A decree of December 4, 1941, made Poles in the annexed territories
subject to a special penal code. Based on the notion of an unlimited duty

of obedience toward the German *Volk,* this law provided the death penalty for offenses such as "inflammatory exercise of an anti-German attitude" or "anti-German statements." Procedures were court-martial-like, sentences were carried out immediately. The special penal code was expanded in January 1942 to include offenses committed prior to the issuing of the decree. It applied not only in the Wartheland and in the *Gau* Danzig–West Prussia, but to all Polish foreign workers throughout the territory of the Reich.

A munitions crisis during the Polish campaign and complaints by the Wehrmacht about inadequate armaments prompted Hitler in March 1940 to appoint Fritz Todt minister for armaments and munitions. Todt seemed the right man for the job: an unbureaucratic technologist (and Nazi since 1922) who had built the *Autobahnen* (highways) and the Western Wall, Germany's defensive line in the west. He persuaded the OKW and its subordinate departments to adopt new structures with which he increased production. The new system was fixed in December 1941 by a decree from Hitler. Five main committees of industry cooperated with military departments under the aegis of an advisory council headed by Minister Todt. In this way a balance was established between industrial efficiency, military needs, and state control. A streamlining program—which cleared up the profusion of designs and models and standardized and simplified production—in conjunction with control of the labor market, the allocation of raw materials, and interventions in production capacity (i.e., the closing of businesses not important to the war and utilization of their capacities) had some success. Still, all these efforts were not able to undo the misjudgments that had been made at the beginning of the war, when the military's armament was neglected because of the blitzkrieg concept, or make up for Germany's inferiority vis-à-vis the Allied powers in terms of resources and productivity.

As a result of the successes against the Red Army and the occupation of Soviet territory, the German war economy gained access to substantial numbers of additional workers. In all, about 15 million Soviet citizens were recruited, in one form or another, into labor services for the German side. Two million eight hundred thousand people were deported into the Reich as civilian "eastern workers," 5.7 million prisoners of war of the Red Army were in German hands, and about 6.4 million Soviet citizens were put to work in the occupied territories. Initially, up to the end of 1941, the deployment of Soviet prisoners of war in the German economy was out of the question on ideological grounds. The ideological war against Bolshevism was about the destruction of the enemy, who was con-

The "partisan war" in the occupied territories of the Soviet Union escalated as a result of the barbaric treatment of the civilian population at the hands of the German occupiers. The German response was ever new punitive actions against civilians. The lower sign reads, "Taking of pictures prohibited!" DIZ, SV-Bilderdienst, Munich.

sidered so inferior that he was not to set foot on German soil even to render auxiliary services. The November trauma of 1918 was still on the minds of the Nazis: the fear that the homeland could be infected by Communism, which might join forces with a resurgent German workers' movement and destabilize the regime. This motivated the political and military leadership to inflict barbaric treatment on Soviet prisoners of war outside of Reich territory, with the goal of decimating and destroying them. Day after day, 3,000–4,000 prisoners died in the camps in the custody of the Wehrmacht. When the number of prisoners of war exceeded 3 million in October 1941, and the need for workers in the German Reich became increasingly acute, Hitler decided to put these "cheapest of labor forces," who had to be fed anyway, to productive use, primarily in excavation work for Organization Todt and in road construction. Prior to the deployment of prisoners in the German Reich, Jews, Asians, and German-speaking Soviet citizens were separated out.

Ukrainian villagers are registered by the Wehrmacht, summer 1942. AKG-images, London.

When Fritz Todt was killed in an airplane crash in early February 1942, Hitler appointed his architect Albert Speer to succeed Todt in all his offices. As minister of armaments and munitions (beginning on September 2, 1943, the department was called Armaments and War Production), Speer displayed a variety of organizational talents that he used to put the production of war materiel on a new footing. The boost in output through efficient management and improved production processes is linked with Speer's name, even though substantial credit for these successes belongs to Speer's predecessors. Still, the advances in production technology were remarkable for their ability to unleash the power of the economy and of bureaucratic management. The effect of this system, which Speer fine-tuned by means of armaments commissions and a centralized planning authority, and over which he acquired more and more power, can be seen in the figures for armament production between January/February 1942 (= 100) and July 1944: the output of tanks rose fivefold (512), the manufacture of munitions nearly tripled (297), the production of weapons more than tripled (323), and the output of planes doubled.

To be sure, these achievements, which reached their high point in the summer of 1944, did not alter the fact that Germany remained far behind the United States and Great Britain in industrial output and productivity. And the gap kept widening, in spite of the mobilization campaigns that Goebbels launched after each major defeat. Its strenuous efforts notwithstanding, economically the Third Reich never had a chance to win the war.

To implement Speer's concepts, the labor of forced workers and concentration camp inmates had to be exploited with utter disregard for their well-being or survival. The collapse of the blitzkrieg strategy drove forward the policy of procuring manpower. Concurrent with the deployment of Soviet prisoners, the regime began the compulsory recruitment of workers, the "eastern workers," in the territory of the Soviet Union. The year 1942 saw the largest deportation of workers from the operational sphere of the German Wehrmacht in the east: in May, 148,000 people were "recruited" for work deployment in the German Reich, in June the number was 164,000. At the end of 1942 and the beginning of 1943 the number of forcibly recruited eastern workers declined, but at the same time the requirements of industry rose. Now the population in the occupied territories was systematically forced to work for the German Reich; the "battle against the partisans" turned into a slave hunt.

Fritz Sauckel, the gauleiter of Thuringia who was appointed to the new post of plenipotentiary-general for labor mobilization in March 1942, described his duty in these words: "I have received my assignment from Adolf Hitler, and I will bring millions of eastern workers to Germany, without any regard for their feelings, whether they want to or not." After some initial recruitment of volunteers, the German occupying authorities operated very much in keeping with this sentiment. For instance, in the Baltic city of Riga in June 1942, a truck drove up to an intersection where pedestrians were randomly loaded up and transported to a reception camp. Another common move was to arrest and deport people who went to the movies. "In front of the central dairy, all of the women standing in line for milk were surrounded, loaded up, and taken off to the reception camp. One woman far advanced in pregnancy gave birth on the way to the camp," one official report noted. If the able-bodied population escaped recruitment into forced labor by hiding in the forests and joining the partisans, draconian punishments followed: the confiscation of grain, the burning of farms, mistreatment, and the transport of captured civilians in chains to work assignments in the German Reich.

The plenipotentiary-general for labor mobilization, who was charged with recruiting "foreign ethnics" (*Fremdvölkische*) as well as motivating German workers to maximum performance, played an important role politically. His office, formally a department within Göring's Four-Year Plan agency, was also used to block the influence of the German Labor Front and rebuff demands by Robert Ley to determine the living conditions of the foreign workers. In equal measures he neutralized the Labor Ministry and the Plenipotentiary for the Four-Year Plan, Göring himself, whose claims to succeed Todt Hitler had passed over. However, Plenipotentiary-General Sauckel's most important function was as part of the triangle of power that included Albert Speer as the armaments chief and the Reich Central Security Office as the police authority in charge of supervising the "foreign ethnics." On one side were the demands from Speer, motivated by the needs of production processes, on the other side were the repressive efforts of the Security Office, initially aimed at keeping foreigners out and then at surveillance and discrimination. Between the two stood the plenipotentiary-general for labor mobilization as the authority who had to reconcile the needs of the armaments industry with the ideological positions of the regime.

The controversy between economic efficiency important to the war effort and Nazi racial policy constituted the central problem in the use of foreign workers during the Second World War. The regime's categorical demand for the highest possible work performance—a claim already embodied in its manner of recruiting slave labor—was not rationalized by giving up any racial principles. An improvement in the living conditions of eastern workers in the spring of 1942 on Hitler's orders was brief. While the recruitment in the east took on the form of slave hunts, the efforts at raising productivity (through a piecework system, bonuses, and food rations tied to output) were counteracted by a system of controls, humiliation, and punishments. The death penalty for sexual intercourse with Germans showed the intransigence of practiced racial ideology, as did the graded discrimination of all "foreign ethnics."

Discrimination expressed itself not only in external identification (a large "P" sewn onto the clothing to mark its wearer as a Pole, or the word "Ost") and living conditions, not to mention the psychology of contempt, as unwise as it was barbaric; it was also evident in the decision to place the "foreign ethnics" under police law or the control of the Reich Central Security Office. However, the clearest sign that racial ideology took precedence over military reason was the fact that the deaths of foreign workers were readily accepted.

At the beginning of 1942, the structure of the concentration camps was adjusted to the necessities of war. The importance of the concentration camps to the war economy rose steadily during the last three years of the

The manufacturing of artificial limbs was one
"armaments trade" preferably kept hidden.
Österreichische Gesellschaft für Zeitgeschichte,
Vienna.

conflict. After Himmler's concept of shifting armament production into
the concentration camps under SS supervision failed, beginning in the
autumn of 1942 a large number of satellite camps were set up in proximity to armaments factories or on the factory grounds themselves. The new
approach, agreed upon in September 1942 at a conference of SS leaders,
was to loan concentration camp inmates to private industry in return for
payment. As a result of this decision, new satellite installations were continually established right up to the end of the war; eventually there would
be 1,200 such branches assigned to industrial enterprises, some of them
with thousands of inmates. I. G. Farben, with its production facilities at
Auschwitz, is just one well-known example.

Inmates in the satellite camps assembled airplanes, produced chemical warfare agents *(Kampfgas),* fashioned field howitzers and ball bear-

Poster for the mobilization of the home front in
total war. It could be seen in armaments factories
beginning in 1943. The text reads, "Hard times,
hard duties, hard hearts." DIZ, SV-Bilderdienst,
Munich.

ings, or dismantled crashed enemy planes. In camp Dora-Mittelbau in the
south Harz, which was not established until August 1943, its original purpose, that of terrorizing and oppressing political and ethnic minorities,
played only a subordinate role. The chief purpose was the assembly of
V2 rockets, the fighter plane program of the air force, and other such armament production, which was carried out mainly by inmates below
ground and with which the regime was hoping to force a "final victory."
To that end even ideological premises were eventually abandoned. Beginning in May 1944, 100,000 Hungarian Jews were deported—in part
via Auschwitz—into the German Reich, which had been declared "free
of Jews" the previous year.

The Nazi regime also demanded maximum performance from German "*Volk* comrades" and especially from the soldiers of the Wehrmacht; this included uniformed, non-combat female helpers, about 300,000 in the reserve army and 20,000 in the field army, as communications and staff assistants. About 130,000 female helpers were employed by the air force. The need for men and materiel rose inexorably and became increasingly difficult to satisfy. The hoped-for military victories had to be replaced by exhortations to stay the course, eventually by the evocation of the "final victory," which made a mockery of the real situation and was somehow to be achieved with the help of secret miracle weapons.

On the eastern front, the Wehrmacht had one last great military success in May 1942 at the encirclement battle of Charkov (taking 239,000 prisoners). Hitler changed the plans for the subsequent summer campaign and had the two army groups march simultaneously—not in succession—to the Volga near Stalingrad and to the Caucasus. Even though the northern army was able to penetrate as far as the Elbrus mountain, it was not able to take Leningrad. In the south, the German Sixth Army under General Friedrich Paulus occupied nearly the entire urban area of Stalingrad in weeks of fighting, but it was not able to break the resistance of the Soviet troops. As early as autumn, the Sixth Army found itself in an increasingly hopeless defensive situation. On November 23, 1942, 250,000 men were encircled and cut off in the Stalingrad area. Breakout attempts toward the west were prohibited by Hitler, who instead held out the prospect of supplies from the air.

In the wake of a leadership crisis in the OKW in September, during which the dismissal of OKW chief Keitel was considered, confusion and dilettantism increased in the top military echelons—a result of the Führer's growing intervention in operative planning and the unquestioning acceptance of his decisions by the opportunistic generals. Stalingrad turned into a military disaster. The Sixth Army surrendered on February 2, 1943; about 100,000 men (91,000 according to German sources, 130,000 according to Russian sources) were taken prisoner. The Soviets counted 146,000 German soldiers killed. The Wehrmacht had now lost the initiative in the east for good. The final attempt was "Operation Citadel" (involving the largest tank battle of the Second World War, near Kursk), which had to be halted. Henceforth the initiative lay with the Red Army.

The destruction of the Sixth Army was presented to the German people as a tragedy comparable to the fate of the Spartan king Leonidas at Ther-

JOSEPH GOEBBELS (1897–1945), rejected for military service in the First World War because of a crippled foot, studied German literature, philosophy, and art history. After earning his doctorate he tried and failed to become a man of letters. In 1924 the "little doctor" joined the NSDAP. A radical ideologue who shook off his upbringing in a Catholic family in the Rhineland and made a name for himself in the left wing of the party, close to Gregor Strasser, he switched to the Hitler camp in 1926 and became gauleiter of Berlin. There he honed his demagogic talent as a speaker and director of political theater. He transformed the young SA man Horst Wessel, who had been killed in an act of jealousy, into the martyr of the movement. A tireless inventor of legends, he became the guiding intellectual force behind the pseudo-religious Führer myth. Appointed propaganda leader of the NSDAP in 1929 and minister of public enlightenment and propaganda and head of the Reich Chamber of Culture in 1933, he dominated the cultural scene of the Third Reich. As the master of mass suggestion he was constantly creating new forms of self-representation for the Third Reich, but he was also a cynical propagandist of hatred toward the Jews and orchestrated the Kristallnacht pogrom. During the war, the worse the military situation became, the more Goebbels turned himself into an agitator who preached a policy of holding out that flew in the face of reality and reason. To prop up morale on the home front, he stoked fears of "Asiatic hordes" and of the "revenge of Jewish Bolshevism," with effects that lasted beyond the end of the Third Reich. In the twilight of National Socialism Goebbels proved himself Hitler's most loyal follower, spending the last days in the the Führer's subterranean bunker in Berlin with his family and following Hitler in death. His diaries, which he wrote to ensure his posthumous fame and promote himself as a genius, instead unmask him as a megalomaniac petty bourgeois.

mopylae. Part of the staging was that Hitler forbade Paulus to surrender and, in expectation of a hero's death, cynically promoted him to the rank of general field marshal (along with 117 officers who were also promoted to the next higher rank). On January 30, 1943, the ten-year anniversary of the seizure of power, Hitler did not dare to appear before the German people, who had a foreboding of the defeat, were beginning to fear that the war was lost, and—as the situation reports of the SD noted—were expecting an uplifting speech by the Führer. Hitler left the speech to Göring and gave Goebbels the task of combating the "psychosis in the population" and restoring the "seriously impaired confidence in victory"

Goebbels and Hitler at the Tempelhof airport
in Berlin in the summer of 1934. This picture
was taken privately and would never have been
approved by the Nazi censors, since Goebbels's
club foot is clearly visible and Hitler at this time
no longer allowed himself to be photographed
with his famous dog whip. DIZ, SV-Bilderdienst,
Munich.

(*Meldungen aus dem Reich,* Reports from the Reich). A secret Führer decree from January 13, 1943, was intended to initiate the complete mobilization of all manpower reserves at home. The result fell far short of expectations. The same was true for the efforts by General Unruh, as part
of "Operation Hero Stealing," to recruit men for the Wehrmacht from
the rear and from state and party offices.

Goebbels during a speech as gauleiter in Berlin, ca. 1931.
AKG-images, London.

The fortunes of war had also turned in North Africa. In May 1942, German and Italian units had pushed as far as El Alamein, one hundred kilometers west of Alexandria. But they were not able to make any further progress, and in the autumn they had to withdraw in the face of the superior forces of the British Eighth Army under General Montgomery. By November only a bridgehead in Tunisia was left. At the beginning of 1943 the German position in North Africa was lost, in May the remnants of the Africa Corps surrendered. On March 9, Hitler had stripped the popular "desert fox," General Field Marshal Erwin Rommel, of his command of Army Group Tunis (although two days later he was awarded the Oak

Goebbels styled the rally on February 18, 1943, in the Sportpalast in Berlin into a national pledge to pursue "total war," delivered by a hysterical and ecstatic crowd that shouted out its devotion to Hitler for several minutes. Goebbels celebrated the dead of Stalingrad as heroes, ignoring those who had been captured. DIZ, SV-Bilderdienst, Munich.

Leaves with Swords and Diamonds of the Knight's Cross). Later Rommel was again used in northern Italy and in France. In October 1944, after his name had appeared on the list of conspirators of the July 20 plot (though he did not belong to the resistance), he was given the option of suicide or trial before the People's Court. He chose to take his own life and was given a state funeral.

The landing of American and British troops in Morocco and Algeria also altered relations between Germany and the Pétain government in Vichy after the latter had agreed to a truce with the Allies in northwest Africa. In response, on November 11, 1942, the Wehrmacht (and in some areas the Italians) moved into previously unoccupied southern France.

From the outset, the conduct of the war and occupation followed the laws of Nazi ideology more than the rules of international law. In the east, soldiers were engaged in a war of ideology, destruction, and plunder, whose manifestations were essentially accepted by the Wehrmacht—notwithstanding widespread critique by officers of the Commissar De-

The "desert fox," Erwin Rommel, commander of the Africa corps, was the most popular German general. He is shown here on his fiftieth birthday. DIZ, SV-Bilderdienst, Munich.

cree, the shooting of prisoners, and the mass killing of Jews. But in the Balkans and other theaters of war, the conduct of the war and the occupying regime became increasingly barbaric as the spiral of violence, once set in motion by the occupiers, was relentlessly accelerated by actions of the resistance and counteractions by the occupying forces. Examples of German "vigorous action," "deterrence," and disproportionate harshness toward uninvolved persons — documented by German records and reports by the perpetrators — are found in (but not limited to) White Russia, the Baltic region, and Russia. Here German police units, operating within the framework of the Wehrmacht and the SS, in conjunction with local "protective detachments" (*Schutzmannschaften*), carried out expeditions against ghettoes, rural settlements, and civilians who had fled into the forests. These actions were intended to pacify the region and were officially directed against partisans and bandits, whereby the smallest shred of suspicion was always accepted as certainty and where torching and mass executions were means to the end of pacification. While the principle in the east was that of prompt and ruthless response by the master race, in the occupied territories of western Europe the occupiers were more discreet in their use of the instruments of coercion. With the Night and Fog Decree of December 7, 1941, the chief of the OKW, Keitel, issued orders that made it possible to deport individuals suspected of resistance to Germany, where they were either tried before special courts or interned in concentration camps without any court sentence (NF inmates). The decree, the primary victims of which where the French and the Belgians, was intended to spread uncertainty and fear, since it was impossible to get any information on the fate of those who vanished during "night and fog."

In September 1944, units of the Sixteenth SS Armored Infantry Division destroyed the small town of Marzabotto near Bologna because partisans in the surrounding hills had been attacking the Germans below, who were constructing a defensive line under General Field Marshal Kesselring. As an act of "reprisal," 1,830 civilians were killed and the houses were riddled with bullets from anti-aircraft guns and torched. Kesselring, SS General Simon, and the directly responsible commander Walter Reder were later tried in Italian military courts for this act of barbarism in violation of the rules of war and international law. In Orodour-sur-Glane in France, units of the Weapons SS Panzer Division "The Reich" carried out a massacre on July 14 in which 642 people were shot or burned alive. On the same day in the Greek village of Distomo, civilians, primarily women, old people, and thirty-eight children ranging in age from two months to ten years were killed as "suspected bandits." This action was the work of men from the Seventh SS Armored Infantry Regiment, who reported that the village had been taken "in combat." In actuality, this combat report, as in so many cases, was falsified to give the slaughter of civilians the appearance of a military action.

Two years earlier in Bohemia, on highest orders, the Germans had given a warning example that set the standards for subsequent behavior. On June 9, 1942, Reinhard Heydrich, the Reich protector in Prague, was buried in Berlin in a splendid funeral. He had been gravely wounded in an assassination attempt on May 7 and had succumbed to his injuries on June 4. Based on vague suspicions that the trail of the assassins led to the Czech mining village of Lidice near Kladno, Hitler ordered all adult men in Lidice shot, the women sent to concentration camps, the children—those who were "capable of being Germanized"—handed over to SS families in the Reich, and the village itself leveled. One hundred and ninety-nine men were shot, 184 women were sent to the Ravensbrück concentration camp (52 died there), and 80 children who did not seem capable of being "Germanized" were murdered in the gas chambers of Chelmno. Lidice (and fourteen days later another Bohemian village, Lezáky) provided the pattern for a policy of retaliation that the commanders in all the territories under German occupation could use as a guide.

Reprisals and deterrence through hostage-taking are justified within the military profession as a way of defining the boundaries in military law between fighting troops and partisans and armed resistance by the population. Blame for the countless violations of the laws of war, the disproportionate reactions, and the crimes toward the civilian population lies not only with the Weapons SS, which grew rapidly in size until it was present in the theaters of war with thirty-six divisions and was infamous for its style of fighting. Wehrmacht units were responsible for many massacres. Among the better known is the "Operation Kalavryta," which was the work of the Seventeenth Fighter Division. During a reprisal action in December 1943, all men from the Greek village of Kalavryta and the surrounding countryside were herded together and cut down by machine gun fire. The list of the victims included 674 men and 22 women and children. The Wehrmacht also bore responsibility for the massacres in Distomon (228 dead) and Klissura (215 dead) in the spring of 1944. Earlier there had been the massacre in Kommeno (near Ioannina), where one hundred men of the 98th Regiment of the 117th Fighter Division carried out an "exemplary surprise action" against the village. Three hundred seventeen men, women, and children were killed, and all the houses in the village were torched.

In Serbia, the village of Kraljevo became a symbol of German occupation policy as early as October 1941. In an act of retaliation against partisans, the local commander had ordered the immediate shooting of 300 civilian hostages, and had announced that "not only will 100 Serbs be shot for each German, . . . their families and property will also be destroyed." For ten days the threat was carried out. Between four and five thousand civilians were cut down by machine guns and buried in mass graves. In the city of Kragujevac, some fifty kilometers away, units of the same Wehrmacht division carried out mass murders of 2,300 civilians, among them schoolchildren and their teachers.

The Allies were only being consistent when they made the legal prosecution of all war crimes one of their war objectives. On October 30, 1943, the three major powers of the anti-Hitler coalition published the principles by which this prosecution would be carried out. All those responsible and involved were to be pursued, arrested, and handed over to the states on whose territory they had committed the crimes. Punishment of the "major war criminals," of the leading Nazis responsible for the war of aggression, and of those responsible for the plundering of occupied countries, the enslavement of individuals, and genocide, was to be accomplished by means of a joint tribunal of the Allies. This was not merely proclaimed: a United Nation's War Crimes Commission drew up the basic principles, while the practical details were worked out by an allied central office beginning in 1943. Since 1941, Thomas Mann, who in regular broadcasts by the BBC in London urged the Germans to distance themselves from Hitler, to send a signal that "German" and "National Socialist" were not synonymous, had repeatedly called attention to the crimes of the Third Reich and to the atonement that would come after the defeat.

Germany prosecuted the war at sea as a trade war against Great Britain, avoiding a direct confrontation with the superior British fleet. The commander in chief of the Navy, Grand Admiral Raeder, and the commander of the U-boats, Dönitz, had different strategic conceptions. Raeder bet on battleships and other large units, while Dönitz considered U-boats the only effective means of modern naval warfare. Eventually, with the help of Minister of Armaments Speer, Dönitz prevailed, replacing Raeder as commander in chief of the navy on January 30, 1943. Naval armaments had been neglected because of the unexpected needs of the army in the eastern campaign. The "Fleet Building Program 43," with an output of forty new U-boats per month, was designed to put an end to the improvisational approach. However, it was not possible to overcome the bottlenecks in production and materials. And when the Allies closed the technical gap to the German U-boats by the middle of 1943, the battle in the Atlantic was decided.

In the meantime, war from the air had long since descended upon the German civilian population. Since May 1940, the planes of the British air force had been dropping bombs from great height on German industrial regions and cities. In February 1942, Air Chief Marshal Arthur Harris became chief of bomber command. He escalated the terror through the area bombing of major cities like Essen, Lübeck, and Rostock. On May 30–31, 1943, he launched a large-scale attack with one thousand planes on Cologne. The intent was to break the morale of the population, but that goal turned out to be illusory. Beginning in the summer of 1942, the Americans participated with their Eighth Airfleet, flying precision raids from Great Britain during the day, while the British continued to drop bombs over Germany at night. The German air defenses had little to put up

Beginning in 1942, Germany's large cities were systematically reduced to rubble by area bombings. The raids were intended to undermine the morale of the German people. DIZ, SV-Bilderdienst, Munich.

against these attacks; from the beginning of 1944, at the latest, Göring's air force was hardly ever seen in the skies above Germany. The German Reich was defenselessly exposed to destruction from the air. The only response still possible was the frenzy of Goebbels's propaganda. Of course the regime did not mention that terror from the sky was first used by the Germans: in September 1939 against Warsaw, in May 1940 against Rotterdam, in March 1941 against Belgrade, for months on end against London in 1940–1941. In June 1943, more than 30,000 people were killed in an Allied air raid on Hamburg. In the months that followed, most large German cities were laid in ruins; more than 600,000 people were killed in the process.

In the summer of 1943, British and American forces landed in Sicily. The military efforts of the Third Reich were now chiefly geared toward

Propaganda was well organized. A "war painting squadron" at work in a studio, where artists took sketches made at the front lines and turned them into battle paintings and heroic images. Österreichische Gesellschaft für Zeitgeschichte, Vienna.

In January 1943, U.S. President Franklin D. Roosevelt (second from left) and British Prime Minister Winston S. Churchill (right) met in Casablanca to discuss Allied war aims. They are shown here in the presence of the rival representatives of the French resistance, General Charles de Gaulle (second from right) and General Henri-Honoré Giraud (left). On January 24, 1943, they formulated their demand for the unconditional surrender of the Axis powers. Österreichische Gesellschaft für Zeitgeschichte, Vienna.

The heads of the anti-Hitler coalition, Stalin, Roosevelt, and Churchill, met in Tehran from November 28 to December 1, 1942, for the first of their Big Three conferences. On this occasion they discussed military questions, such as the invasion of France, and political issues, such as the future world order. The problem of how Germany should be treated after the war was delegated to the European Advisory Commission. AKG-images, London.

defending Fortress Europe. At the same time, the regime's system of alliances started to show cracks, and more and more forces were tied up to keep allies in line or occupy their ground. On July 24, 1943, Mussolini was forced by the Grand Council of Fascism to resign and was arrested. Although the new Italian prime minister, Marshal Pietro Badoglio, declared Italy's intent to continue the war on Germany's side, the Fascist system utterly collapsed within a very short period. The population was war weary: at the beginning of September, Italy signed a truce with the Allies.

Once again the Nazi regime, with weakening forces, opened a secondary theater of war when the Wehrmacht occupied Italy, disarmed the Italian units, and set up defensive positions against the British and the Americans near Naples. German paratroopers had rescued Mussolini from his prison at the mountain resort of Gran Sasso in the Apennines. Under German protection he emerged as the head of a Fascist "Repubblica Sociale Italiana" at Lake Garda (the Salò Republic). Northern and central

Mussolini with German paratroopers after his liberation from the ski resort in the Apennine mountains where he was being held, September 12, 1943. DIZ, SV-Bilderdienst, Munich.

Italy was de facto a German occupied region. In May 1944 the Allies began their advance through Italy; in June they occupied Rome. By November they stood south of the Po valley.

After Stalingrad, Rumania, which at Germany's side had declared a "holy war" on the Soviet Union in June 1941, sought a political way out of its alliance with Germany, as did Hungary. The Rumanian dictator Antonescu assured Hitler of his loyalty to the alliance, but his downfall in August 1944 was followed immediately by a declaration of war on Germany. Hungary, which had joined the Three Powers Pact in November 1940, also looked about for alternatives after Mussolini's end, which is why German troops occupied the country in March 1944. The people of Slovakia rose up against the German allies at the end of August, and Bulgaria left the alliance in September 1944. At the same time Finland concluded an armistice with the Soviet Union, as part of which it had to commit itself to drive out the German Lapland army. August 1944 had seen a Polish national uprising in Warsaw aimed at freeing the Polish capital before the imminent invasion of the Red Army. SS units put down the Polish resistance before the eyes of the Soviets, who stood by passively with a wait-and-see attitude. Following the evacuation of the civilian population at the beginning of October 1944, the deserted Warsaw was systematically destroyed. The death throes of the Nazi system of rule began with a scorched-earth policy as German forces retreated from the annexed and occupied territories.

13

THE MURDER OF THE JEWS

THE ADVANCE OF THE WEHRMACHT into Poland was accompanied by outrages against the Jewish civilian population. Even before the surrender of Warsaw on September 27, 1939, the *Einsatzgruppen* (task forces) of the security police and the SD, which followed behind the Wehrmacht, had received detailed instructions from Gestapo headquarters in Berlin on how to deal with the Polish Jews. They were to be concentrated in larger cities favorably located with respect to transportation facilities and herded into ghettoes under the administration of Jewish Councils (*Judenräte*), at the head of each of which a Jewish elder was placed to act as an agent of the German occupation authority. In Warsaw, half a million people were packed together into a very small area. Hermetically sealed off from the outside world, the Jews, living in abysmally unsanitary conditions and with completely inadequate provisions, were forced to work in factories and workshops producing armaments for the Reich. In Lodz (after April 1940 called Litzmannstadt), about 160,000 Jews lived in the ghetto; a similar situation prevailed in many other Polish cities, such as Radom and Kielce, Cracow and Tschenstochau (modern Czestochowa). Part of the misery was the humiliation inflicted on the Jews. After the synagogues had been destroyed, Polish Jews were forced, beginning in November 1939, to wear a mark of identification on their clothes, first a yellow armband and then a Jewish star. But ghetto life was only a prelude to much worse to come. Over the next three years, Poland was the main theater for the "final solution to the Jewish question."

The outbreak of war on September 1, 1939, also served as a pretext for new harassment of the Jews in Germany. They were barred from leaving

The painter Felix Nussbaum was born in 1904 into an upper-middle-class German Jewish family in Osnabrück. In 1932–1933 he was a fellow at the Villa Massimo in Rome. After 1935 he lived in exile in Brussels, at the end in hiding, until he was denounced in July 1944. He was murdered at Auschwitz a short time later. His *Selbstbildnis mit Judenpaß und Judenstern* (Self-Portrait with Jewish Passport and Jewish Star"), painted in August 1943, has come to symbolize Jewish life in the time of Nazi persecution. Felix-Nussbaum-Haus, Osnabrück.

their apartments and houses after 9:00 P.M. in the summer and 8:00 P.M. in the winter. As "enemies of the Reich" they were prohibited from owning radios after September 20; from July 19, 1940, the same applied to telephones. Starting in September 1939, Jews could obtain their food rations (substantially reduced compared to what "Aryans" received) only in special shops; in Berlin an ordinance passed in July 1940 stipulated that they could do so only between 4:00 and 5:00 P.M., when many goods were no longer available. Mean-spirited bureaucrats dreamed up ever new nastiness, such as prohibitions against keeping pets and using lending libraries.

Beginning in December 1938, Jews were obligated to perform forced labor. In the armaments industry they replaced the men who had been drafted into the Wehrmacht, working under discriminatory conditions in "closed work deployments" separated from the "Aryan" workforce. On September 1, 1941, the regime issued a police ordinance on the identification of Jews: as of September 15, all Jews age six and older would have to wear a yellow star sewn onto their clothes. This put the finishing touches on public humiliation and stigmatization and perfected the surveillance of the persecuted minority. As of July 1, 1943 (by virtue of the Thirteenth Decree to the Reich Citizenship Law), Jews were placed under police law, which meant they no longer had any possibility of legal appeal. But by this time very few Jews were still living in Germany. About half had emigrated, the others had been "evacuated," which means they had been deported east in collective transports. Officially the German Reich was "free of Jews." A few had taken refuge in clandestine existence, others lived with the dubious protection afforded by "mixed marriages" with non-Jewish partners, ever fearful of sharing the fate of the majority of the German Jews.

Why did Germany's Jews as a whole not flee from the impending catastrophe of Hitler and Nazi rule in a timely escape? The reasons why they did not include the economic and administrative obstacles to emigration, as well as the political barriers that potential host countries erected for Jews from Germany (and later for Jews from all over Europe). Other obstacles were the almost inevitable loss of status that came with emigration and the lack of professional qualifications for a new life in the countries of exile. The self-conception of the highly assimilated German Jews was a significant—at first even the most significant—reason not to emigrate. German Jews could not help but realize that their service for the fatherland in the First World War, their love for Germany, and their roots in German culture and intellectual life counted for nothing. Even so, very

In June 1940, 157,000 people lived in the ghetto in Lodz (Litzmannstadt). The German administration was headed by Hans Biebow, a coffee dealer from Bremen. Beginning in October 1939, Mordechai Chaim Rumkowski was the Jewish elder (*Judenältester*). In October 1941, 20,000 Jews arrived, some of them from Germany and Austria. The residents of the ghetto also included 5,000 "gypsies" from Burgenland (a province in the east of Austria). Jüdisches Museum, Frankfurt am Main.

few believed the threats that the Hitler government would solve the "Jewish question" by force, and in the beginning many even refused to accept the announced measures as reality.

After its annexation in the spring of 1938, Austria became the testing ground for the forced emigration of the Jewish minority. According to the census of March 1934, Austria was home to 191,481 persons of the "Israelite faith" (after the definitions introduced by the Nuremberg Laws there were a few thousand more Jews, their total number estimated at 206,000). About 130,000 Austrian Jews left the country between the *Anschluss* and the outbreak of the Second World War. Some fled on their own initiative. Others took that step in response to pressure exerted after August 1938 by the Central Office for Jewish Emigration, which was set up in Vienna by Adolf Eichmann on orders from the Reich Central Security Office and the commissioner for the reunification of Austria with the Reich, Josef Bürckel. In return for a fee of 5 percent of a person's assets, the Central Office issued passports and organized the departure in a process that involved

Forced labor in the saddlery of the Lodz ghetto. One of 450 slides made by an amateur German photographer who documented ghetto life from the perspective of the perpetrators. Jüdisches Museum, Frankfurt am Main.

further plundering of the émigrés. As an agency concerned purely with driving Jews out, it did not bother with visas and passages or other details pertaining to entry into a country of exile. In the beginning its sole aim was to finance the emigration with Jewish money and to drive forward the departure also of poor Jews with the help of forced levies.

The Central Office in Vienna, which organized the deportations to the extermination camps beginning in 1941 and thereby had a major role in the genocide, provided the model for the Reich Central Office for Jewish Emigration in Berlin, which was established in January 1939 and was run by Eichmann from October 1939.

Until 1939, the Nazi state simultaneously pushed and slowed down the emigration of German Jews. The displacement of Jews from economic life made them more willing to leave, but the plundering to which they were subjected by the confiscation of assets and ruinous fees and levies obstructed emigration. One piece of insidiousness on the part of the regime was that it was hoping to export anti-Semitism if the impoverished Jews driven from Germany became a social problem in their host countries. In July 1938, an international conference devoted to the problem of Jewish emigration from Germany took place in Evian on the French shores of Lake Geneva. Invitations had been issued by U.S. President Franklin D. Roosevelt, representatives from thirty-two countries attended, nothing was done.

Heightened pressure to emigrate exerted by the Nazi state in early 1939 was followed by massive obstructionism, culminating in the prohibition of emigration in the autumn of 1941. At the last moment, after the Kristallnacht pogrom, many German Jews, who now recognized the seriousness of the situation, tried to obtain the necessary papers, battled bored bureaucrats, and negotiated with unscrupulous profiteers hawking visas and passages of dubious quality as a chance to save oneself. There was a flourishing trade in questionable tickets and useless entry visas to South American countries. Many countries, Cuba being one of them, required "presentation money" as starting capital upon arrival; because of German foreign currency regulations, this money could be furnished only by relatives or friends abroad.

An application for a passport could be submitted to the police only after the applicant had procured certificates of non-objection from various tax offices stating that all taxes had been paid, including the "Reich Escape Tax" and one's proper share of the "Atonement Payment," the special tax cynically imposed on German Jews following the November pogrom. The necessary money was difficult to raise even for those who still had wealth, because Jewish assets had been sequestered since the end of April 1938.

Great Britain, because it did not eventually fall under German rule as did most of the emigration countries of Europe, was home to the largest number of German Jewish immigrants, temporarily and permanently. By the autumn of 1938, about 11,000 Jews had taken themselves to safety in the British Isles; after Kristallnacht another 40,000 were allowed to enter. British aid for Jewish children from Germany, which began immediately after the November pogrom, was swift and generous: thousands were saved by the Children's Transports (*Kindertransporte*).

The most important and most desirable countries of emigration were Palestine and the United States. However, for a variety of reasons it was particularly difficult to get to either one. Palestine was under the British Mandate, and the Zionists eager to immigrate, mostly young Jews preparing for a life together as settlers, were admitted only in small numbers on the basis of a complicated quota system. Under the official aegis of the Jewish Agency, that is to say, legally, a maximum of 29,000 Jews from Germany emigrated to Palestine between 1933 and 1936; from 1937 to 1941, approximately another 18,000 emigrated. Illegal immigration (*alijah beth*) was fraught with risks and only a few thousand individuals in all were successful at it.

Immigration quotas were for many the insurmountable barrier to the United States, but up until 1939 the yearly quotas were not even met. The reasons for this were both the foreign currency controls in Germany and the restrictive policies of the American immigration authorities. Although the restrictions were loosened following the November pogrom of 1938, for many it came too late. If the initial concern in the United States was that of being inconvenienced by impoverished Jews from Central Europe, once the war broke out there was the added fear that Nazi spies could infiltrate the stream of refugees. In any case, to obtain an immigration permit to the United States one had to surmount considerable bureaucratic hurdles. Still, the United States became by far the most important emigration country, a place where more than 130,000 German-speaking Jews found refuge.

The outbreak of the Second World War spelled an end to most emigration options as diplomatic representations were closed and opportunities for transportation disappeared. Only 15,000 Jews managed to leave Germany in 1940; another 8,000 followed in 1941. In spite of the prohibition on emigration issued on October 23, 1941, six weeks after the police ordinance requiring the wearing of the Jewish star, another 8,500 Jews escaped between 1942 and 1945. The final phase of Nazi policy toward the Jews began in the fall of 1941 with the systematic, bureaucratically organized, and meticulously planned deportation of Jews from Germany. This policy was now single-mindedly and exclusively aimed at the extermination of European Jewry. Since the end of July 1941, Heydrich had been in possession of an ordinance from Hermann Göring, who in formal terms had the final say on anything concerning the "Jewish question" in Germany. The authorization contained two tasks: first, Heydrich was "to make all necessary preparations with regard to organizational, practical, and financial aspects for a comprehensive solution [*Gesamtlösung*] to the Jewish question in the German sphere of influence in Europe"; second, Heydrich was to present Göring "promptly" with an overall plan for the execution of the intended "final solution [*Endlösung*] to the Jewish question."

The preparations were complete by the middle of October 1941. Jews everywhere now received mimeographed orders to appear at collection sites for "evacuation." They were sent rules of conduct on what to take along for "settlement in the east," in what condition to leave their apartments and houses (electricity, gas, and water bills had to be paid before departure). Along with being assigned an "evacuation number," Jews had been informed that their entire assets had been confiscated by the state police retroactive to October 15, 1941, and that "dispositions of assets (gifts or sales) made since that time were invalid." In addition, they were ordered to draw up a declaration of property that had to include objects sold or given away in the interim, along with the names and addresses of the new owners. All relevant documents, such as promissory notes, stock certificates, insurance policies, purchase contracts, and so forth, had to be appended to the declaration.

In formal terms the robbing of Jewish wealth and property, a process that forced Jews to lend a bureaucratic helping hand in their own victimization, was based on the Eleventh Decree to the Reich Citizenship Law, one of the Nuremberg Laws of 1935. Step by step these implementation decrees had curtailed the rights of the Jews, in the end driving all those who had not been able to escape into ghettoes and extermination camps. The Eleventh Decree, which came into force on November 25, 1941, stipulated the conditions under which Jews lost their German citizenship and specified the details; the loss was automatic with "relocation of the habitual residence to other countries." The purpose of the decree was made plainly evident by the following statement: "Upon the loss of citizenship the assets of the Jews become the property of the German Reich." To preclude every possibility of circumventing this regulation, the section of the Reich Central Security Office in charge of Jewish affairs, IV B 4, had issued restraints on the disposal of movable Jewish property. This ordinance, dated November 27, 1941, was also retroactive to October 15. Its purpose was to prevent transfers of property prior to the deportation of the Jews.

As if these retroactive legal constructions were not dubious enough, one must add the fact that relocation of one's "habitual residence" to another country was no longer in any way a matter of choice for Jews. In order to close the last gap in the system designed to rob German Jews first of their wealth and freedom, then their civic existence, and finally their lives, at the beginning of December 1941 the Interior Ministry, in a secret directive on the implementation of the Eleventh Decree, defined the phrase "other countries" (*Ausland*) as it related to deportation: "The loss of citizenship and the confiscation of property applies also to those . . . Jews whose habitual residence is, or will be in the future, in territories occupied by German troops or placed under German administration, including the Generalgouvernement and the Reich Commissariats of Ostland and Ukraine."

With these legislative acts the regime had created the framework for the expulsion of the Jews from Germany. Moreover, the deportation of Jews from Reich territory had already been tested in various places: the expulsion of a Jewish population on a large scale had occurred in the immediate aftermath of the assault on Poland when western Polish territories were annexed. Polish Jews living in the annexed *Gau* Wartheland had been moved to the environs of Lublin and to other areas of the General-gouvernement, where they led a miserable existence in camps. Six months after the outbreak of war, the first deportation of German Jews took place in Pomerania: on February 12, 1940, one thousand Jews from Stettin and environs were taken from their homes in the middle of the night and sent to three villages near Lublin. The same fate befell three hundred and sixty Jews from the Prussian administrative district of Schneidemühl in March 1940. The action was justified on the grounds that the residential space was "urgently needed for reasons of the wartime economy." Few survived these deportations; most fell victim to the mass murders that began in the spring of 1942.

As late as the summer of 1941, the goal of Nazi policy toward the Jews had not yet been fixed in its final consequence. Although there was no lack of public threats, including that of the "destruction" of the "Jewish race," uttered for example by Hitler in his speech to the Reichstag in January 1939, until the attack on the Soviet Union it was not clear what it all meant. Some historians have argued that the regime was radicalized during the Second World War. This argument cannot be brushed aside, but neither can the emphasis placed on the anti-Jewish intentions in the ideology and practice of National Socialism, which ended in genocide.

Ideas for the Final Solution included a plan to deport the Jews from the German sphere of power to the island of Madagascar, a French colony. Following the defeat of France in 1940, the Foreign Ministry took up the plan, with Eichmann at the Reich Central Security Office in charge of the details. The idea to deport Jews to Madagascar could be found in the anti-Semitic literature of the nineteenth century; considering just the climate of the island, we should see it more as an expression of the desire to annihilate the Jews than as a project to set up a Jewish state. In the discussions about the expulsion of the Jews, a reservation near Lublin was considered for a while. This project was undone not least by the opposition of Governor-General Hans Frank in Cracow, who wanted the part of occupied Poland he governed to be "free of Jews." The Madagascar plan, pursued under the catchphrase "territorial final solution," was filed away in August 1940. The attack on the Soviet Union offered new options for the Final Solution, namely straightforward destruction. In the summer of 1941, the phrase "final solution"—like "special treatment," or "resettlement," one of the euphemistic expressions of what Victor Klemperer called the "lingua tertii imperii" (the language of the Third Reich)—took on the exclusive meaning of genocide. It no longer meant evacuation or deportation.

The decision to physically destroy European Jewry had been made by this time. It required neither a written order from Hitler nor the protocol of a conference in the dictator's closest circle of leadership. Tacit agreement was sufficient for the order to Himmler as the man in charge of the necessary personnel in the SS and the police. Within official channels, the planning and implementation of genocide was the responsibility of the chief of the Reich Central Security Office, Reinhard Heydrich, and after 1943 of his successor, Ernst Kaltenbrunner.

Himmler himself had repeatedly spoken bluntly about the murder of the Jews to high functionaries of the regime and generals of the Wehrmacht. For example, in October 1943, he said in a speech in Poznan, "The sentence 'The Jews have to be exterminated,' just a few words, is easily uttered, gentlemen. From the person who has to carry it out, it demands the harshest and gravest thing there is. . . . We had to ask ourselves the question What about the women and children? I have decided to find a clear solution also in this regard. You see, I did not feel justified in exterminating the men—meaning, to kill them or have them killed—and having their avengers, in the shape of their children, grow up for our sons and grandsons. The grave decision had to be taken to make this people disappear from the earth."

One part of the machinery of destruction had already been in action since the beginning of the Russian campaign. The task forces (*Einsatzgruppen*) of the security police and the SD were units placed under the supreme command of Reichsführer SS Himmler and authorized, as an order in the spring of 1941 put it, "to take executive measures against the civilian population on their own responsibility within the framework of their task." Their task was to execute "ideological enemies," namely functionaries of the Communist party of the Soviet Union, "Jews holding positions in the party and the state," and other "radical elements."

This had already been tested in the war against Poland, but also after the *Anschluss* of Austria and the invasion of Czechoslovakia, when task forces of the security police liquidated potential opponents such as intellectuals, clergymen, and politicians. Following the assault on the Soviet Union, beginning in the summer of 1941, four *Einsatzgruppen,* to-

Einsatzgruppen (literally, Special Task Groups; in reality, mobile SS killing units) in the Soviet Union.

taling 3,000 men, were operating as murder units carrying out massacres of a nearly unimaginable magnitude among the civilian population in the Baltic region, White Russia, Ukraine, and on the Crimea. Between June 1941 and April 1942, nearly 560,000 people were murdered by the *Einsatzgruppen,* among them virtually the entire Jewish civilian population of the conquered territories. Men, women, and children were driven into forests or open fields, shot, and buried in mass graves.

While the *Einsatzgruppen* of the SS in the east and the Baltic had long since begun carrying out the large-scale mass murder of Polish, Russian,

Reinhard Heydrich (1904–1942, on the left), who in 1931 organized the Security Service (SD) on the model of the Secret Service, was Himmler's most important collaborator in setting up the system of terror. He died from injuries suffered during an assassination attempt by the Czech resistance. DIZ, SV-Bilderdienst, Munich.

and Ukrainian Jews, the Reich Security Central Office was preparing the Final Solution. On July 31, 1941, Göring had passed the formal order to that effect to Himmler's right-hand man, SS Obergruppenführer Reinhard Heydrich, who, as chief of the Reich Central Security Office, held the office where all the threads of the terror apparatus came together. The thirty-seven-year-old SS general was considered the prototype of the ice-cold, intelligent, and cultivated technician of power, who, unlike the "old fighters" with their emotional ties to Hitler and Nazi ideology, pursued his career and implemented plans with a distanced and cool demeanor. In September 1941, Heydrich also took over the duties of the Reich protector in Prague in order to secure the Czech armament potential by disciplining Czech workers.

Heydrich had sent out invitations to a "conference followed by breakfast" in his villa on the Große Wannsee in Berlin. The meeting was supposed to have taken place in December 1941, but it had to be postponed on short notice. The invitation was urgent, "since the questions up for discussion do not permit any further delay." On January 20, 1942, at noon, fifteen important men gathered, with Heydrich presiding: high officials with the rank of undersecretaries of state from the Interior Ministry, the Foreign Ministry, the Ministry of Justice, the Reich Chancellery, the Eastern Ministry, and the administration of the Generalgouvernement, representatives of the NSDAP apparatus, and officers from the highest levels of the SS. The Reich Transportation Ministry, the Reich Railroad, and the

Adolf Eichmann at his trial in Jerusalem, 1961. DIZ,
SV-Bilderdienst, Munich.

Reich Finance Ministry were not represented, and nobody from the Wehrmacht was present. SS Obersturmbannführer Eichmann kept the minutes of the meeting with the help of an unknown secretary, the only
woman present.

On the agenda was the murder, if possible, of all the Jews living in Europe. This had long since been decided upon at the highest levels. The issues in January 1942 were merely the logistics of genocide, the "paral-
lelization of approaches," as Heydrich put it, temporal and regional
preferences, and finally, the circle of individuals affected: whether, and if
so, how *Mischlinge* or Jewish partners in "mixed marriages" should be included in the program of murder. Although the debate about *Mischlinge*
and family members had no immediate consequences, it did reveal the
determination of the Nazi regime to murder all the Jews it could lay its
hands on in a planned, cold-blooded, bureaucratic, and calculated manner. The first issue, as Heydrich explained, was eleven million Jews all over
Europe who had to be exterminated.

In the minutes of the conference, the murderous intent of the Nazi
regime was little changed with respect to language, and little effort was
made to conceal it. The central passage reads as follows: "Under proper
leadership the Jews shall now be put to work in the framework of the

A report from Himmler to Hitler from December 1942, reporting the execution of 362,211 Jews (under section 2, "Guerilla helpers and suspected guerillas," line c, Jews executed). Bundesarchiv, Koblenz.

Final Solution. The Jews shall be taken into the eastern areas, building roads in large work crews, separated by sex. There is no doubt that a large number will become natural casualties. . . . The Jews who remain will have to be given special treatment. These Jews are undoubtedly the most resistant group because they represent a natural elite that, when free again, could be the germ cell of a new Jewish revival."

There was hardly any discussion about the genocide of Europe's Jews. The high officials and officers were all in agreement and were eager to outdo each other in their approval for the Final Solution. Nobody expressed doubts or skepticism, let alone objections. When Eichmann was on trial in Jerusalem two decades later, he described the mood of the assembled gentlemen: "On this point one could note not only a happy agreement from all sides, but beyond that also something quite unexpected, I would call it an effort to outdo and trump each other with respect to the demands for the final solution to the Jewish question."

The erroneous idea that the murder of the Jews was decided on at this conference is widely held. An agreement to exterminate millions of human beings would have far exceeded the competencies of the participants. Moreover, the tragedy of the mass murder of Jews was long since a reality. Murders were already being carried out in Soviet territory, and reports of them were regularly and properly conveyed to Berlin. For example, Activities Report No. 6 of the *Einsatzgruppen* of the Security Police and the SS recorded the following in October 1941: "In Kiev all Jews were arrested and a total of 33,771 Jews were executed on September 29 and 30. Money, valuables, and clothing were secured." This crime in the ravine of Babi Yar on the outskirts of Kiev was only one incident among many. Murders by means of poisoned gas had also been going on in the camp at Chelmno since the beginning of December 1941. The phase of pogroms, massacres, and excesses was at this time replaced by the period of systematic, industrially perfected murder. At least half a million Jews had been killed by the time the Wannsee conference took place in January 1942.

The shootings and killings, however, were unnerving to the perpetrators, even if they found plenty of willing helpers in the form of Ukrainian, Lithuanian, and Latvian militias. In response the SS began looking for new ways to kill human beings on a mass scale. In the fall of 1941, participants in the euthanasia "Action T 4," who had experience with the planned murder of the sick and disabled, began the construction of extermination camps at three remote locations on Polish soil: Belzec, Sobibor, and Treblinka. Residents of the Jewish ghettoes were transported to these camps and immediately murdered in gas chambers. The gas came from the exhaust of diesel motors operated by Ukrainian auxiliaries. Between March 1942 and October 1943, about 1.75 million Jews died in these three camps, first Jews from Poland, then Jews from other countries. "Action Reinhard," the code name for this mass murder, also yielded material booty worth at least 180 million reichsmarks, all of it stolen from the victims. The traces of these places of murder were covered up as early as 1943.

The largest extermination camp, Auschwitz, had been set up in the spring of 1940 as a concentration camp on annexed Polish territory. In 1941, the original camp (called the *Stammlager* or Auschwitz I) was expanded with the addition of two new areas: the extermination camp Birkenau (Auschwitz II), and Monowitz (Auschwitz III), the site of forced labor in the buna factory owned by I. G. Farben and the center for forty satellite camps (*Aussenlager*) in Upper Silesia. In the summer of 1941,

HEINRICH HIMMLER (1900–1945) was shaped by his upbringing in a pious Bavarian Catholic family devoted to the monarchy. After studying agriculture he worked for a time as a fertilizer salesman and ran a chicken farm near Munich. In 1923 he participated in the Hitler putsch; following his appointment as head of the SS in January 1929, he devoted himself exclusively to politics. In his capacity as Munich police president, he set up the Dachau concentration camp at the beginning of March 1934 and with expanded powers he organized the political police in all of the states. Following the elimination of the SA in 1934, he moved into the top echelons of power. After the merger of the SS and the police, Himmler, who controlled the Gestapo and the concentration camps, had all the instruments of terror at his disposal. As "Reich Commissioner for the Strengthening of Germandom" (from October 1939), he was responsible for "Germanization" of the occupied territories. Beginning in August 1943 he was also minister of the interior, and in July 1944 he was appointed commander-in-chief of the Reserve Army. Loyal and submissive toward Hitler, implacable and patriarchal as commander of the SS, Himmler, who had the personality of a narrow-minded bookkeeper, was not very popular. His power protected him from becoming a laughingstock, even though, as Joachim Fest has written, he had "a tendency toward institutionalizing his foolishness." A hypermoralistic pedant who was pitiless in his persecution of corruption, Himmler was also a fantast who dreamed of living in an imaginary world peopled by figures from Germanic prehistory and the German Middle Ages. He combined the character traits of a small-minded bureaucrat with those of a pathological mass murderer. The genocide of the European Jews, for which he bore ultimate responsibility, was something he regarded as a difficult duty proudly carried out: "This is a glorious page in our history, one that has never been written and shall never be written."

Himmler had summoned the commander of Auschwitz, Rudolf Höss, to Berlin and informed him that his camp would be given a central role in the Final Solution. With Eichmann's help, Höss prepared for mass extermination.

Gas was chosen as the method of mass murder, since shooting would be "simply impossible and also too great a strain on the SS men who would have to carry it out, in view of the women and children," Höss wrote in his memoirs. Murders with carbon monoxide from the exhaust of motors took place in many places in the east: in fixed locations like Treblinka, and in mobile fashion with "gas trucks," specially fitted vehicles where the ex-

Hermann Göring and Heinrich Himmler dressed
as "Old Fighters" at the anniversary march on
November 9, 1937. Münchner Stadtmuseum,
Munich.

haust fumes were directed into the holds of the trucks, which were crammed
with people. These kinds of murder machines, which unloaded the bodies into mass graves after driving around for twenty to thirty minutes, had
been in use since the autumn of 1941. At least thirty "gas trucks" were operating in the sphere of the *Einsatzgruppen,* especially in the territory of
the Soviet Union, but also in Serbia. In Chelmno (Kulmhof) in the Warth-
gau, stationary "gas trucks" were the transition to the extermination camp.

Cyclon B eventually emerged as the most suitable instrument of mass
murder because it was the easiest to transport and use. Rudolf Höss tested
it in Auschwitz in September 1941. Because the method worked so
smoothly, he built gas chambers and crematoria in which the killing of
human beings and the burning of bodies was carried out like an indus-

Heinrich Himmler during a visit to the Auschwitz extermination camp. Next to him is the chief engineer of the I. G. Farben installations at Auschwitz; behind them is Rudolf Höss, the commander of Auschwitz. DIZ, SV-Bilderdienst, Munich.

trial operation. The installations at Auschwitz-Birkenau were destroyed at the end of October 1944 and inmates who were still fit for transportation were evacuated into the interior of the Reich on death marches. On January 27, 1945, the Red Army liberated Auschwitz.

One million victims are documented for Auschwitz; 900,000 were killed in Treblinka between July 1942 and August 1943, 600,000 in Belzec, 250,000 in Sobibor, 152,000 in Chelmno, and at least 60,000 in Lublin-Maidanek. But even though extermination camps existed, the atavistic methods of mass murder through pogroms and massacres, executions in front of ditches that the victims themselves were forced to dig, and every manner of sadistic killing continued on a daily basis. "Actions" is what the murderers called their deeds, and they gave them code names such as "Harvest Feast." In the camps of Trawniki, Poniatowa, and Maidanek, more than 40,000 Jews were killed under this code name at the beginning of November 1943 alone.

One group of German Jews seemed to be privileged over those who were transported directly to the death camps of the east. In northern Bo-

Inmates in a barracks at the Buchenwald concentration camp. AKG-images, London.

hemia, in a fortress dating to Austrian times, the regime had set up a ghetto that was declared a preferred camp and old-age home for Jews from Czechoslovakia, Austria, and Germany (a substantial number also came from Denmark and the Netherlands): Theresienstadt. But the "old-age ghetto" for decorated war veterans and other prominent Jews, eventually home to 40,000 German Jews, was in practice a concentration camp with Jewish self-administration and for most merely a transfer station on the way to one of the extermination camps—Auschwitz, Treblinka, Sobibor, Belzec.

The cynical Nazi regime had not shied away from robbing the ghetto inmates in Theresienstadt with purchase contracts promising them a peaceful retirement home, and deceiving the public by staging artistic presentations and social events that gave the impression the inmates were leading a carefree, happy, urban existence when international delegations came to visit. For Jews from German-speaking regions, the highly assimilated bearers of German culture, the reality of Theresienstadt had to

The gate to the Auschwitz concentration camp. The words above the gate read, "Work liberates." DIZ, SV-Bilderdienst, Munich.

become a synonym for the betrayal of the Germans: with their faith in emancipation, they had felt safe even after 1933, because they could not imagine that their service to what they believed was a common fatherland would be ignored, their patriotism disparaged, their consciousness of German culture despised, and their civic existence no longer recognized— indeed, that it should cease to exist.

Of the roughly 500,000 German Jews, about 278,000 emigrated, though emigration did not by any means save all of them from the Holocaust. Somewhere between 160,000 and 195,000 were murdered, about 15,000 survived as spouses in "mixed marriages," fewer than 6,000 outlived the camps in the east (most of these were freed from Theresienstadt). A handful survived by living an illegal existence, especially underground in Berlin and Vienna. Their number, usually estimated at 5,000, can be determined with even less certainty than that of the murdered victims. The number of murdered German Jews is far surpassed by the victims of the genocide who were Soviet or Polish citizens. At least six million human beings were deliberately and systematically murdered because they were Jews.

There was another group that fell victim to the racial madness of the Nazis. By the mid-1930s, the traditional discrimination against gypsies turned into persecution. The Nuremberg Laws of 1935 demoted Sinti and Roma, along with Jews, to that status of citizens with lesser rights. In 1938, a Reich Central Office for Combating the Gypsy Nuisance was set up within the Reich criminal police, and on December 8, 1939, Himmler decreed that the "regulation of the gypsy question" would have to arise "from the nature of this race." Ghettoization into camps, as in Berlin, Frankfurt am Main, and other large cities, had begun in 1936; Sinti and Roma were often sent to concentration camps for being "asocial elements."

The organized deportation of Sinti and Roma from the territory of the German Reich via collection camps to Poland began in May 1940. Following internment in ghettoes and forced labor camps, the regime ordered in January 1943 that they be sent to Auschwitz. The "gypsy camp" in Auschwitz-Birkenau was liquidated in August 1944 and all its inmates were murdered in the gas chambers. Sinti and Roma were also killed in the extermination camps of Treblinka and Maidanek. In the Baltic region, Ukraine, Croatia, and Serbia, they were murdered in mass executions by the SS and the Wehrmacht as well as by local accessories to German racial policy. It is difficult to determine the number of victims, but it rose into the hundreds of thousands. Compensation for the survivors created a scandal lasting well into the 1970s, because officials, in conjunction with politicians and the media, argued along the lines of traditional discrimination and prejudice, claiming that the gypsies had been interned as criminals and asocial elements and had not been victims of racial persecution.

Auschwitz has become synonymous for the collapse of civilization represented by the crime committed against the Jews and other ethnic minorities. The genocide, carried out by dutiful servants of the Third Reich with the tacit complicity of those not directly involved, was unique for its cold-blooded planning and execution as an act of supposed raison d'état. The fact that natives in Ukraine and Lithuania, Latvia and White Russia were brought in as helpers, and that autochthonous anti-Semitism was used for pogroms and excesses against the Jews, diminishes neither Germany's guilt nor its obligation for restitution.

14

RESISTANCE

TRANSLATION OF THE PAMPHLET of the White Rose:

Leaflets of the Resistance Movement in Germany.

A call to all Germans!

The war is nearing its certain end. As in 1918, the German government is trying to shift all attention to the growing U-boat danger, while in the east the armies are continually streaming back, and in the west the invasion is expected. America's armament has not reached its peak, but today it already surpasses anything ever seen in history. Hitler is leading the German people into the abyss with mathematical certainty. *Hitler cannot win the war, only prolong it!* His guilt and that of his helpers has infinitely exceeded every measure. Just punishment is getting closer and closer!

But what are the German people doing? They do not see and they do not hear. Blindly they follows their seducers into destruction. Victory at any cost, they have written on their flag. I fight to the last man, says Hitler—meanwhile the war is already lost.

Germans! Do you and your children want to suffer the same fate that befell the Jews? Do you want to be measured with the same yardstick as your seducers? Shall we be forever the people hated and cast out by all the world? No! Therefore separate yourselves from the National Socialist sub-humanness! Prove by your deeds that you think differently! A new war of liberation is dawning. The better part of the people is fighting on our side. Tear off the mantle of indifference you have wrapped around your heart! Decide, *before it is too late!*

While the majority of the Germans—either seduced by propaganda and blandishments, beaten down by coercion and terror, or content with the achievements of the ideology and practice of Nazi rule—lived in harmony with the regime of the Third Reich, had taken their place within the "*Volk*

Flugblätter der Widerstandsbewegung in Deutschland.

A u f r u f   a n   a l l e   D e u t s c h e !

Der Krieg geht seinem sicheren Ende entgegen. Wie im Jahre
1918 versucht die deutsche Regierung alle Aufmerksamkeit auf
die wachsende U-Bootgefahr zu lenken, während im Osten die Armeen
unaufhörlich zurückströmen, im Westen die Invasion erwartet wird.
Die Rüstung Amerikas hat ihren Höhepunkt noch nicht erreicht,
aber heute schon übertrifft sie alles in der Geschichte seither
Dagewesene. Mit mathematischer Sicherheit führt Hitler das deutsche
Volk in den Abgrund. H i t l e r   k a n n   d e n   K r i e g   n i c h t
g e w i n n e n ,   n u r   n o c h   v e r l ä n g e r n ! Seine
und seiner Helfer Schuld hat jedes Mass unendlich überschritten.
Die gerechte Strafe rückt näher und näher !

Was aber tut das deutsche Volk? Es sieht nicht und es hört
nicht. Blindlings folgt es seinen Verführern ins Verderben. Sieg
um jeden Preis, haben sie auf ihre Fahne geschrieben. Ich kämpfe
bis zum letzten Mann, sagt Hitler - indes ist der Krieg bereits
verloren.

Deutsche! Wollt Ihr und Eure Kinder dasselbe Schicksal erleiden,
das den Juden widerfahren ist? Wollt Ihr mit dem gleichen Masse
gemessen werden ,wie Eure Verführer? Sollen wir auf ewig das von
aller Welt gehasste und ausgestossene Volk sein? Nein! Darum
trennt Euch von dem nationalsozialistischen Untermenschentum!
Beweist durch die Tat, dass Ihr anders denkt! Ein neuer Befreiungs-
krieg bricht an. Der bessere Teil des Volkes kämpft auf unserer
Seite. Zerreisst den Mantel der Gleichgültigkeit, den Ihr um Euer
Herz gelegt! Entscheidet Euch, e h '   e s   z u   s p ä t   i s t !

"A Call to All Germans," the fifth pamphlet disseminated by the White Rose resistance group in January 1943, was written against the backdrop of the catastrophe in Stalingrad. Several hundred copies were distributed at the University of Munich, and it was the group's penultimate pamphlet. Gedenkstätte Deutscher Widerstand, Berlin.

community," and had succumbed to the Hitler myth, there were still many who had reservations and were skeptical. In the face of overwhelming approval and enthusiasm for the foreign policy successes of the Nazis, the minority of critics of the regime had withdrawn into "internal emigration" and displayed opposition on the outside at most through discreet acts of noncompliance.

Even among critics of the regime, patriotism and the sense of duty, German virtues rehearsed for many generations, impaired the willingness to take an oppositional stance, because such a stance seemed to violate values such as nation and fatherland. But moral outrage on the part of individuals at the unparalleled corruption of the rulers as well as the daily acts of violence gradually intensified. Beginning in 1938—the year of the Kristallnacht pogrom and the Sudeten crisis—this outrage solidified into political opposition. Unease arose among high military officers, in the Bavarian nobility, among civil servants and diplomats, and in quite disparate circles of the traditional elites who had either been stripped of power by the Nazis or who had come to recognize the true nature of the regime after initially supporting it. It was unease, first, about the radicalization of Nazi policy, especially toward minorities, and second, and more importantly, about Hitler's expansionist foreign policy, which was obviously aimed at war. After the military successes—the blitzkrieg against Poland in 1939 and the triumph over France in 1940—resistance was nowhere in sight. Resignation and paralysis had settled upon the discontented and the enemies of Nazi rule. But the hardships of everyday life in wartime were being felt. The dilettantism of Nazi functionaries and empty promises regarding the course of the war gave rise to doubts and criticism. This criticism crystallized in various circles in which members of the traditional elites, liberals and conservatives, military men and diplomats, set the tone.

Carl Goerdeler, born in 1884, came from a civil servant family rich in tradition. After studying law he joined the civil service and was appointed lord mayor of Leipzig in 1930. His reputation as an eminent expert in administration and a superb organizer spread far beyond Leipzig, and on several occasions he was mentioned as a possible candidate for the office of chancellor. In December 1931 he was appointed Reich price commissioner. Unlike his colleague Konrad Adenauer, whose tenure as lord mayor of Cologne came to an abrupt end with the Nazis' accession to power, Goerdeler, a politician with a national-conservative bent, was not forced to leave his post in Leipzig. He was also reappointed price commissioner in January 1934, even though he had made no concessions to the new Reich government and had not joined the NSDAP.

Soon, however, Goerdeler found himself in opposition to Nazi finance and economic policy. He disapproved of the risky creation of credit by Hjalmar Schacht, the minister of economics, which was used to finance rearmament, and he criticized the anti-Jewish policy of the Third Reich because of its negative repercussions for Germany's reputation abroad. In two expert opinions on the financial situation (dated 1934 and 1935), which Hitler had solicited, Goerdeler did not hide his criticism. It turned into open protest when the Nazis, in November 1934, forced through the removal of the monument to Jewish composer Felix Mendelssohn-

Carl Goerdeler, the lord mayor of Leipzig, at
the festivities at the Gewandhaus celebrating
the fiftieth anniversary of Richard Wagner's
death, 1933. DIZ, SV-Bilderdienst, Munich.

Bartholdy from its place in front of city hall. On April 1, 1937, Goerdeler
resigned as lord mayor of Leipzig.

At this point, however, Goerdeler's oppositional attitude was not yet
a stance of resistance aimed at getting rid of the Hitler regime. Even if he
and many other conservatives disapproved of the Nazis' methods, the re-
peal of the Versailles treaty and the restoration of the 1914 borders of the
Reich were goals they all shared. Furnished with a consulting contract by
the Stuttgart industrialist Robert Bosch, Goerdeler, with the full knowledge of Hermann Göring, undertook extensive business trips outside of
Germany in the years following his resignation as mayor. One result of
these trips was that he repeatedly warned Göring that German foreign
policy leaders should not underestimate France and Great Britain. At the
same time, he called attention to the negative impression that the policy
toward the churches and the persecution of the Jews were creating
abroad. Another purpose of these trips was to awaken and promote sympathy and understanding for opposition to the Reich government.

The Berlin Wednesday Club (*Mittwochgesellschaft*), a traditional circle of liberal and conservative personalities from academia and public life, which had been meeting every other Wednesday since 1863 for scholarly conversation, became a meeting place for critics and opponents of the Nazis. Here Goerdeler met others of like intellect who shared his critique of Hitler, men like the chief of the army general staff, Ludwig Beck, the German ambassador to Rome, Ulrich von Hassell, Prussian Finance Minister Johannes Popitz, and economist Jens Jessen. They were all in agreement that the war Hitler was openly pursuing would be disastrous for Germany. Until the summer of 1938, General Beck tried to influence Hitler with memoranda and presentations about the risk that a war posed to Germany. However, when he realized how little support his concerns enjoyed among high officers, he tendered his resignation on August 18, 1938.

With his far-ranging contacts to opponents all over Germany, Goerdeler became the center of a circle of resistance that expanded in various directions and was closely linked with the military opposition through Ludwig Beck. After the outbreak of war in the autumn of 1939, unionists like Jakob Kaiser and the Social Democrat Wilhelm Leuschner joined the Goerdeler circle. The industrialists Robert Bosch and Paul Reusch sympathized with the plans of the Goerdeler circle. The network of like-minded individuals—mostly men from the conservative and national-liberal bourgeoisie and Christian politicians—was growing.

The activities went in two directions. First, Goerdeler urged a coup, the overthrow of Hitler by the military to prevent the widening of the war. Second, he was working on blueprints for a political and social order whose foundation would be constitutionality, morality, civic decency, and a Christian worldview. The ideas of the Goerdeler circle were characterized more strongly by authoritarian traits than democratic ones, and national-conservative longings oriented toward the Bismarckian empire are impossible to overlook.

At the end of 1941, Carl Goerdeler and Ludwig Beck co-authored an essay entitled "Das Ziel" (The Goal). Alongside the "Grundsätze für die Neuordnung" (Principles for the New Order) that emerged from the Kreisau circle, this essay was the most important constitutional blueprint of the resistance. The time of its composition—the period of Hitler's greatest military triumphs—explains its assumption that the German Reich would be able to continue to exist within its territorial boundaries of 1938 (including Austria, Alsace, the Sudeten region, and the Polish territories). The political stance of the Goerdeler circle is revealed nowhere better than in this essay. Characteristic are the statements on voting rights, the structure of the Reich from the bottom up, the notion of self-government, and the dominant position of the chancellor. The people's assembly appears in last place among the constitutional institutions, almost as an appendix to the Reich government. Alongside the indirectly elected Reichstag there would be an unelected Reichsständehaus (composed of representatives of professional groups, the universities, and individuals appointed by the "leader of the state") with equal authority. The minister of defense headed the list of necessary ministers. A minister of labor was deliberately rejected, since all ministries were to participate in equal measure in this important area of civic life.

Patriarchal features in Goerdeler and Beck's conception combine with calls for moral enlightenment. A sense of responsibility and "mutual trust among decent men" were more important to the authors of the essay than democratic notions of participation. "The dictatorial or tyrannical Führer state" seemed to them "as much out of the question as unchecked hyperparliamentarism." At the head of the state they considered options such as a hereditary emperor, an elective emperor, or a "Reich leader" (*Reichsführer*) elected for a specific term, but they showed a clear predilection for a hereditary monarch.

In the winter of 1941–1942, the plans took on more concrete shape. Following Hitler's violent overthrow, a directorate would initially exercise governmental power: General Ludwig Beck as Reich leader, Goerdeler as chancellor, and General Field Marshal von Witzleben as commander in chief of the army. Lists of ministerial appointments were worked out; later these fell into the hands of the Gestapo, with fatal consequences for many. A program of government was drawn up in the summer of 1944 in expectation of the imminent coup. That required long negotiations and the bringing to bear of influence on the military opposition. In 1942, Goerdeler tried in vain to win over a popular, high-ranking troop commander like the chief of Army Group Middle on the eastern front, General Field Marshal Kluge. Because the popular frontline fighters refused to join the effort, this left only the officers of the reserve army, especially in offices in Berlin, who would be able to accomplish the coup militarily. The most important contact was General Friedrich Olbricht, head of the Army Central Administration Office.

As time passed and the number of failed assassination plans by the military grew and Germany's military situation deteriorated, it became increasingly clear that a coup could no longer serve the goal of political renewal but would merely end the war. Another goal, moreover, was to send the world a signal that there had been resistance to National Socialism.

The Goerdeler-Beck government that was to assume power following Hitler's removal could not have done much more than conclude an unconditional armistice.

Even before July 20, 1944, Goerdeler came under suspicion and went underground. He was informed on and arrested on August 12, 1944. Sentenced to death on September 8, 1944, he was executed at the Berlin-Plötzensee prison on February 2, 1945, after countless interrogations. His fate was shared by Johannes Popitz, estate owner Ewald von Kleist-Schmenzin, Eugen Bolz, Ulrich von Hassell, the former German ambassador to Moscow, Graf von der Schulenberg, and many others.

In Kreisau in Lower Silesia, on the estate of Graf Moltke, a few men and women gathered at Pentecost in 1942 to discuss topics ranging from the relationship between state and church to education, university reform, and the training of teachers. Prominent leaders of the "Kreisau Circle" were Helmuth James Graf von Moltke and Peter Graf Yorck von Wartenburg. Moltke had studied law and was familiar with the Anglo-Saxon world. Politically liberal and with a deep Christian conviction, he despised the Nazis. After passing his second state examination in 1933, he decided to give up his goal of becoming a judge and settled as a lawyer in Berlin. At the beginning of the Second World War he became an expert on international law in the *Abwehr* of the Army High Command (OKW). Peter Graf Yorck von Wartenburg was likewise the bearer of a famous Prussian name. He too was a lawyer, had risen in the civil service to the level of senior government councillor, and after 1942 worked in the War Economy Office of the OKW.

Even before the war, the two men had gathered opponents of the regime around themselves. Among these like-minded individuals was Eugen Gerstenmaier, a Protestant theologian from the Swabian petty bourgeoisie who during the war was drafted into service in the Department of Cultural Policy of the Foreign Ministry. Other Kreisau members were Adam von Trott zu Solz, a lawyer in the Foreign Ministry and a cosmopolitan patriot with connections abroad; Hans Lukaschek, the former Oberpräsident of the Prussian province of Upper Silesia, whom the Nazis had thrown out of office; and Theodor Steltzer, who had been a Landrat in Rendsburg until 1933. The Kreisau Circle was made up of men of very diverse social, ideological, and political backgrounds. Alfred Delp and Augustin Rösch were Jesuit fathers, Adolf Reichwein was an educator and Social Democrat, Hans Peters was a professor of administrative law and a committed Catholic and Democrat, Harald Poelchau was a Protestant clergyman and religious Socialist, Theo Haubach, Julius Leber, and Carlo

Helmuth James Graf von Moltke before the People's Court in the fall of 1944. An estate owner in Silesia, von Moltke became an opponent of the Nazis out of Christian and liberal convictions. DIZ, SV-Bilderdienst, Munich.

Mierendorff had made names for themselves as Social Democratic politicians and suffered for it in the concentration camps. Many members of the circle had been influenced and shaped by the youth movement; social commitment was something they all had in common.

The "Principled Declaration," which they drafted in May of 1942, is a key document of the resistance against Hitler. It expresses the intention of giving the state and society a new order and new orientation following the defeat of National Socialism: "We see in Christianity supremely valuable forces for the religious and ethical renewal of the *Volk,* for overcoming hatred and lies, for rebuilding the west, for the peaceful cooperation of nations."

In three larger meetings, the Kreisau Circle discussed the foundations of a humane and social order of coexistence within a national and European framework, ideas that were put into their final form in 1943 in the "Principles of a New Order." Seven indispensable demands were to form the basis of inner renewal and of a just and lasting peace. The reestablishment of the constitutional state (*Rechsstaat*), the guarantee of freedom of religion and freedom of conscience, and the right to work and property stood at the top of the list. Self-determination and responsibility would once again take the place of the principle of command and obedience. Instead of dictatorship and subjugation, the principles of the political and social order would be political responsibility and the participation of every person, including participation in decision-making in the workplace and the economy. The Kreisauers were more interested in establishing a community of nations in the spirit of international tolerance than they were in preserving the sovereign rights of single states.

The "Principles of a New Order" constituted a program for rebuilding Germany at the heart of which were the workers and the churches. It also offered an interesting variation on voting rights: every head of a household would receive an additional vote for each child that was not yet entitled to cast a ballot. Political officials and men under arms were not eligible for the Reichstag, which was to be indirectly elected by the *Landtage* (state parliaments). The economic program was dominated by the leitmotifs of state guidance of the economy, socialization of key industries, and the notion of participation in decision-making. Against Nazi rule, which was based on coercion, subjugation, and irrationality, the Kreisauers set up a social and political order founded on humanity, Christian ethics, justice, and the overcoming of class barriers. The goal of the Kreisau Circle was to reestablish a humane state based on the rule of law, which was to be rebuilt with a democratic constitution once the Nazi criminals had been punished.

Graf von Moltke was driven to resistance primarily by the Nazi crimes against the Jews, prisoners of war, and the population of the occupied eastern territories. Although he was intent on supplanting the Nazis and doing away with the totalitarian state and racial thinking, for a long time he rejected the idea of a violent removal of Hitler. His misgivings about the murder of the tyrant were not only moral in nature. The Kreisauers, like many other opponents of National Socialism, feared that the violent overthrow of the regime during a war could give rise to myths. After Germany had lost the First World War, those who could not accept the defeat had created the legend of the "stab in the back": betrayal had decided the outcome of the war when the brave and victorious German army was stabbed in the back by forces at home. The Kreisauers were very reluctant to encumber the political and social renewal with a similar burden, which the assassination of Hitler could have given rise to.

Graf von Moltke was arrested by the Gestapo in January 1944. Without Moltke as its intellectual center, the Kreisau Circle was at an end. The most active members joined the resistance surrounding Goerdeler and participated in the attempted assassination of Hitler on July 20, 1944. In the middle of August 1944, while interrogating the many accessories to the July 20 event, the Gestapo stumbled upon the Kreisau Circle. After physical abuse and torture, its leading members were put on trial before the

People's Court. To protect as many friends as possible, Moltke's strategy of defense was to claim that no coup had been planned, no organizational steps had been taken, there had been no discussions with anybody about offices and posts in a post-Hitler government. Those involved had merely engaged in theoretical musings.

Helmuth James von Moltke was sentenced to death on January 11, 1945. He was executed at the Berlin-Plötzensee prison on January 23, 1945, three months before the collapse of the Hitler state. Very few from the core of the Kreisau Circle escaped the Nazi executioners. Some were involved in the democratic reconstruction of Germany after Hitler. The legacy of the Kreisauers was their idea, set down in documents and letters, of a humane and social society after Hitler.

During the war years, resistance groups from the workers' movement expressed public criticism of the regime. The Communists, with a new tactic and largely independent of their leadership abroad, disseminated leaflets, called for sabotage of the war efforts, and circulated information about the military situation. The group surrounding Robert Uhrig and Beppo Röhmer had more than two hundred members in Berlin and Munich, with branches in Leipzig, Hamburg, and Mannheim. In February 1942 it became a victim of the Gestapo. In October 1942, the Bästlein group in Hamburg was smashed. A proletarian circle operated in Berlin until July 1944, led by machinist Anton Saefkow and former KPD deputy Franz Jacob, who built a network of resistance in Berlin's factories.

Youth protests existed for a variety of motives. Some young people simply avoided the Hitler Youth because they got nothing out of the drills and the uniformed tedium of the organization. Others, calling themselves "Edelweiß pirates," "Meuten" (gangs), and "swing youths," rebelled against the political and social strictures. Their numbers ran into the thousands. These young people irritated the authorities by the mere fact of their existence, even if political goals aimed at overthrowing the regime are barely detectable in most cases.

The youthful members of a Communist group in Berlin named after Herbert Baum, an electrician by trade, numbered about a hundred and came from a working class background. What made this group unusual is the fact that most of its members came from the Jewish youth movement and included many young girls and women. The high point and end of the activities of the Herbert Baum Group was an arson attack on the anti-Communist propaganda exhibit "The Soviet Paradise." This show had opened on May 8, 1942, in the Lustgarten in Berlin. Ten days later Herbert Baum and his friends tried to set fire to the exhibit, which com-

In 1938, in response to the Sudeten crisis and social developments in Germany, the Swabian carpenter Georg Elser (1903–1945), a loner with a pronounced sense of justice and fairness, resolved to kill Hitler. He planted a bomb in the Bürgerbräukeller in Munich, where Hitler was due to deliver a speech commemorating the putsch of 1923. But on the evening of November 8, 1939, Hitler left the hall earlier than planned, ten minutes before the bomb went off, killing eight and wounding many others. After his arrest at the Swiss border Elser confessed, but Nazi propaganda spread the story that he had acted on behalf of the British Secret Service. As a "special prisoner," Elser was interned in the concentration camp at Sachsenhausen and later in Dachau, where he was murdered on April 9, 1945. For a long time the legend that he was a Nazi agent and an instrument of the regime delayed Elser's recognition as a resistance fighter. DIZ, SV-Bilderdienst, Munich.

bined racial, cultural, and political prejudices into a primitive picture of the Soviet Union. The fire and a concurrent leafleting action, which also involved members from other resistance groups, such as the Red Chapel, were intended as a signal that resistance to National Socialism was still alive. The leaflets read "Permanent exhibit—the Nazi paradise—War. Hunger. Lies. Gestapo. How much longer?" The fire caused only minor damage and was quickly extinguished, but the Gestapo struck back at the perpetrators a few days later. In several trials, more than twenty members of the group were sentenced to death. Herbert Baum died in prison after being severely tortured.

On July 12–13, 1943, in Krasnogorsk, German prisoners of war and Communist émigrés, under Soviet direction, established the National Committee Free Germany, which called for the rescue of the fatherland through the overthrow of the Hitler regime. After initial hesitation, a large number of officers from the Stalingrad army participated, led by General Walter von Syedlitz-Kurzbach. Gedenkstätte Deutscher Widerstand, Berlin.

The student protest articulated by the Munich group the White Rose on leaflets distributed between June 1942 and February 1943 was clearly recognizable as a Christian-humanist appeal for resistance to war. Eventually the White Rose, pointing to the hopeless military situation following the catastrophe of Stalingrad, called for an active struggle against the crimes of the Nazi state. The five students who made up the core of this morally uncompromising resistance group—Hans and Sophie Scholl, Willi Graf, Christoph Probst, and Alexander Schmorell—and their mentor, the philosopher Kurt Huber, were arrested in February 1943, sentenced to death, and executed.

At the end of 1941, various groups of oppositional officers existed within the Wehrmacht, men who placed their sense of justice, morality, and political reason above military obedience. To be sure, they constituted a small minority. One member of these groups was Claus Graf Schenk von Stauffenberg. Gravely wounded in Africa, he was appointed chief of staff to the commander of the reserve army in 1944. Since the spring of

Members of the White Rose in Munich, 1942: left to right, Willi Graf, Hans Scholl, Sophie Scholl, and Alexander Schmorell. DIZ, SV-Bilderdienst, Munich.

1942 he had been urging a coup to eliminate Hitler and put an end to the crimes of the regime.

All previous attempts on Hitler's life had failed in almost grotesque fashion. After a number of plans miscarried, one was devised by which Hitler was to be shot during a visit to Army Group Middle in Smolensk. However, concern for the safety of uninvolved officers prevented the assassination from being carried out; afterward, Colonel Henning von Treschkow had a bomb placed in Hitler's plane, but the detonator failed. In March 1944, the *Abwehr* officer Colonel Rudolf-Christoph von Gersdorff smuggled a bomb into the Berlin arsenal, where Hitler was to inspect captured Russian war materiel. But Hitler left the exhibit earlier than expected, just as he had escaped Georg Elser's attempt on his life at the Bürgerbräuhaus in Munich in 1939 when he left the hall early. At the beginning of 1944, two young officers, Axel von dem Bussche and Ewald von Kleist, were planning to eliminate Hitler during the presentation of new uniforms. Since Hitler did not show, this plan too failed.

By the summer of 1944 the military situation had long since become hopeless. The Allies had landed in Normandy, the eastern front had collapsed in the center, and Germany's defeat was only a matter of time. The oppositional officers were facing the question of whether a violent overthrow still made sense, since it was foreseeable that the fate of the Ger-

Göring and Bormann inspect the site of the attempt on Hitler's life on July 20, 1944, the "Lagebarracke" (large wooden hut for meetings) at the Wolfschanze near Rastenburg (East Prussia). AKG-images, London.

mans would be decided by the victors after the war. Colonel von Stauffenberg was determined to carry out the attempt on Hitler's life, if for no other reason than to send a moral signal. He was encouraged to do so by Henning von Treschkow, who believed that it was no longer a question of practical purpose but one of whether "the German resistance movement . . . dared the decisive move before the world and history."

The coup had long since been planned. A government declaration, to be signed by Beck as the provisional head of state and Goerdeler as chancellor, had already been drafted. It was to be published immediately after the violent overthrow of the Hitler regime. To get control of the country, General Friedrich Olbricht, together with Stauffenberg and his friend Mertz von Quirnheim, drew up the operational plan "Valkyrie," which was based on an already existing plan on how to put down a potential uprising by foreign forced laborers. A web of trustworthy officers in the important military control centers was spun.

The attempt on Hitler's life was postponed three times because Himmler and Göring were not present at the conferences at the Berghof near

After an initial flirtation with National
Socialism, Colonel Claus Graf Schenk
von Stauffenberg became a driving force
of military resistance after 1938. DIZ,
SV-Bilderdienst, Munich.

Berchtesgaden on July 6, 11, and 15; as Hitler's most dangerous and important followers and holders of the highest offices in the state, they were to be killed along with Hitler. Although they were also absent on July 20, Stauffenberg and his aide-de-camp Lieutenant Werner von Haeften decided to wait no longer. In the early morning hours they left Rangsdorf airport outside of Berlin and flew to Hitler's headquarters, "Wolf's Lair," at Rastenburg in East Prussia. Shortly before 12:30 in the afternoon, Stauffenberg tripped the timer of the bomb and went to the barracks where Hitler conducted his daily situation conference. He set his briefcase with the bomb close to Hitler and left the room on a pretext. The bomb went off around 12:45, killing five of the twenty-five men present. Hitler suffered only slight injuries. Stauffenberg, who witnessed the explosion, believed the attempt had been successful and flew back to Berlin. There the co-conspirators had been waiting for hours in the offices of the High Command of the Army in the Bendlerstraße to alert the defense districts according to the "Valkyrie" plan. Friedrich Fromm, commander in chief of the reserve army, could not be persuaded to join the side of the resistance. Stauffenberg had him arrested. His place was taken by General Erich Hoepner, whom Hitler had dismissed in 1942. But hesitation on the part of the commanders of the defense districts to join the conspirators, along with the quick radio broadcast that Hitler had survived, led to the collapse of the attempted coup.

In Prague, Paris, and Vienna the conspirators were briefly successful.

They took control of the situation and took SS leaders into custody. In Berlin the resistance collapsed on the evening of July 20. Shortly before midnight, General Fromm, who had been freed by officers loyal to Hitler, arrested the leaders of the resistance. He offered Generals Beck and Hoepner the option of suicide (Hoepner declined); Olbricht, Stauffenberg, Mertz von Quirnheim, and Haeften were shot after midnight in the courtyard of the High Command office building.

During the next few days, the Gestapo arrested thousands of opponents of the regime in a large sweep. Their trials began in early August before the People's Court and went on until the collapse of the Nazi regime in May 1945. The exact number of those convicted is not known; hundreds became victims of Hitler's revenge and were executed in cruel fashion. Many of their relatives who had nothing to do with the attempted coup were taken into "Sippenhaft" (detention by reason of family liability) and sent to prison or concentration camps.

Against the blanket accusation that the German people had offered too little resistance to the Nazi regime too late, many responded, after the collapse of the Third Reich, that they had not known about the crimes, or that they had disapproved of many things but could do nothing about them, that they had to be accommodating to avoid becoming victims, that the terror had been too much. Needless to say, these justifications ignore the fact that the system of oppression did not exist from the very outset, it had to be built. The Nazis had time to do that because their successes allowed them to rely on the growing approval of the majority of the German citizens. It is also not true that the Germans, as some foreign observers speculated, were predestined to accept totalitarian rule because of a special predisposition to authoritarianism. Just as they were hardly powerless victims of Nazi oppression, a strong effect was exerted by their agreement with the goals of the regime even though they may have condemned its methods in specific instances. There were multitudinous forms of noncompliance and quiet opposition, but also patriotic loyalties that took priority over all else during the war. Many officers and social elites lived with a dilemma: while they despised the Hitler regime, they felt duty-bound to defend the state and their people against external enemies, an obligation that did not permit open outrage and violent overthrow of the government.

15

COLLAPSE

LONG BEFORE ITS MILITARY and political downfall, the Third Reich was an administrative and constitutional chaos. The orderly exercise of government power had gradually vanished during the war. From September 1939, Hitler, whose unconventional and sporadic work habits had always been antithetical to well-ordered administration and governance, was fixated on his role as general. The last session of the Reich cabinet had taken place in February 1938. The department chiefs, unless they had a personal relationship to Hitler, ceased to have access to the head of the government. Moreover, their powers were rendered void by plenipotentiaries directly accountable to the Führer, by commissioners, and by a profusion of new offices and authorities. The Ministerial Council for the Defense of the Reich, established on August 30, 1939, as a kind of regency council for the duration of the war and composed of the five holders of the key posts in the government, the party, and the Wehrmacht under the chairmanship of the Reich marshal, had no practical significance because of Göring's laziness and lack of interest.

Power in the bureaucratic sense in the end lay in the hands of three men who had the qualities of subordinate secretaries: Hans Heinrich Lammers, chief of the chancellery with the rank of minister; Martin Bormann, Hitler's omnipresent personal secretary and head of the party chancellery; and Wilhelm Keitel, chief of staff of the High Command of the Armed Forces (OKW), who was, his title of general field marshal notwithstanding, merely a desk officer with a servile attitude toward the dictator. Every document that acquired the force of law as a command, directive, or decree of the Führer was examined, edited, and put into final form by these

Soldiers of the Red Army hoist the Soviet flag on the Reichstag building in Berlin, May 2, 1945. DIZ, SV-Bilderdienst, Munich.

three secretaries. With complete loyalty and lack of imagination they made sure that every expression of their master's will was followed.

Hitler had long since ceased to inhabit reality. Filled with a deep distrust of the generals, sealed off by Bormann from ministers, gauleiters, and NSDAP chiefs, even though they formed the elite of the Third Reich as "old fighters" and companions, the Führer had given himself over to his delusions and outbursts of rage, to the fears and fantasies that filled his days and nights. Since the beginning of the war he had been spending a good deal of time in the well-equipped and fortified command centers from which he directed the military operations. He spent the longest stretches of time at "Wolf's Lair" in Rastenburg in East Prussia, where the attempt on his life took place on July 20, 1944. As he had done before the war, he often held court in Obersalzberg. In December 1944 he directed the Ardennes offensive from "Eagle's Aerie" near Bad Nauheim. On January 16, 1945, he withdrew to the bunker beneath the chancellery in Berlin, which he would not leave alive.

While Göring had progressively lost power and prestige following the failed Battle of Britain in 1940, three of the dictator's other paladins remained powerful and important—and rivals—right up to the edge of the abyss. Their guile and skills made them indispensable: the liar Goebbels, the executioner Himmler, and the technician Speer. Himmler's loyalty, however, did not last until the very end. At the last minute the Reichs-führer SS, Reich interior minister, and commander in chief of the reserve army tried to save himself and sought to negotiate a partial surrender with the western powers in the grotesque hope they would accept him as a com-rade in arms against the Soviet Union. Albert Speer, the Führer's personal architect and minister of armaments, to whom Hitler had a deeper emo-tional attachment than to anyone else, took the risk of obstructing the scorched-earth policy at the last moment. During the last days of the Third Reich he calculated his options and was perhaps already preparing for the role of the chastened Nazi, which he successfully played out after the col-lapse at the trial of the chief war criminals in Nuremberg, as an inmate in Spandau, and in his literary self-portrayal following his release.

Goebbels—though he had no other choice—remained fanatically loyal to his idol. On July 25, 1944, he had been appointed plenipotentiary-general for total war, a position that was tailor-made for the notorious firebrand. Finally he had power that went beyond issuing exhortations to hold out and inventing campaigns that extended the war: now he could order the closing of luxury restaurants and other businesses not vital to the war and was the organizer of "national resistance" to the reality of the lost war. Consistent to the last, Goebbels staged his own end at the Führer's side, down to his suicide in the bunker of the chancellery, a fate his wife and six children had to share.

The long-awaited invasion of Normandy by the western Allies was the beginning of the end for the Third Reich. Under the supreme command of U.S. General Dwight D. Eisenhower, 619,000 soldiers went ashore on June 6, 1944. With protective cover from a gigantic fleet, little impeded by the Atlantic Wall, and supported by their superior air force, the Allies opened the Second Front Stalin had long awaited and began their un-stoppable advance on "Fortress Europe." Paris was liberated on August 25; on September 3 the Allies marched into Brussels, and on October 21 they took their first larger German city, Aachen.

While the invasion of France was under way, the Red Army on the eastern front launched a large-scale offensive against Army Group Mid-dle on June 22, the third anniversary of the German attack on the Soviet Union. Within a few days, twenty-eight German divisions had been smashed. With a loss of 350,000 men, this was a greater catastrophe even

ALBERT SPEER, born in Mannheim in 1905, studied architecture in Karls-ruhe, Munich, and Berlin, where, fascinated by Hitler, he joined the NSDAP in 1931. As an unemployed architect he kept himself afloat with small projects for the party until 1933, when he was asked to renovate the Propaganda Ministry and given the job of providing designs and decorations for the party's mass rallies. Staging marches with the help of lighting effects and flags, he created a Nazi aesthetics and attracted the attention of Hitler, who held him in high regard and regarded the fellow artist as a kindred spirit. Hitler assigned Speer the task of designing the New Chancellery in Berlin and the Party Palace in Nuremberg. In 1937 he was appointed general architectural inspector of Berlin and given the assignment to plan the German capital's large-scale rebuilding and transformation into the megalopolis Germania. In 1938, at age thirty-three, he was awarded the title of professor and became a Prussian state councillor. A second career, which would take him into the top echelon of Nazi leadership, began in February 1942, when he was appointed to the offices held by Fritz Todt, who died in a plane crash: minister of armaments and munitions (after 1943 called armaments and war production), general inspector of roads, and head of an army of workers called the Todt Organization. In spite of the war-induced scarcity of infrastructure and resources, Speer was able, through dictatorial intervention and controls, to spur industry to maximum performance levels and achieve enormous increases in the production of war materiel. It was not least the unscrupulous exploitation of foreign forced labor and concentration camp inmates that allowed the talented organizer Speer to achieve these successes. In the final phase of the war, Speer, bound to Hitler by sentimental friendship, blocked the Führer's scorched-earth policy. At the war crimes trial in Nuremberg he was sentenced to twenty years in prison, which he served in Spandau, the prison for war criminals. In his memoirs (1969) and in other books, Speer depicted himself as the contrite, chastened Nazi, though he tried to deny his involvement in the crimes of the regime to the last. At first the "general provisioner of the regime," as Joachim Fest has called him, then the self-assured technocrat of many talents, with which he willingly served Hitler, Speer was one of the most important guarantors of the functioning of the Nazi state. He died in London in 1981.

In October 1943, at a meeting of NSDAP functionaries in Posen, where Himmler described the murder of the Jews in unvarnished language, Speer, whose rhetorical skills were modest, got into a fight with the gauleiter when he destroyed illusions about armaments production with a threatening tone. Later Speer would point to his all-absorbing job as chief of the mammoth armaments ministry when he claimed, as he did to the end of his life, that he had been completely unaware of the Holocaust. The fact that he left the meeting prior to Himmler's speech is, needless to say, not proof of his claim. A few days later, on October 18, 1943, he called upon apprentices of the armaments industry in Berlin to do their utmost in support of the fighting troops. Here he is shown in the company of Reich Youth Leader Axmann greeting young Germans wearing the uniforms of the Hitler Youth and the League of German Girls. DIZ, SV-Bilderdienst, Munich.

than Stalingrad. The Red Army began its advance against the German Reich. By October it had reached West Prussia.

In the autumn of 1944, the Third Reich mustered its final strength. Under the political auspices of the NSDAP and the military leadership of Himmler as commander in chief of the reserve army, the regime called out a *Volkssturm*, a people's army. What these last reserves lacked in fighting power the gauleiters were to make up for with ideological appeals. Wherever the *Volkssturm* saw action it suffered horrendous casualties, wherever it was supposed to halt the advancing Allies with anti-tank obstacles and other improvised measures it proved ineffective.

Albert Speer on Hitler's right in the hour of the
triumph over France in June 1940. On his tour of
Paris, Hitler surrounded himself with his favorite
artists, who were dressed in uniform for the occa-
sion. To Hitler's right: Speer, the sculptor Arno
Breker, and the architect Hermann Giesler; second
row: SS Group Leader Karl Wolff, Major General
Keitel, Chief Adjutant Wilhelm Brückner, Karl
Brandt (personal physician to Hitler and his staff),
Martin Bormann, and Reich Press Chief Otto
Dietrich. DIZ, SV-Bilderdienst, Munich.

Bombing had reduced German cities to ruins. Hildesheim, Stuttgart,
Heilbronn, Munich, Krefeld, and Kassel were destroyed. Cologne counted
53,000 war dead among its inhabitants, 20,000 of them victims of the
bombing raids. Three-quarters of the housing stock was destroyed.
Cologne's rubble, heaped into a single pile, would have risen nearly twice
the height of the towers of its cathedral. The area bombing of civilian targets, intended as a strategy of psychological attrition, instead had the effect of stabilizing the population's will to hold out. At the least, the mil-

Dresden after the air raid of February 13–14, 1945. DIZ, SV-Bilderdienst, Munich.

itarily unnecessary destruction from the air provided Nazi propaganda with an argument to call out the last reserves for the defense of the home-land and to demand the exertion of whatever strength was left. On Jan-uary 2, 1945, the old quarter of Nuremberg was destroyed under a hail of bombs. An air attack on Berlin on February 3 claimed 22,000 lives. On February 13–14, Dresden was consumed by a sea of flames in which 35,000 inhabitants lost their lives. Würzburg was destroyed on March 16, Pots-dam in the middle of April by one of the last bombing raids, before that Chemnitz—the inferno was everywhere.

In his last radio address to the German people on January 30, 1945, Hitler declared that the "horrific fate" that was playing itself out in the east would, in the end, be "averted and mastered by us in spite of all set-backs and severe tests." That same day the film *Kohlberg,* with its message of holding out, premiered. This lavish cinematic production, using the example of citizens resisting Napoleon, was to be a model in a hopeless situation, an appeal to loyalty to one's homeland and to discipline. Three weeks later, February 24, 1945, Hitler, on the occasion of the twenty-fifth anniversary of the founding of the NSDAP, had a proclamation read that

Poster from November 1944: "For freedom and
life. The People's Army." DIZ, SV-Bilderdienst,
Munich.

closed with the prophecy that the Third Reich would be victorious in the
end: "If the homeland continues to fulfill its duty, as it is now doing, indeed, if it rises even higher with the will to do the utmost, if the frontline soldier follows the example of the homeland and risks his entire life
for this new homeland, the whole world will shatter against us!" To the
very end, Goebbels, too, invoked the hope of a miracle that would decide the war.

As the superiority of the Allies became more and more obvious and
palpable, Nazi propaganda increasingly revolved around the theme of miracle weapons. To assuage the anxieties of the Germans, there was talk right
up to the end of secret developments of weapons with terrible destruc-
tive power. Two weapons saw action: the "Diligent Lieschen," a gun with
a range of 150 kilometers, and especially the "Retribution Weapons" V1
and V2 (V standing for *Vergeltung,* retribution). The V1, the Luftwaffe's

pilotless, jet-propelled aircraft that carried a ton of explosives, was aimed at London beginning in June 1944 and at Antwerp and Lüttich after the withdrawal of German troops from the channel coast, but it did little damage to the supply lines of the Allies. Its larger sister, the army's V2 rocket, was fired at London and Antwerp beginning in September 1944, but its accuracy and explosive power left something to be desired. Likewise, the jet-propelled planes Messerschmidt 262 and Heinkel 162, technical innovations that were to make true the claim that German ingenuity would defeat the material superiority of the Allies, did not bring about a change in the fortunes of war. Small weapons such as a one-man torpedo and the *Panzerfaust* (an anti-tank rocket launcher), represented the final, desperate logic of the collapsing regime.

Among the legends of the Third Reich is that of the "Alpine Redoubt" in which the regime would be able to continue the fight or hold out for some time to come. After both the elaborately constructed Western Wall and the improvised lines in the east had proved useless against the assault of the Allied forces, Hitler's approval of the project "Core Redoubt Alps," once those around him finally dared to present it to him in April 1945, was nothing more than a farce.

Eventually Goebbels replaced the miracle weapons with invocations of history. In his last public speech on the eve of Hitler's fifty-sixth birthday, he drew a parallel between Roosevelt's death on April 12, 1945, and the reversal of Frederick the Great's fortune in the Seven Years' War after the death of Tsarina Elizabeth of Russia. The regime reinforced its propaganda of holding out with draconian measures and orders. On February 15, courts-martial were introduced in "Reich areas threatened by the enemy"—their purpose was to strengthen the population's will to fight by imposing death sentences.

Resistance after Germany's defeat and a guerilla campaign against Allied occupation troops was to be the mission of "Werewolf," an organization of guerilla fighters set up in the final days of the war. In actuality these activities were chiefly fabrications. But as a result of the propaganda noise, the Allies, believing the rumors of sabotage, attacks, and massacres, were very cautious for quite some time after all fighting had come to an end. They also believed in continuing resistance—which did not materialize—because they had to assume that most of the Germans who had remained loyal to Hitler for so long were fanatical Nazis. The only sensational action by "Werewolf" was the murder of the Allied-appointed lord mayor of Aachen at the end of March 1945. The Allied media took this deed as evidence of the drawn-out partisan war on German soil that

When British troops liberated the concentration camp Bergen-Belsen on April 15, 1945, they found, apart from 56,000 inmates (14,000 of whom died in the following weeks), 10,000 unburied corpses. For sanitary reasons, all barracks were burned and the bodies buried in mass graves. AKG-images, London.

awaited the victorious armies; as late as April 1945, Goebbels, broadcasting from a "Station Werewolf," tried to prevail upon the Germans to hold out by threatening the revenge of the underground army. But the Germans, despite the sense of duty that had kept them for so long at the side of their criminal regime, were exhausted and longed for peace. And the "functionaries" and "officials" of the regime, the gauleiters, district leaders, local group leaders, and block wardens of the party, along with other ideologically committed Nazis, who at the very end had "cowards," "traitors" and the "war-weary" sentenced to death by courts-martial and shot to set an example, now tore off their uniforms and took refuge in false identities or the pretense of being honest citizens who had always kept their distance from the Hitler regime.

The advancing Allied troops made discoveries that caused sheer horror. In July 1944, the Red Army in Poland encountered for the first time the remnants of a Nazi extermination machine when it liberated Lublin-Maidanek. Even though the SS had tried its best to cover up the traces of organized murder, more and more of the Third Reich's terrible secrets were revealed to the world. In Auschwitz the soldiers of the Red Army found about 8,000 inmates in the early afternoon of January 27, 1945. The SS had burned a large portion of the camp's files, the crematoria at the extermination camp Auschwitz II (Birkenau) had been dynamited, and tens of thousands of inmates had been evacuated toward the interior of the Reich on death marches.

Over the next three months the horror of the victorious armies would be multiplied many times over, until the last concentration camps were liberated: Buchenwald near Weimar on April 11, four days later Bergen-Belsen, where the British found conditions that defy description. There all help came too late for about 14,000 inmates, who died in the following weeks from exhaustion, dysentery, and typhus. Dachau, where 33,000 inmates were liberated by the Americans on April 29, offered the sight of mountains of corpses. One death march of concentration camp inmates from the Harz region ended in Gardelegen (Anhalt): on April 13, 1945, one day before the arrival of the Americans, 1,016 people were burned alive in a barn. In the Bay of Lübeck, 7,000 inmates from the concentration camp Neuengamme were killed when the boats in which they were to be evacuated were sunk by British fighter-bombers.

At the same time there unfolded the tragedy of the refugees fleeing their homelands in East Prussia, Silesia, and Pomerania before the advancing Red Army, people leaving the annexed Polish lands where they had been settled as "ethnic Germans" only a few years before. They fled westward in treks over land and across the Baltic Sea with the help of the navy. On January 30, 1945, the twelfth anniversary of the assumption of power by the Nazis, the overloaded steamer *Wilhelm Gustloff* was hit by Soviet torpedoes near Stolpmünde off the coast of eastern Pomerania. The sinking of this former Kraft durch Freude (Strength through Joy, a Nazi recreation program) cruiser, which had a place among the myths of National Socialism as the symbol of the state's concern for the "*Volk* community," pulled more than five thousand people to their deaths.

The great offensive by the Red Army, launched on January 12, 1945, opened the final phase of the military collapse. By the end of January Soviet units were crossing the Oder, thus isolating East Prussia from the German Reich; the industrial region of Upper Silesia was lost. By the middle of February, Breslau was surrounded, and shortly thereafter the last great offensive by the Allies began in the west. In early March the left bank of the Rhine from Emmerich to Koblenz was in the hands of British, Canadian, and American units. On March 7 the Americans captured the un-

From the end of 1944, the civilian population in the
eastern territories of the German Reich fled westward
from the Red Army. The evacuation was badly planned,
began too late, and claimed many casualties. DIZ, SV-
Bilderdienst, Munich.

damaged Rhine bridge at Remagen. The Americans, surprised at the unexpected speed of their success, set up the first bridgehead on the right
bank of the Rhine. An ugly fate awaited the hundreds of thousands of
German soldiers who were taken prisoner there. Since the advancing Allies were not prepared for so many captives, the latter were huddled in
improvised camps on bare earth under the open sky, under catastrophic
sanitary conditions, suffering from hunger and cold. About 10,000 prisoners did not survive this internment. Decades later, right-wing radicals
used this to concoct the story that the Americans had deliberately allowed
one million soldiers to die in the meadows along the Rhine.

In the last week of March, the thrust across the Rhine began in the

Soldiers of the Wehrmacht marching to the prisoner of war camp near Gießen, while American tanks roll eastward on the *Autobahn*. DIZ, SV-Bilderdienst, Munich.

west, while in the east the Red Army was gearing up to cross the Oder. Now the heart of the Reich was threatened. The capital Berlin, where Hitler had gone into hiding in the bunker of his chancellery, came within range of Soviet artillery. The situation was hopeless, but the German war machine was still running. German troops were still in Italy, in the Protectorate of Bohemia and Moravia, in the Netherlands, Denmark, and Norway. Hitler was appointing and dismissing generals, and on March 20 he welcomed "battle-tested" Hitler youths and was filmed in their company. He issued orders and—interrupted by bouts of hysteria and depression—indulged in fantasies of final victory, which he himself no longer believed in.

In the Ruhr region, the Allies took 325,000 prisoners—including 30 generals—when 21 divisions surrendered. The Allied threat to the Ruhr region had prompted Hitler to issue the notorious Nero Decree on March 19: "The battle for the existence of our *Volk*" compelled the destruction of all "military, transportation, communications, industrial, and supply installations, as well as all property within the Reich territory" that could be of use to the enemy in the conduct of the war. What this

On April 25, the day the Red Army and the U.S. Army met in Torgau, the United Nations was established in San Francisco. To make President Roosevelt's dream a reality, delegates from fifty states assembled to lay the foundation of the organization that was to guarantee a future without war. DIZ, SV-Bilderdienst, Munich.

meant was that the German troops, on their withdrawal into the interior of the Reich, were to leave behind scorched earth, a wasteland. At least now Hitler's minister of armaments, Albert Speer, was wise enough to heed the signs of the times. He did everything within his power to thwart or minimize implementation of the decree. His action, as he emphasized at the Nuremberg trials and would repeat to the end of his life, saved the German people industrial and transportation installations as well as other valuable properties for the postwar period. It was also Speer who recorded Hitler's reasoning behind the scorched-earth policy in his own country. It was not necessary, Hitler said on March 18, "to show any regard for the basic necessities that the German *Volk* will need to continue existing in its most primitive form. On the contrary, it is better to destroy even these things. For the *Volk* has shown itself to be the weaker one, and the future belongs exclusively to the stronger eastern *Volk*. What is left after this war are, in any case, only the inferior people, for the good ones have been killed in action." The social Darwinism of Nazi ideology was now turned against its own people. The departure of the Führer who for twelve years had preached to his followers a consciousness of supe-

For all the native humor of the Berliners, this banner on the occasion of Hitler's fiftieth birthday on April 20, 1944, was not meant to be ironic: "We greet the first worker of Germany: Adolf Hitler!" Österreichische Gesellschaft für Zeitgeschichte, Vienna.

riority, the ideology of the master race, could not have been any more cynical and pitiful.

On April 11, the western Allies reached the Elbe River. Two days later the Red Army occupied Vienna. On April 18 and 19, the Americans took Magdeburg and Leipzig. Nuremberg, the city of the party rallies, fell on Hitler's birthday, April 20, after intense street fighting. On April 22 the French marched into Stuttgart. The Soviet advance on the capital of the Reich had begun on April 16; by April 25, Berlin was surrounded. That same day, in Torgau on the Elbe River, soldiers of the U.S. Sixty-ninth Infantry Division shook hands with their brothers in arms from the Soviet Fifty-eighth Guard Division.

The military collapse had become inescapable on all fronts. The purpose of operations in the east was now merely to keep open the road to the west for the millions of people fleeing from the advancing Red Army. The political collapse of the Third Reich was swift. On April 15, when it

Berlin, the capital of the Reich, in its last days
defended against the Red Army by children and
old men. DIZ, SV-Bilderdienst, Munich.

became clear that the Allied advance would cut the Reich in half from
west to east, Hitler dictated a Führer order: "In case of an interruption
of land contact in Central Germany," Grand Admiral Dönitz would become commander in chief of the northern region and General Field Marshal Kesselring commander in chief of the southern region. At the same
time he issued a proclamation to the "soldiers of the German eastern
front," that is, above all the defenders of Berlin. In the usual style it spoke
of the final assault of the "Jewish-Bolshevik mortal enemy," who would
be drowned in a bloodbath, and prophesied that with the death of Roosevelt, "at the moment when fate has removed the greatest war criminal of
all times from the earth," the fortunes of war were about to turn.

Even his most loyal paladins no longer believed it. On April 23, Hermann Göring, who was in Obersalzberg, sent a telegram to Berlin, in-
quiring whether he could now take Hitler's place, as provided for in the
secret decree of June 1941. Hitler ranted and raged and ordered the arrest of Göring, until then the second man in the Third Reich. When Hitler
dictated his political testament in the morning hours of April 29, 1945,

Göring and SS leader Himmler were expelled from the NSDAP and stripped of all their offices: "Göring and Himmler, quite apart from their disloyalty to me personally, have done immeasurable harm to the country and the entire *Volk* by secret negotiations with the enemy, which they have conducted without my knowledge and against my wishes, and by illegally attempting to seize state power for themselves."

In place of the outcasts, Goebbels was to become chancellor and Grand Admiral Dönitz president, minister of war, and commander in chief of the Wehrmacht. The testament went into effect when Hitler shot himself in the afternoon of April 30, 1945, in the bunker of the chancellery. Prior to doing so he had married Eva Braun, evidently because he felt the need to legitimize his relationship with the lover he had always concealed from the public.

On the evening of May 1, Goebbels, too, committed suicide. The other occupants of the bunker fled, among them Martin Bormann, who was killed in the attempt to escape. At the outermost edge of the northern region of Germany, the head of the German navy was now in charge as Hitler's successor, first at the naval headquarters, a collection of barracks on the Plöner Sea but with good communications links, and after May 2 in Flensburg. Admiral Dönitz had been informed via radio of his new position, and since Hitler's death was not reported at the same time, he had immediately sent a devotional telegram to Berlin: "My Führer! My loyalty to you will be inalienable. I will therefore continue every effort to relieve you in Berlin. But should fate compel me to lead the German Reich as the successor designated by you, I will carry out this war to the end in the manner demanded by this unparalleled heroic battle of the German *Volk*." It matters little how seriously the grand admiral meant these phrases, for in actuality there was nothing left for him and his "Reich government" to do but offer Germany's unconditional surrender.

When the Third Reich came to an end, eight million Germans were prisoners of war in the hands of the victorious powers of the Second World War. The last POWs did not return from Siberian camps until 1956. At least thirteen million people had lost their lives to crimes of the Nazi regime, not to acts of war: among them were six million Jews, more than three million Soviet prisoners of war, at least two and a half million Poles, hundreds of thousands of forced laborers, and many others, including Sinti and Roma, Yugoslavs and Dutchmen, Norwegians and Greeks, and citizens of nearly all other European nations.

The balance sheet of the Third Reich included more than seventeen million soldiers killed on the Allied side, more than four million on the

German side. Many millions lost their homeland in the German eastern regions; in addition, the number of deaths caused by the flight and expulsion of ethnic Germans reached a million. All told, the result of Nazi rule in Europe was more than fifty million dead.

Hitler and Goebbels were not the only Nazi potentates who tried to escape the Third Reich. Heinrich Himmler, the Reich leader SS, condemned by Hitler and rebuffed by the Dönitz government, roamed about disguised as a soldier with a pay book under a false name in his pocket, until he was captured on May 23 by British troops in the Lüneburg Heath. When he was recognized he took his own life by swallowing poison. Foreign Minister Ribbentrop was able to hide in Hamburg until June 14. Göring had first been interned by an SS unit in Tyrol and had then been taken into custody by the Allies. Some Nazi functionaries committed suicide, others managed to go underground or even escape to South America.

The military existence of the Third Reich ended with the surrender on May 7 in Reims and on May 9 in Berlin-Karlshorst, its political existence with the Berlin Declaration issued by the four Allied commanders, who assumed the power of government in Germany on June 5, 1945. Many contemporaries—accessories and passive supporters, opportunists and the indifferent—had trouble comprehending how they could ever have believed in the promise of the Third Reich. The socio-revolutionary dynamic of the "movement" that wanted to renew Germany had petrified into a regime of uncontrollably corrupt bosses. In the end the "*Volk* community," defined by the exclusion of and discrimination against outsiders, was nothing more than a community of fate of the oppressed and the disenfranchised, who had submitted to the seductions of a totalitarian ideology before they began to feel its coercion. The legal system and constitutional order, civic spirit and humaneness had been destroyed, along with cities and houses and the happiness and lives of millions of victims. After the Götterdämmerung of the Third Reich, the lives of Germans were for a long time dominated by occupation and national division, alienation and powerlessness. Following an excess of national pride and racial blindness, the next generations also found themselves confronted with the crimes and consequences of a regime their parents and grandparents had done too little to resist.

EPILOGUE

FOLLOWING GERMANY'S CAPITULATION, the "government" of Grand Admiral Dönitz, which derived its legitimacy solely from Hitler, continued until May 23, 1945, to indulge its illusions by holding cabinet meetings and carrying out other phantasmal acts of government at the Mürwik naval school near Flensburg, largely ignored by everybody. In the meantime, Allied troops were occupying all of Germany. Anticipating future decisions, the Soviets placed the area east of the Oder under Polish administration; the rest of Germany was divided into four zones of occupation, each headed by a military governor. The extent and shape of the zones had long since been determined by the Allied European Advisory Commission. At the Yalta Conference in January 1945, Roosevelt, Stalin, and Churchill had agreed that France would be the fourth occupying power and would receive a zone in southwestern Germany, chiefly at the expense of the Americans.

Occasional confusion during the establishment of the occupational governments (for example, the French did not wish to hand Stuttgart over to the U.S. Army), and the fact that the military advance had not everywhere proceeded in tandem with planning for the future occupational administrations, gave rise to legends of missed opportunities and political omissions. The fantasy that immediately following the defeat of Germany, the western Allies would launch a campaign against Stalin's Communist Soviet Union in conjunction with the remnants of the Wehrmacht (intact divisions of which were still on Czech and Norwegian soil) seemed to acquire a veneer of reality after the fact, during the cold-war era. And many residents of Saxony and Thuringia considered the withdrawal of the Americans from that region in the early summer of 1945 not only regrettable but a political mistake, irrespective of the fact that the borders of the zones of occupation had been firmly agreed upon by the Allies, that

The first German postwar film, Wolfgang Staudte's *Die Mörder sind unter uns* (The Murderers Are among Us, DEFA, 1946), dealt with the war experience and the question of guilt. Deutsches Historisches Museum, Berlin.

there was no reason for them to break their agreements, and that the desire of the Germans to live under American rule rather than be exposed to the arbitrariness of the Red Army, to Soviet requisitioning commandos, or to plundering and raping Russian soldiers was of no concern to the Allies.

Berlin, divided into four sectors and jointly governed by the Allies, became the seat of the Allied Control Council. The council, conceived of as a collegial organ of government consisting of the four military governors, supported by an enormous four-layer bureaucracy (British, American, French, and Soviet), was supposed to determine the fate of the Germans, but in reality it was incapable of taking any action.

The Big Three, the heads of state of the Soviet Union, the United

States, and Great Britain, met in Potsdam in the second half of July 1945, their third meeting after Tehran and Yalta. This conference was supposed to have taken place in the capital of vanquished Germany, but Berlin was too badly destroyed. The topics of discussion were Germany, its structure and borders, reparations, and the European order. As the precondition for everything else, Germany was to be demilitarized and de-Nazified, democratized and decentralized—on this the Allies were in agreement. They also agreed that those responsible for world war and genocide should be punished, that the Nazis should be held accountable, and that Germans as a whole should be examined as to their political attitudes and then educated to be democrats. Of course, how this was to be done remained an open question. Likewise, there was no universally agreed-upon concept of democracy. Added to this was the ideological difference between the Soviet Union and the west, which during the war had not played the role it was to assume later on.

Under the occupational governments, the zones quickly developed in very different directions. In the cold war that soon broke out, the confrontation between the superpowers was projected onto the constellations in Germany: very quickly, the western zones and the eastern zone confronted each other with contrasting ways of life. The division of Germany, enshrined by the establishment of the Federal Republic of Germany and the German Democratic Republic in 1949 (a division that was to last forty years but that for a long time seemed it would be permanent), had its beginning at the Potsdam Conference. The Big Three were unable to reach an agreement on German reparations and laid down the principle that the occupying powers would extract what reparations they could from their respective zones. France and the Soviet Union made excessive use of this to compensate themselves for the losses and destruction in their own countries.

The Potsdam Conference was a congress of helplessness and disunity. While nothing was settled in terms of international law, the agreements and compromises that were reached had significant ramifications, even though the Potsdam Agreement was merely a conference communiqué. The expulsion of Germans from east-central Europe, intended as ethnic cleansing and a measure that would promote lasting peace, was the terrible result of Potsdam. The number of people who lost their homeland, including those who had fled during the war, eventually topped fifteen million. In made no difference to their collective fate that they had been used as instruments of the Nazi ideology of conquering living space, or that most of them were innocent individuals. In the countries liberated

The Potsdam conference took place between July 17 and August 2, 1945, in Cecilienhof castle. The round table for the plenary sessions had been built in Moscow and transported to Potsdam, where it turned out to be too big and had to be cut down. The conference was interrupted for British parliamentary elections. Following their defeat at the polls, Churchill and Foreign Secretary Eden did not return to the conference table. The new British prime minister, Atlee, and his foreign secretary, Bevin, were not equal to the task: in the second round of the conference, Stalin and Molotov, as well as President Truman (he, too, a newcomer to the international stage) and the American Secretary of State, J. F. Brynes, articulated the differences between west and east. Zentrum für Antisemitismusforschung, Berlin.

from Nazi occupation, few took pity on the Germans who were forced to leave the Sudeten region, Silesia, Pomerania, East Prussia, or the German settlement areas in Hungary, Yugoslavia, and Romania, and who were abused, humiliated, and robbed during the process of expulsion.

One of the tragic legacies of the Third Reich were the displaced persons: freed from concentration camps and forced labor camps, from the Wehrmacht and from other, mostly involuntary circumstances, they were, like the Jews, in search of a new home, a process that usually involved years of waiting in camps. Many Soviet citizens who had ended up as German prisoners of war or had been conscripted as forced labor (and some had volunteered their services) anxiously awaited forced repatriation into Stalin's realm. Former functionaries and elites of the Third Reich had been placed in automatic detention in the western zones and were awaiting de-Nazification or trial. The situation was especially bad in the special camps of the eastern zone, where arbitrariness ruled; not only former Nazis were interned there, but many others who had opposed the establishment of Communist rule in the Soviet zone of occupation or who, having been branded as Fascists, were conscripted as laborers for reconstruction work in the Soviet Union.

By the spring of 1945, all political life for which Germans had any responsibility had come to an end. Occupation officers commanded and supervised all Germans' activities. Beginning at the lowest level, Germans of known anti-Nazi sentiment were installed as representatives of the military governments; they were permitted to act as mayors or district administrators but had no sphere of independence.

In November 1943, in the Moscow Declaration, the Allies had announced their intention to put all war criminals of the Axis powers on trial before an international tribunal. An agreement to that effect was signed in August 1945 by representatives of twenty-three states. The international court, made up of prosecutors and judges from Great Britain, the United States, the Soviet Union, and France, was to rule on conspiracies against peace, crimes against peace, war crimes, and crimes against humanity. This referred specifically to crimes such as murder and torture, deportation into slave labor, persecution, and destruction of human life. New in legal history was the first charge, "conspiracy against peace," which declared the act of preparing for and carrying out an offensive war a crime against the community of nations. However, what the Allies conceived of as an advance in international law was seen by many Germans as victors' justice, as arbitrariness and revenge.

After the solemn opening of proceedings in Berlin on October 18, 1945, the court was in session in Nuremberg from November 20, 1945, and issued its verdicts on October 1, 1946. Twenty-four men stood accused, and with them six "criminal organizations": the Reich government, the corps of political leaders of the NSDAP, the SS, the Gestapo, the SA, and the General Staff and High Command of the Wehrmacht. Only twenty-one defendants were actually put on trial: Robert Ley had committed suicide, Martin Bormann was tried in absentia (he was no longer alive, but for years many believed he had escaped to South America), Gustav Krupp von Bohlen und Halbach was not fit to stand trial. Of those in the dock, the highest-ranking member of the Nazi regime was Göring, stripped of his pomp, emaciated following treatment for his morphine addiction, and much more agile than in the previous years. Rudolf Hess, the former "deputy of the Führer," had been brought over from a British prison. They were joined by Foreign Minister Ribbentrop; General Field Marshal Keitel; Gestapo Chief Kaltenbrunner; party ideologue and Minister of the East Rosenberg; the publisher of the "Stürmer," Julius Streicher; Minister of Economics Walther Funk; Grand Admirals Karl Dönitz and Erich Raeder; the former head of the Hitler Youth, Baldur von Schirach; Plenipotentiary-General for Labor Mobilization Fritz Sauckel; Interior Minister Frick; Minister of Armaments Speer; Major General Alfred Jodl; the governors of the occupied territories, namely Governor-General Hans Frank (Poland), Reich Commissioner Seyß-Inquart (the Netherlands), and Reich Protector von Neurath (Bohemia and Moravia); Propaganda Ministry Department Chief Hans Fritzsche; former Vice Chancellor Franz von Papen; and Reichsbank President Hjalmar Schacht. To the surprise of many observers, the last three were acquitted, in spite of the considerable services they had rendered to the Third Reich. Hess was sentenced to life in prison and served until his death in August 1987. Schirach and Speer were given twenty years, Dönitz ten, Neurath fifteen (he was pardoned after eight). Funk, who was supposed to serve a life term, was released in 1958. All others were sentenced to death and executed by hanging at dawn on October 16, 1946. Göring committed suicide right before the execution by swallowing poison.

The trial of major war criminals in Nuremberg was followed by other tribunals under the jurisdiction of individual countries. The best remembered are the twelve trials conducted by the United States following the international proceedings, also in Nuremberg. These lasted until the middle of 1949 and brought charges against 184 individuals. Based on a mountain of documentary evidence, these trials were a first inventory of Nazi rule: they dealt with the perversion of medicine and with war preparations, forced labor and robbery, the war in the Balkans, terror and genocide, diplomacy, and violations of international law. Those called to account for their actions were the Nazi elite on the level of the generals and gauleiters, SS leaders, and state secretaries.

At many locations in all zones there were trials of concentration camp personnel; functionaries of the German occupational power were sentenced in the Netherlands, Italy, Poland, and Czechoslovakia. German courts did not deal with larger Nazi crimes in the immediate postwar years; the Allies were not confident that the German justice system, which first had to be democratized and rebuilt, was ready to do so. The process of

The trial of major war criminals in Nuremberg in 1945–1946 assembled once more high-ranking members of the Nazi elite, this time in the dock. Front row, left to right: Hermann Göring, Rudolf Hess, Joachim von Ribbentrop, Wilhelm Keitel; second row: Grand Admirals Dönitz and Raeder, Baldur von Schirach, and Fritz Sauckel. Albert Speer is just entering the courtroom. DIZ, SV-Bilderdienst, Munich.

working through Nazi injustice before German courts did not begin until the 1960s—scandalously late because the passage of time was creating an ever greater gap between the legal charges, on the one hand, and memory, the possibility of proof, and fitness to stand trial, on the other. The Auschwitz trial in Frankfurt am Main, the Treblinka trials in Düsseldorf, and many other proceedings were attempts at rendering temporal justice that dragged on to the end of the century.

But many perpetrators escaped prosecution by flight or cunning. The most sensational case was that of Adolf Eichmann, the organizer of the Final Solution. Like many others he disappeared to South America, but the Israeli secret service tracked him down and abducted him to Israel, where he was put on trial in 1961. Others, like Joseph Mengele, the chief medical officer at Auschwitz, who died in Argentina in 1979, remained untouched. That Anton Burger, the former commander of Theresienstadt, was able to live in Essen unpunished until his death in 1991, in spite of various lackluster prosecutions, remains as unforgivable as the aid that church leaders from both Christian denominations extended to escaping Nazi mass murderers after the collapse of the Hitler state.

The Allies believed that drastic interventions in the institutional and structural framework of German society were necessary. These measures— for example, the dissolution of the largest German state, Prussia—were carried out jointly under the sovereignty of the Control Council, or were at least begun by general agreement, as with the dismantling of industrial installations. An important turning point was the end of the inflation that had been caused by the Nazis' ruinous armament and war policy. But the monetary reform of 1948, carried out in the three zones controlled by the western powers, drew a vehement reaction from the Soviets in the form of a blockade of Berlin and contributed indirectly to the division of Germany. Other projects, such as land reform or the attempt to restructure the civil service, remained projects at the zonal level and also deepened the division.

The Germans yielded to the occupiers' ideas about reform with remarkable alacrity and quickly embraced the accomplishments of the new era. Secretly, but more likely after the fact, some resisted the Allies' goal of democratizing Germany, a resistance aimed more at the American reforming zeal than the Soviets' desire to rebuild society, and they disparaged what was officially called "reorientation" as "reeducation." They protested against the alleged charge of the collective guilt of all Germans, a charge that was never officially raised by the governments of the occupying powers and did not serve as a guideline of occupation policy.

Although it was tedious and unpleasant and only moderately successful overall, the de-Nazification procedure, carried out in all four zones, is the best evidence that only individual entanglement in the Nazi system was examined and punished. With questionnaires and before de-Nazification tribunals and courts, all members and functionaries of the NSDAP and its branches and associated organizations had to explain their political past. Ultimately they either had sanctions imposed on them or were classified as a "less incriminated person" or a "passive supporter." In the eastern zone, de-Nazification—which, as a process of political cleansing, was a mixture of discrimination and rehabilitation—was officially concluded in 1948; in the western zones the proceedings continued somewhat longer. While some regarded them as unfairly lenient and others as excessively draconian, they undoubtedly had the intended cleansing effect.

The years after the Third Reich, the period between the end of the war and new statehood under foreign guardianship, in the form of the Fed-

In German postwar society, the churches were regarded as the only organizations that were morally intact, and their influence was correspondingly large. Church procession in Cologne, 1948. Bildarchiv Preußischer Kulturbesitz, Berlin.

eral Republic of Germany centered on Bonn and the German Democratic Republic governed from Berlin, were years of humiliation, despair, and misery. But the humiliation was certainly recognized as self-inflicted. The acceptance of Nazi rule, the sustained and willing agreement with and devotion to Nazi ideology, the horror at the crimes of the regime, which were not only suspected but known by most—all this the Germans now had to come to terms with. They had to justify it, deny it, or treat it with stubborn silence. Even without the drastic assistance of the Allies, who brought Germans into the liberated concentration camps to force them into self-reflection by confronting them with the mountains of corpses, the feelings of humiliation and shame would have made themselves felt.

The silent denial of the Germans was utterly puzzling to the officers of the occupying forces, who had nearly unlimited power in Germany. One Englishman observed that there was one man most of the officers of the military government were eager to meet, namely the Nazi who stood by his convictions, who admitted that he once believed in Hitler and had followed him. By now the occupying officers had met many former party members, "but they all said they belonged to the party only because they had to keep their jobs and feed their families. Evidently nobody believed in its politics, let alone approved of it. And yet they all worked on its behalf." The flight of the Germans into an apolitical condition, their attempt, in the face of the catastrophe, to claim to have been indifferent nonparticipants, was perplexing not only to this British officer: "After all the years of fighting against Germany, we had expected to find it thoroughly intertwined with National Socialism. And what did we find? A German people who almost unanimously rejected any connection with or sympathy for National Socialism. What are we to make of this? Is this an almost universal inner dishonesty or cowardice? A people which like a herd of sheep is incapable of resisting its shepherd or its watchdog, and which gives no thought to where it is being led, even if it is to the slaughterhouse? Or is this a people which is quite consciously waiting for any kind of opportunity to fall upon a peaceful world to its own imagined advantage?"

The Allies were puzzled: the Germans they had been told would continue the fanatical struggle as guerrilla fighters after the fall of the Hitler state now claimed that they never had anything to do with Nazi ideology. The Germans who had instigated the Second World War and fought it as a merciless racial and ideological conflict now bowed their heads humbly and picked up the cigarette butts discarded by Allied troops to greedily smoke the last bit of tobacco in them. The self-proclaimed "master race" was now earning a few pennies shining boots, and was feeling miserable and victimized. All this was strangely unsettling to the Allies and distasteful to the Germans themselves.

A shortage of living space, cold and hunger, concern for family members who had not yet returned from the war and who might never return if they had not been taken prisoner—these problems were enough to fill the daily lives of the Germans after 1945. Moreover, the flood of displaced persons and refugees that poured into a smaller Germany from the lost eastern territories and from east-central Europe created seemingly insurmountable problems. On April 1, 1947, the British zone recorded an increase in population of 3.67 million (or 18 percent) over the 19.8 million who had lived there in 1939. The population in the American zone grew by 3.25 million (23 percent), that of the Soviet zone by 3.16 million (16 percent); the French zone accepted very few refugees and did so very reluctantly. The largest portion of the migration movement had to be absorbed by the agrarian states of Mecklenburg–West Pomerania, Schleswig-

Holstein, Lower Saxony, and Bavaria, because the prospects of housing and feeding the refugees were better there than in the industrialized regions.

Worst of all was the hunger. The winter of 1946–1947, brutally cold and long, had used up the last reserves, afflicted the people with hopelessness, and, through the collapse of the infrastructure in three cold spells, turned the food and economic crisis into a permanent one. Supplies and raw materials saved from the war years were sufficient for modest production up to the end of 1946. But with the onset of winter the catastrophe became clear: the food and energy supply, as well as transportation, essentially collapsed. Only aid from Great Britain and especially the United States prevented the situation from becoming even worse, but the support fell far short of meeting the needs and expectations of the Germans.

In 1936, the average daily consumption of calories in Germany was 3,113, higher than the norm of 3,000 calories established by the League of Nations. By the spring of 1945, it had dropped to 2,010 calories. The low point was reached in 1946 and 1947, depending on the zone. Each of the military governments officially established the number of calories for its sphere: in 1946, the number was 1,330 for the American zone, 1,083 for the Soviet zone, 900 for the French zone, and 1,050 for the British zone. These numbers for the "normal" consumer were fixed with food rationing cards. Workers engaged in heavy or very heavy labor and coal miners received supplements or were at least entitled to them. The distribution of items that were in short supply was controlled with food rationing and purchasing cards, and cards for fuel and shoe resoling. Rations and calories, needless to say, are abstractions not well suited to demonstrating the reality of everyday life in postwar Germany.

The dismantling of industrial installations was something the Germans experienced as an oppressive burden. What the victors had intended as a measure of demilitarization, with the added purpose of reparations, struck them as an act of revenge. When the Germans demonstrated against the destruction of their jobs—the most heavily affected was the steel industry, whose capacity the Nazi state had vastly expanded for its rearmament—they were also protesting against the humiliation they experienced from the demolition of factory installations and the removal of machinery. In retrospect, the psychological injury was worse than the economic damage. In the British and American zones, where 682 businesses were on the dismantling list of October 1947, the benefit of subsequent modernization outweighed the economic damage.

Only a single remnant is left of the project for the new capital "Germania":
the large load structure in the area of the planned triumphal arch, which was
erected in 1941 to test the load-bearing capacity of the soil. Angelika Benz.

The contribution of the Allies—especially Great Britain and the United
States—to the reconstruction and democratization of Germany was soon
forgotten and repressed. The humiliation and sense of powerlessness of
the postwar years disappeared beneath the proud memory of the accom-
plishment of rebuilding the nation. And many soon misperceived the success of rebuilding in the west and of social reorientation in the east as an
act of atonement, one that evidently allowed them to forget the causes of
the war, the destruction, and the misery.

The discrepancy between the propagated ideals of the Third Reich—
national greatness, prosperity, and security in a national community without class barriers—and its reality—terror and persecution, unlimited
control of human lives, a lust for power, and unprecedented corruption
at all levels—was greater than the gap between political goals and reality
in any other period of German history.

The blueprint of the Third Reich was simple, so simple that it intoxi-
cated some, and others failed to recognize its effect until it was too late.
The radical social and national renewal it promised proved to be a rupture of civilization. One of the decisive prerequisites of what Friedrich

Meinecke called the "German catastrophe" was the fact that the departure from democracy and the constitutional state, the relapse into barbarism, was so quick to meet with the approval of those who at first had laughed at Hitler and his followers and then had deluded themselves into thinking they could use Hitler for their purposes. Many of those who had willingly submitted at the time later—after the collapse of the Third Reich—considered themselves innocent and abused.

The price for twelve years of Nazi rule was the loss of freedom and autonomy by the majority, and the disenfranchisement and discrimination, and eventually even the physical destruction, of minorities and undesirables. The ostensible benefits of jobs, economic security, and sense of community did not last or were merely an illusion of "modernization."

SELECT BIBLIOGRAPHY

Ackermann, Joseph. *Heinrich Himmler als Ideologe*. Göttingen, 1976.

Arad, Yitzhak, Shmuel Krakowski, and Shmuel Spector, eds. *The Einsatzgruppen Reports*. New York, 1989.

Arad, Yitzhak, Yisrael Gutman, and Abraham Margaliot, eds. *Documents on the Holocaust*. Jerusalem, 1981.

Barkai, Avraham. *From Boycott to Annihilation: The Economic Struggle of German Jews 1933–1945*. Hanover, N.H., 1989.

Bartov, Omer. *Hitler's Army*. New York, 1991.

Benz, Wolfgang, ed. *Dimension des Völkermords: Die Zahl der jüdischen Opfer des Nationalsozialismus*. Munich, 1991.

——. *The Holocaust: A German Historian Examines the Genocide*. Trans. Jane Sydenham-Kwiet. New York, 1999.

——, ed. *Die Juden in Deutschland, 1933–1945*. Munich, 1988.

Benz, Wolfgang, Hermann Graml, and Hermann Weiß, eds. *Enzyklopädie des Nationalsozialismus*. Stuttgart and Munich, 1997.

Benz, Wolfgang, and Walther Pehle, eds. *Encyclopedia of German Resistance to the Nazi Movement*. Trans. Lance W. Garmer. New York, 1997.

Bracher, Karl Dietrich. *The German Dictatorship*. Trans. Jean Steinberg. London, 1970.

Broszat, Martin. *Hitler and the Collapse of Weimar Germany*. Trans. V. R. Berghahn. New York, 1987.

——. *The Hitler State*. Trans. John W. Hiden. London, 1981.

Browning, Christopher. *Ordinary Men: Reserve Battalion 101 and the Final Solution in Poland*. New York, 1993.

——. *The Path to Genocide*. Cambridge, 1992.

Burleigh, Michael. *Death and Deliverance: Euthanasia in Germany c. 1900–1945*. Cambridge, 1994.

——. *The Third Reich: A New History*. New York, 2000.

Conway, J. S. *The Nazi Persecution of the Churches 1933–1945*. London, 1968.

Domarus, Max, ed. *Hitler: Speeches and Proclamations 1932–1945*. 3 vols. London, 1990–1997.

Eichholtz, Dietrich. *Geschichte der deutschen Kriegswirtschaft 1939–1945*. 3 vols. Munich, 1999.

Falter, Jürgen W. *Hitlers Wähler.* Munich, 1991.

Fest, Joachim. *The Face of the Third Reich.* Trans. Michael Bullock. London, 1979.

———. *Hitler.* Trans. Richard and Clara Winston. New York, 1974.

———. *Plotting Hitler's Death: The Story of the German Resistance.* Trans. Bruce Little. New York, 1996.

———. *Speer. Eine Biographie.* Berlin, 1999.

Freeman, Michael. *Atlas of Nazi Germany: A Political, Economic, and Social Anatomy of the Third Reich.* 2nd ed. London, 1995.

Friedländer, Saul. *Nazi Germany and the Jews.* Vol. 1, *The Years of Persecution, 1933–1939.* New York, 1997.

Gilbert, Martin. *Atlas of the Holocaust.* Oxford, 1988.

Gill, Anton. *An Honourable Defeat: A History of German Resistance to Hitler, 1933–1945.* New York, 1994.

Graml, Hermann. *Europas Weg in den Krieg: Hitler und die Mächte 1939.* Munich, 1990.

———. *Reichskristallnacht: Antisemitismus und Judenverfolgung im Dritten Reich.* 3rd ed. Munich, 1998.

Gruchmann, Lothar. *Totaler Krieg: Vom Blitzkrieg zur bedingungslosen Kapitulation.* Munich, 1991.

Hackett, David, ed. *The Buchenwald Report.* Boulder, 1996.

Herbst, Ludolf. *Das nationalsozialistische Deutschland 1933–1945: Die Entfesselung der Gewalt: Rassismus und Krieg.* Frankfurt a. M., 1996.

Hildebrand, Klaus. *Das Dritte Reich.* Munich, 1995.

Hilger, Andreas. *Deutsche Kriegsgefangene in der Sowjetunion, 1941–1956: Kriegsgefangenenpolitik, Lageralltag und Erinnerung.* Essen, 2000.

Hoffmann, Peter. *The History of German Resistance to Hitler 1933–1945.* 3rd ed. Montreal, 1996.

Horwitz, Gordon J. *In the Shadow of Death: Living Outside the Gates of Mauthausen.* London, 1991.

Kater, Michael H. *The Nazi Party: A Social Profile of Members and Leaders, 1919–1945.* Cambridge, Mass., 1983.

Kehr, Helen, and Janet Langmaid. *The Nazi Era 1919–1945: A Selected Bibliography of Published Works from the Early Roots to 1980.* London, 1982.

Kershaw, Ian. *Hitler 1889–1936: Hubris.* London, 1998.

———. *Hitler 1936–1945: Nemesis.* New York, 2000.

———. *The "Hitler Myth": Image and Reality in the Third Reich.* Oxford, 1987.

———, ed. *Weimar. Why Did German Democracy Fail?* London, 1990.

Klee, Ernst. *"Euthanasie" im NS-Staat.* Frankfurt a. M., 1983.

Krohn, Claus-Dieter, Patrik von zur Mühlen, Gerhard Paul, Lutz Windckler, eds. *Handbuch der deutschsprachigen Emigration 1933–1945.* Darmstadt, 1998.

Kube, Alfred. *Pour le mérite und Hakenkreuz: Hermann Göring im Dritten Reich.* Munich, 1986.

Laqueur, Walter, ed. *The Holocaust Encyclopedia.* New York, 2001.

Lifton, Robert Jay. *The Nazi Doctors.* New York, 1986.

Marrus, Michael. *The Holocaust in History.* London, 1989.

Mosse, George L. *The Crisis of German Ideology: Intellectual Origins of the Third Reich.* New York, 1981.

——. *Nazi Culture: Intellectual, Cultural, and Social Life in the Third Reich: A Documentary History.* New York, 1966.

Müller, Ingo. *Hitler's Justice: The Courts of the Third Reich.* Trans. Deborah Lucas Schneider. Cambridge, Mass., 1991.

Müller, Klaus-Jürgen. *The Army, Politics, and Society in Germany 1933–1945.* Manchester, 1987.

Noakes, Jeremy, and Geoffrey Pridham, eds. *Nazism 1919–1945: A Documentary Reader.* Exeter, 1983–1988.

Orth, Karin. *Das System der nationalsozialistischen Konsentrationslager: Eine politische Organisationsgeschichte.* Hamburg, 1999.

Overy, Richard J. *Göring: The Iron Man.* London, 1983.

——. *Why the Allies Won.* London, 1995.

Parker, R. A. C. *Struggle for Survival: The History of the Second World War.* Oxford, 1989.

Pätzold, Kurt, and Manfred Weißbecker. *Rudolf Hess: Der Mann an Hitlers Seite.* Leipzig, 1999.

Peukert, Detlev J. K. *Inside Nazi Germany: Conformity, Opposition, and Racism in Everyday Life.* Trans. Richard Deveson. New Haven, 1987.

Proctor, Robert N. *Racial Hygiene: Medicine under the Nazis.* Cambridge, Mass., 1988.

Pulzer, Peter G. *Germany 1870–1945: Politics, State Formation, and War.* Oxford, 1997.

——. *The Rise of Political Antisemitism in Germany and Austria.* New York, 1964.

Reichel, Peter. *Der Schöne Schein des Dritten Reiches: Faszination und Gewalt des Faschismus.* Munich, 1991.

Reuth, Ralf Georg. *Goebbels.* London, 1993.

Ruck, Michael. *Bibliographie zum Nationalsozialismus.* Cologne, 1995.

Schleunes, Karl. *The Twisted Road to Auschwitz: Nazi Policy toward German Jews, 1933–1939.* University of Illinois Press, 1990.

Stern, Fritz. *Dreams and Delusions: National Socialism in the Drama of the German Past.* New York, 1987.

——. *The Politics of Cultural Despair: A Study of the Rise of Germanic Ideology.* Berkeley, 1961.

Thamer, Hans-Ulrich. *Verführung und Gewalt: Deutschland 1933–1945.* Berlin, 1986.

Todorov, Tzvetan. *Facing Extremes: Moral Life in the Concentration Camps.* New York, 1997.

Turner, Henry Ashby, Jr. *Hitler's Thirty Days to Power: January 1933*. London, 1996.

Ueberschär, Gerd R. *Der Nationalsozialismus vor Gericht: Die allierten Prozesse gegen Kriegsverbrecher und Soldaten 1943–1952*. Frankfurt a. M., 1999.

Ueberschär, Gerd R., and Winfried Vogel. *Dienen und Verdienen: Hitlers Geschenke an seine Eliten*. Frankfurt a. M., 1999.

Weinberg, Gerhard L. *A World at Arms: A Global History of World War II*. Cambridge, 1988.

Weiß, Hermann, ed. *Biographisches Lexikon zum Dritten Reich*. Frankfurt a. M., 1998.

Wendt, Bernd-Jürgen. *Großdeutschland: Außenpolitik und Kriegsvorbereitung des Hitler-Regimes*. Munich, 1987.

Wistrich, Robert. *Who's Who in Nazi Germany*. London, 1982.

Yahil, Leni. *The Holocaust: The Fate of European Jewry*. Oxford, 1987.

Zentner, Christian, and Friedemann Bedurftig. *The Encyclopedia of the Third Reich*. New York, 1997.

INDEX

Text:	10/13 Galliard
Display:	Helvetica Neue Light
Compositor:	Integrated Composition Systems
Printer and binder:	Maple-Vail Manufacturing Group